FOUR MIDDLE
ENGLISH ROMANCES

Sir Isumbras, Octavian,
Sir Eglamour of Artois, Sir Tryamour

 MIDDLE ENGLISH TEXTS SERIES

The Middle English Texts Series is designed for classroom use. Its goal is to make available to teachers and students texts that occupy an important place in the literary and cultural canon but have not been readily available in student editions. The series does not include those authors, such as Chaucer, Langland, or Malory, whose English works are normally in print in good student editions. The focus is, instead, upon Middle English literature adjacent to those authors that teachers need in compiling the syllabuses they wish to teach. The editions maintain the linguistic integrity of the original work but within the parameters of modern reading conventions. The texts are printed in the modern alphabet and follow the practices of modern capitalization, word formation, and punctuation. Manuscript abbreviations are silently expanded, and *u/v* and *j/i* spellings are regularized according to modern orthography. Yogh (3) is transcribed as *g*, *gh*, *y*, or *s*, according to the sound in Modern English spelling to which it corresponds; thorn (þ) and eth (ð) are transcribed as *th*. Distinction between the second person pronoun and the definite article is made by spelling the one *thee* and the other *the*, and final *-e* that receives full syllabic value is accented (e.g., *charité*). Hard words, difficult phrases, and unusual idioms are glossed on the page, either in the right margin or at the foot of the page. Explanatory and textual notes appear at the end of the text, often along with a glossary. The editions include short introductions on the history of the work, its merits and points of topical interest, and brief working bibliographies.

FOUR MIDDLE ENGLISH ROMANCES

Sir Isumbras, Octavian,
Sir Eglamour of Artois, Sir Tryamour

Edited by
Harriet Hudson

SECOND EDITION

Published for TEAMS
(The Consortium for the Teaching of the Middle Ages)
in Association with the University of Rochester

by

MEDIEVAL INSTITUTE PUBLICATIONS
Kalamazoo, Michigan
2006

Library of Congress Cataloging-in-Publication Data

Four Middle English romances / edited by Harriet Hudson. -- 2nd ed.
 p. cm. -- (Middle English texts)
 Commentary and notes in English; poems in original Middle English with extensive
glossing.
 Includes bibliographical references.
 ISBN-13: 978-1-58044-111-7 (pbk. : alk. paper)
 1. Romances, English. 2. English poetry--Middle English, 1100-1500. 3. English
poetry--England--Midlands. 4. Knights and knighthood--Poetry. I. Hudson, Harriet
(Harriet E.) II. Series: Middle English texts (Kalamazoo, Mich.)
 PR2064.F68 2006
 821'.1--dc22

 2006018041

ISBN 1-58044-111-7

Printed in the United States of America

P 6 5 4 3 2

❦ Contents

 ACKNOWLEDGMENTS

ACKNOWLEDGEMENTS FOR THE FIRST EDITION

I would like to acknowledge the financial support from the Indiana State University Research Committee, and the gracious and learned editorial assistance of Alan Lupack and Russell A. Peck. Pauline Alma at the University of Rochester read the edition carefully against xerox copies of the medieval sources, and Jennifer Church formatted the volume for publication and saw it through various stages in the preparation of camera-ready copy. I am grateful to the National Endowment for the Humanities for its assistance in bringing the project to fruition, and I wish to thank Tom Seiler and Juleen Audrey Eichinger for their final proof reading. I also wish to thank the Syndics of Cambridge University Library for permission to use Cambridge University MS Ff. 2.38 in the editing of *Octavian*, *Sir Eglamour*, and *Sir Tryamour*; Lincoln Cathedral Library for permission to use the Thornton manuscript in the editing of *Sir Isumbras*, *Octavian*, and *Sir Eglamour*; and the British Library for permission to use Cotton Caligula A.ii in the editing of *Sir Isumbras*, *Octavian*, and *Sir Eglamour*.

ACKNOWLEDGEMENTS FOR THE SECOND EDITION

I am grateful to have the opportunity to revise and reformat this edition. Thanks are due to Leah Haught of the Middle English Texts Series for reformatting the edition, and to both her and Leila K. Norako for reviewing current scholarship and researching additional explanatory notes.

GENERAL INTRODUCTION

Sir Isumbras, *Octavian*, *Sir Eglamour of Artois*, and *Sir Tryamour* are important works in a major literary development of the fourteenth century: the flourishing of Middle English popular romance. These four narratives were among the most popular; all survive in multiple manuscripts and continued to circulate in prints through the sixteenth century. All were composed in the northeast Midlands in the fifty years between 1325 and 1375, and they appear together in several manuscripts. Furthermore, they employ the same style, stanza form, and plot elements. The basic story concerns the separation and reunion of a family accompanied by a fall and rise in social and/or spiritual status. Sometimes called family romances, these narratives can be distinguished from those of the earlier hero alone pattern that originated in twelfth-century France. Stephen Knight notes that the family-based romances grant a larger role to women and embrace a wider range of values than the earlier works, adapting the feudal ideology to a different social context.[1]

The tale the romances tell — of exiled queens, orphaned children, and penitent fathers — was one of the most prevalent medieval stories. Sometimes called the Constance/ Eustace legend (after two well-known pious versions), its influence can be seen in numerous romances. In addition to the four works in this volume, there are *Emaré*, *Sir Degaré*, *The King of Tars*, *The Erle of Toulous*, *Florence of Rome*, *Sir Torrent of Portengale*, *Chevalier Assigne*, *Robert of Sicily*, *Sir Gowther*, and others. Fourteenth- and fifteenth-century audiences must have found the story compelling. Individual treatments may emphasize the vicissitudes of the wife, the tribulations of the father, or the adventures of the children, or a combination of all three. The wife's story often conforms to the type known as the calumniated queen, the husband's follows the pattern of the man tried for his faith. The calumniation takes three well-defined forms: the heroine is falsely accused of sexual misconduct and exiled by either her jealous, sometimes incestuous father (*Eglamour*), her jealous mother-in-law (*Octavian*), or her seducing steward (*Tryamour*). The man tried for his faith is tested by exile and poverty (*Isumbras*). Frequently exile is accomplished by a voyage, children are carried off by animals and raised by foster parents, sons engage in combat with their fathers and are married at the reunion of their parents. The romances' composers developed various possibilities inherent in the formulaic plot: *Isumbras* is a lesson in penance and family devotion, *Octavian* deals in exotic romance and social comedy, *Tryamour* focuses on loyalty and combat, *Eglamour* combines chivalric adventure with family conflict.

With the exception of Octavian's story, which was first composed in French, these four romances are all original English compositions. They have no direct sources, but similar stories had long circulated in pious legends of Sibelle, Charlemagne's exemplary queen, and

[1] Knight, "Social Function," p. 111.

tales of Constance were current in England at the time, as evidenced by Gower's story of Constance in Book 2 of the *Confessio Amantis*, Chaucer's *Man of Law's Tale*, and a variant in the *Gesta Romanorum*. Legends of St. Eustace exist in numerous English manuscripts; some version of this saint's life was doubtless the model for *Isumbras*.

Almost nothing is known of the authors who fashioned these four narratives. The southern version of *Octavian* (which is not the one printed here) is sometimes attributed to Thomas Chester, author of *Sir Launfal*, and L. H. Loomis, following Sarazzin, indicates that *Isumbras* and northern *Octavian* are by the same author, but we know nothing of him.[2] It used to be assumed that these romances were the work of minstrels; however, that now seems unlikely. More probably, the poems were composed by clerics, both ecclesiastical and secular, since they could read, write, and have access to books and patrons. It is possible that some of the romances were composed in association with bookshops, as Loomis has suggested of the earlier romances in the Auchinleck manuscript.

All the authors wrote in an indigenous English verse form, tail-rhyme, which was used almost exclusively for romances and, from the mid-fourteenth century on replaced the French-derived couplet of earlier Middle English narratives.[3] The basic unit of the tail-rhyme stanza is the triplet rhyming *aab*; in general, the couplet lines have four stresses, the tail (or tag) lines have three. The form may be derived from the French octosyllabic couplet. The stanzas consist of from two to five triplets, all with the same rhyme in the tail line, though six and twelve line stanzas are the norms. The shorter is more common in poems in southern dialects, the longer in those from eastern regions. Usually the stanzas are fairly discrete units relating individual episodes, exchanges of dialogue between characters or descriptions of particular things. Enjambment is the exception. Each line tends to be a clause; often each three-line unit constitutes a loose sentence.

The tail-rhyme romances are notable for their use of syntactic and lexical formulas. Susan Wittig's analysis of their language shows *Isumbras* to be 22% formulas, *Octavian* 25%, *Tryamour* 25%, and *Eglamour* 29%.[4] Because the romances are highly formulaic, and because the tail lines lend themselves to conventional rhyming expressions, there are many instances of repetition and near repetition. Sometimes the tail lines are mere filler, but they also serve to emphasize, to regulate the pace of the narration, and to establish a relationship between the narrator and the audience.

The oral style of narration, based on formulas of direct address to the audience, suggested to early scholars that the romances were composed by minstrels, or by others writing for minstrel performance. While minstrels undoubtedly did recite romances, evidence suggests that such performances declined in the fourteenth century (when our romances were composed), as the roles of minstrels changed.[5] Indeed, the minstrel style may be a nostalgic feature of genre validation. The texts in the fifteenth-century manuscripts edited here were probably copied from written exemplars and owe little to minstrel performance, though there are some signs of oral transmission. The audiences would have heard the story read from a manuscript. The romances' lengths and episodic structures are such that they could be conveniently related in a couple of sessions.

[2] Loomis, *Medieval Romance*, p. 269.

[3] The Chester cycle plays and a life of St. Eustace also make use of tail-rhyme.

[4] Wittig, *Stylistic and Narrative Structures*, p. 18.

[5] Southworth, *English Medieval Minstrel*, pp. 96–98.

Texts of these romances survive in many of the same manuscripts. They were frequently included in compendium-type manuscripts — those large collections of diverse instructional and entertaining works common in the fifteenth century. Often texts of the four romances occur near each other, as though they circulated together in the scribes' exemplars. Murray Evans, in his study of romances in their manuscript contexts, identifies them as part of an "*Isumbras* group."[6] In the Lincoln Thornton Manuscript, one booklet[7] (fols. 53–153) contains *The Alliterative Morte Arthur*, *Octavian*, *Isumbras*, *Erle of Toulous*, *Sir Degrevant*, and *Eglamour of Artois*. Cambridge Manuscript Ff. 2.38, folios 63–102, contains *Erle of Toulous*, *Eglamour*, *Tryamour*, and *Octavian*. Manuscript Cotton Caligula A.2 contains *Eglamour*, *Octavian*, and *Isumbras*. *Isumbras* and *Eglamour* appear together in the sixteenth-century manuscript Douce 261. In the seventeenth century *Tryamour* and *Eglamour* were copied together in the Percy Folio.

The principal manuscripts postdate the composition of the romances by fifty to one hundred years. Despite the names found in the manuscripts, few specifics are known about their original owners or the romances' original audiences, with the exception of the Lincoln Thornton Manuscript, which was compiled by Robert Thornton, a knight of Yorkshire. But we do know something about the social class to which the audiences belonged, namely the gentry (used in the broad sense to include professionals and members of the upper bourgeoisie as well as landed families). The gentry class was evolving and proliferating in the fourteenth and fifteenth centuries, and it is tempting to see a relationship between this and the simultaneous proliferation and evolution of romance in English. This class seems to have been particularly concerned with social advancement. Through the ownership of books, especially works of chivalric literature and private devotion, they aligned themselves with the aristocracy. Many of the romance manuscripts contain items of instruction in etiquette and appropriate behavior bespeaking a concern for gentility. The romances themselves doubtless served as exemplars of courtesy. The anonymous eulogy for John Berkeley, a Leicestershire knight of the fifteenth century evokes something of the romances' cultural function. He is described as a generous host with whom one could hunt or read romances in the company of fair ladies — the very picture of a gentleman. Larger romance manuscripts also contain works for religious instruction and devotional use, including saints' lives, and items of a domestic nature as well. Such volumes contained material for all members of the family and provide a fascinating glimpse of the tastes and interests of their owners.

A note on stanza form and punctuation: in the manuscripts, stanzas and tag lines are not indicated, though some do have brackets to mark rhymed tail lines. I have followed the fairly standard editorial practice of printing the stanzas separately and indenting tail lines. Punctuation has been introduced for clarity; the manuscript texts are not punctuated.

[6] Evans, *Rereading Middle English Romance*, p. 56.

[7] A booklet is a series of quires forming a self-contained unit. Often composed of several texts, booklets were produced independently but could be bound together in one larger volume. See Robinson, "Booklet," pp. 46–64.

INTRODUCTION TO *SIR ISUMBRAS*

Sir Isumbras is one of the most popular Middle English romances, surviving in more manuscripts and prints (nine and five, respectively) than any other romance. It relates a version of one of the most widespread stories of the European Middle Ages, the man tried by fate. This plot was often developed in hagiographic narratives. Indeed, *Isumbras* is a secularized retelling of the legend of Saint Eustace, which circulated widely in England in martyrologies, legendaries and homilies. No immediate source for the romance of *Sir Isumbras* has been found. However, certain treatments of the Eustace story, such as that in the Middle English *Gesta Romanorum* where the concluding martyrdom is omitted, or that in Digby MS 86, which employs tail-rhyme, may have suggested ways in which the story could be cast as romance. The romance was circulating in England before 1320, when William of Nassington referred to it in his *Speculum Vita*. His comment is revealing, for he disparages stories of Isumbras as vanities (along with those of the equally popular and pious Guy of Warwick and Bevis of Hampton), an indication that he saw a generic difference between it and the legends of saints. However, in several manuscripts, *Isumbras* is grouped with saints' legends and other religious materials.

Isumbras is aptly described as a "homiletic romance," a term used by Dieter Mehl to refer to narratives that occupy a middle position between the genres of saint's legend and romance.[1] The author of *Isumbras* adapted his hagiographic material to the patterns of romance. The Eustace legend consists of three main episodes: the visionary conversion of a Roman officer including the foretelling of his suffering and eventual martyrdom; his exile and separation from his family; and their reunion and martyrdom in battle against the Romans. Isumbras is not converted, for he is already a Christian; rather his vision warns him of his separation from God through pride and gives him the choice of atoning for it in youth or age. The alteration in the terms of the heroes' suffering — Eustace suffers for his faith, Isumbras for his sins — casts the romance's hero in a more worldly light. The "choice of woe" motif, too, has been adapted to a worldly frame of action; by converting, Eustace rejects well-being in this life for joy in heaven. Isumbras knows his atonement in youth will be followed by well-being in this life. The romance also elaborates the episode of the separated family, which was the basis for numerous other romances. There it is often a vehicle for the exploration of secular problems relating to social status and family structure, but the composer of *Isumbras* focused on more spiritual matters. Unlike the families of Octavian, Tryamour, and Eglamour, which are separated by internal conflicts, Isumbras' and Eustace's families are separated by causes which lie outside the family, in spiritual relationships. *Isumbras* follows the formulas of romance in its secular comic ending. There is no martyrdom. Rather, the

[1] Mehl, *Middle English Romances*, p. 121.

family is reunited and restored to wealth and exalted social status. *Eustace*, of course, concludes with the spiritual comic vision of the hero freed from earthly ties, and the soul reunited with God in heavenly bliss.

Though they follow the patterns of romance, some parts of *Isumbras* seem to challenge the values of romance. At the beginning of the story, Isumbras is described as a paragon of chivalry and renowned patron of minstrels, living lavishly with his beautiful wife and three sons. However, he has become estranged from God by his "pryde of golde and fee" (line 45), as he is told in his vision. "Gold and fee" is a formula common to tail-rhyme romances; it is almost always used in a positive sense. Pride, of all the seven deadly sins, is the one most suited to treatment in romance, since it was usually depicted as the sin of nobles and other members of the wealthy and powerful classes. Following his vision, the hero is stripped of his chivalric accoutrements: his hawks fly away and his hounds and horse die; his estates are ravaged, the buildings burned and his workers and their chattel destroyed. The episode culminates in an emotional scene of Isumbras' simultaneous relief to learn of his family's survival, and his pity to see them running naked toward him "that erste were comely cladde" (line 105).

The adventures which follow are related with little attention to features often embellished in romances such as romantic love, combats, and occasions and objects of chivalric display. His only battles are against the enemies of Christendom. The closest *Isumbras* comes to armorial description is the cross the hero carves on his own shoulder as a badge of his pilgrim status. Isumbras humbly submits to God, acknowledging His power and accepting His punishment: "All the sorow that we ben inne, / Hit is for owre wykked synne, / Worthy we be well more" (lines 112–14). The family sets out for the Holy Land, but two children are carried off by animals. Isumbras approaches a sultan's ship to beg for food and is spurned. When a courtier points out his noble features, the sultan offers to make Isumbras his knight in his campaigns against Christendom. The hero refuses to forsake his faith, but is unable to prevent the sultan from buying his wife to make her queen. Before her departure, she is able to give him food, a ring, and promises of aid if he can undertake to kill the sultan. The next day, an eagle carries off Isumbras' payment, and a unicorn abducts his remaining son.

Bereft of worldly goods and human ties, Isumbras prays for guidance, and from this point on, his fortunes slowly reverse themselves. The mechanism of reversal is a kind of economic initiative seldom found in the heroes of romance or saint's legend.[2] Havelok, the industrious cook's knave, comes to mind, but that romance is exceptional for its realistic and sympathetic treatment of laborers. Isumbras is one of the few romance heroes who actually earns his way back to chivalric status. Coming upon some ironworkers, he asks for food, appealing to their charity. The smiths propose instead that he work for his food as they do. For seven years he labors with them, progressing from lowly stone carrier to apprentice to paid craftsman. Eventually he is able to make himself a suit of armor, giving new meaning to the term "self-made knight." This episode contains precise references to various smelting operations and to the trade hierarchy of smiths. The author chose to embellish the motif of hero, unrecognized, performing lowly tasks, and to embellish it in this particular way, while other, more chivalric episodes such as combats are not embellished at all.

When the sultan attacks Christendom, Isumbras rides to battle on a blacksmith's horse. The homemade armor and inferior mount are conventional in tales of knights in reduced circumstances, and here, as in other tales, they play a role in the initial combats by which

[2] Crane, *Insular Romance*, pp. 116 and 129.

the hero demonstrates his prowess, but are then replaced by proper arms, signifying his achievements and restoration of status.

Vanquishing the enemies of Christendom and killing the sultan who had seized his wife would seem to prepare the way for Isumbras' reunion with her and rule in the sultan's lands, but this culmination is delayed until he has fulfilled his vow of pilgrimage. Significantly, he maintains his humble identity, telling the king he is a smithy man, and leaves the court before he can be knighted. Only after seven years of begging and doing God's will does he complete his penance. Arriving famished at Jerusalem, he stops at a well where an angel appears to tell him his sins are forgiven and that he may return home. He journeys to the castle of a great queen renowned for her generosity to the poor; from among a crowd of beggars, he is brought into the hall and fed.

Throughout this episode of penance, and in the earlier episode of exile, the many references to hunger heighten the pathos of the hero's suffering. At every encounter Isumbras begs food and drink. Embarking on their exile, he tells his family to trust to God to "sende us our lyves fode" (line 132). The angel who brings him news of God's forgiveness also brings him food. This hunger can be read allegorically, as a spiritual hunger (just as Jerusalem has allegorical significance), but it is always treated simply as a physical need so its larger implications are not dwelt upon; rather it is a measure of the hero's misery and humility.

Pathos is a major feature of the reunion episode as well. Seated in the joyous hall, Isumbras is overcome by memories of his former happiness and weeps, unable to eat. Remarking this, the lady inquires of his journeys, then takes him into her court. The reunion of husband and wife seems imminent, but it is postponed, offering another depiction of Isumbras' suffering for the loss of his family. In a wood one day, he discovers the mantle and the sultan's gold taken from him by the eagle. He keeps these in his chamber, meditating upon his loss; his sadness and isolation are noted at court, and their causes sought. His treasure is found and brought to the queen. Recognizing it, she asks the palmer to tell how he acquired it and he relates the story. Thus, in large part, Isumbras regains his wife, not as a result of combat, or of courteous service, but because his grief attracts the lady's sympathetic notice.

The bond between husband and wife is both spiritual and emotional, a model of Christian union rather than romantic love. They are faithful, not only to each other (the sultan sends the wife to rule his countries in his absence; they never cohabit), but also to God and the sacrament of marriage. When the sultan asks to buy his wife, Isumbras replies that he can not sell her because he has "weddyd her in Goddys lay [law]" and will "holde here to myn endyng day, / Bothe for wele or woo" (lines 283–85). To be parted from her willingly is tantamount to forsaking his faith. His wife affirms this, saying she prefers to meet her end rather than live apart from him. Later, when they have been reunited (and remarried), she insists on being armed and fighting the infidel beside her husband so that, by God's grace, they might die together.

This battle is the culminating step in the hero's spiritual career as well as the occasion of the family's complete restoration. The couple is about to be slain when three knights arrive riding a lion, a leopard, and a unicorn. They vanquish the remaining 20,003 Saracens before identifying themselves to Isumbras as his children. After a celebration, father and sons conquer and convert three kingdoms. At their deaths, we are told, their souls go to heaven. The near-martyrdom of the parents, coupled with the more conventional reference to their souls' destination, may have been suggested by the apotheosis of the martyrs at the end of St. Eustace's legend.

Isumbras' adventures are spiritually motivated, but his sufferings and his reward are presented in material terms of poverty and wealth. He interprets his choice of woe economically, asking to be given poverty in youth and wealth in age, and comforts his ravaged tenants saying ". . . God bothe geveth and taketh / And at His wyll ryches maketh / And pore men also" (lines 94–96). The sultan's attempt to buy Isumbras' wife, and the importance of his treasure as an identifying token have no counterpart in the Eustace legend. At the end of the story it is explicitly stated that Isumbras is even richer than he was before his loss. The restoration to wealth and high social status can be read spiritually, but they are employed as literally as the hunger of earlier episodes.

Sir Isumbras is among the shortest of the Middle English romances. At 771 lines, it is half the length of most romances of separated and reunited families. Events unfold at a brisk pace in very regular stanzas of twelve lines. There is little elaboration, no doubling or tripling of episodes, and few descriptive details. The composer limits the narration to the father's adventures, providing no information about the careers of the sons or of the wife, apart from her husband. *Isumbras'* brevity heightens the plot's symmetry. The structure is bipartite, consisting of the fall and rise of Isumbras. The turning point comes halfway through the romance when he prays for guidance. Each half is comprised of two main episodes: Isumbras loses his worldly goods and then his family in the first; he becomes a smith and then a palmer in the second. Both episodes in the second half conclude with battles against the infidel.

As was mentioned earlier, *Sir Isumbras* survives in nine manuscripts and numerous prints. The earliest manuscript, Gray's Inn, is a 104-line fragment dated around 1350. This text closely resembles that of Gonville and Caius College, Cambridge MS 175, the second oldest manuscript, dating from 1425–50, which is the basis for the present edition. These texts differ significantly from the Thornton, Ashmole, and Advocates' manuscripts, which give the story a more "heroic" treatment. The Cotton and Naples manuscripts form a third group; their versification closely resembles that of the Gonville and Caius text. For that reason the Cotton was chosen to supply the lines of folio 91, which is missing from the Cambridge volume.

The Cambridge manuscript was produced in the southeast Midlands; its text of Isumbras shows a mixture of dialectal forms, as the poem itself was composed in the northeast Midlands. Characteristic northeast Midland features include the use of *are* (rather than more southerly *bee[n]*) for the indicative present plural of *to be*: the use of *-ande* (not *-ing*) for the participial ending, as in *wayvande*; and the spellings *swyche* and *mekyll*, among others. However, characteristically southeast Midland forms are present in the third-person plural pronouns, which begin with *h- (hem)*, not northerly *th- (them)*, and in the initial spelling *sch- (schal)* rather than *s- (sall)*.

MANUSCRIPTS AND PRINTS

Indexed as item 1184 in Boffey and Edwards, eds., *New Index of Middle English Verse*:

- London, Gray's Inn MS 20 (1350), fol. 228, 104-line fragment corresponding to Gonville and Caius, MS lines 216–308.
- Cambridge, Gonville and Caius College MS 175 (1425–50), fols. 98r–106 [Base-text for this edition].
- Lincoln, Lincoln Cathedral MS 91, called the Thornton MS (c. 1440), fols. 109r–114v.

- Naples, Biblioteca Nazionale MS 13 B 9 (1457), fols. 114r–115r, a fragment containing the first 122 lines.
- London, British Library MS Cotton Caligula A.ii (1450–1500), fols. 130r–134r.
- Oxford, Bodleian Library MS Ashmole 61 (1475–1500), fols. 9r–16r.
- Edinburgh, National Library of Scotland Advocates' MS 19.3.1 (1475–1500), fols. 48r–56v.
- Oxford, Bodleian Library MS Douce 261 (1564), fols. 1r–7v.
- Oxford, University College MS 142 (end 14 c), fol. 128r, a 17-line fragment.

- Oxford, Bodleian Library Douce fragment f 37. London: Wynkynde Worde or W. Copland, 1530? 1550? (*STC* 14281), one leaf.
- Oxford, Bodleian Library 1119. London: William Copland?, c. 1530 (*STC* 14282), one leaf.
- London, British Library C 21c61, Garrick Collection. London: William Copland, c. 1530 (*STC* 14282), fifteen leaves.
- Boston, Harvard University Library. London: John Skot, c. 1525 (*STC* 14280.1), eight leaves.
- Boston, Harvard University Library. London: I. Treveris, c. 1530 (*STC* 14280.2), one leaf.

SIR ISUMBRAS

Hende in halle and ye wole her *Gentlefolk; if you; hear*
Off eldres that before us wer *Of*
 That lyfede in are thede. *earlier times*
Jhesu Cryst, hevene kynge,
5 Geve hem alle hys blessyng *them*
 And hevene unto oure mede. *reward*
I wold yow telle off a knyght
That was bothe hardy and wyght *able*
 And doughty man of dede. *valiant*
10 Hys name was callyd Sere Ysumbras;
So doughty a knyght as he was
 There levyd non in lede. *among those folk*

He was mekil man and long *powerful; lean*
With armes grete and body strong
15 And fair was to se.
He was long man and heygh, *lanky; tall*
The fayreste that evere man seygh; *saw*
 A gret lord was he.
Menstralles he lovyd wel in halle
20 And gaf hem ryche robes withalle, *gave them rich robes, moreover*
 Bothe golde and fe. *property*
Off curteysye he was kyng *courtesy*
And of his mete never nothyng *meat (hospitality)*
 In worlde was non so free. *generous*

25 A fayr lady hadde hee
As any man myghte see,
 With tungge as I yow nevene. *tell*
Bytwen hem they hadde chyldren thre,
The fayreste that myghte on lyve be *alive*
30 Undyr God off hevene.
Swyche pryde in his herte was brought,
On Jhesu Cryst thoghte he nought
 Ne on His names sevene. *Nor*
So longe he levede in that pryde

35 That Jhesu wolde no lenger abyde;
 To hym he sente a stevenne. *voice (summons)*

 So hit byfell upon a day
 The knyghte wente hym to play,
 His foreste for to se.
40 As he wente by a derne sty, *secret; place*
 He herde a fowle synge hym by
 Hye upon a tre. *High*
 He seyde, "Welcome Syr Isumbras,
 Thow haste forgete what thou was
45 For pryde of golde and fee.
 The kynge of hevenn the gretheth so: *greets you thus*
 In yowthe or elde thou schall be wo, *age; afflicted*
 Chese whedur hyt shall be." *choose which*

 With carefull herte and sykynge sore *sighing*
50 He fell upon his knees thore, *there*
 His hondes up he helde.
 "Worldes welthe I woll forsake,
 To Jhesu Criste I wyll me take, *entrust myself*
 To Hym my sowle I yelde.
55 In yowthe I may ryde and go, *walk*
 In elde I may noght do so, *old age*
 My lymes wyll wex unwelde. *limbs will become unsteady*
 Lorde, yf it Thy wyll be,
 In yowthe sende me poverté
60 And welthe in myne elde."

 Away that fowle toke hys flyghte
 Alone he lette that drurye knyghte, *left; dejected*
 Full sone he wente his wey;
 And whenne he that fowle had lore, *bird; lost sight of*
65 His steede that was so lyghte byfore,
 Dede under hym ley. *Dead*
 His hawkes and his howndes bothe
 Ronne to wode as they were wrothe *Fled; forest as if crazy*
 And eche on taketh here weye. *one; their*
70 What wonder was thowgh hym were wo?
 On fote byhoveth hym to go, *foot obliged*
 To peyne turned his pleye. *pain*

 And as he by the wode wente
 A lytyll knave was to hym sente,
75 Come rennynge hym ageyne. *Came running toward*
 Worse tydynges he hym tolde,
 "Syr, brent be thy byggynges bolde, *burned; buildings*

 Thy menne be manye sleyne.
 Ther is noght lefte on lyve
80 But thy children and thy wyfe, *Except*
 Withouten any delayne." *delay*
 He seyde, "If they on lyve be,
 My wyfe and my children thre,
 Yet were I never so fayne." *happy*

85 Forth he wente hymself alone;
 His herdemen he mette eche one,
 He seyde, "What eyleth yowe?" *troubles*
 "Owre fees ben fro us revedde, *livestock; taken*
 There is nothynge ylevedde, *left*
90 Nowghte on stede to thy plowe." *one horse for*
 The wepte and gaf hem yll, *They; were upset*
 The knyghte badde they schold be styll: *still*
 "I wyte nowght yow this wo, *caused*
 For God bothe geveth and taketh
95 And at His wyll ryches maketh
 And pore men also."

 A dolfull syghte thenne ganne he se,
 His wyfe and his chylderen thre
 Owte of the fyre were fledde.
100 As naked as they were borne
 There they stode hym byforne,
 Were browghte out of here bedde.
 Yette chaunged no thyng his ble *expression*
 Tyll he sawe his wyfe and children thre
105 That erste were comely cladde. *before*
 The lady badde her children be blythe;
 "For yette I se your fader on lyve, *alive*
 For nothynge be ye dradde."

 They wepte and gafe hem ylle, *were upset*
110 Her fader badde they sholde be stylle *Their*
 And wepe nowghte so sore; *sorely*
 "All the sorow that we ben inne,
 Hit is for owre wykked synne;
 Worthy we be well more. *We deserve even more suffering*
115 And we full evell kan wyrke, *poorly*
 Owre frendes of us wyll yrke, *will be annoyed with us*
 Of londe I rede we fare. *From [this]; advise we depart*
 Of myselfe have I no thowghte
 But that I may geve my menn noghte,
120 For hem is all my kare."

	He toke his mantell of ryche pall	*cloth*
	And over his wyfe he lette hit fall	
	With a drewrye mode.	*dejected spirit*
	His ryche sirkote then toke he	*surcoat*
125	To his pore chyldren thre	
	That naked byfore hym stode;	
	"Do ye shull after my rede,	*as I advise*
	To seke God wher He was quykke and dede	*seek; lived and died*
	That for us shedde His blode.	
130	For Jhesu Criste that is so fre	*gracious*
	Hym to seche wher it be,	*seek*
	He sende us our lyves fode."	*sustenance*

	With his knyfe he share	*cut*
	A crosse on hys sholder bare	
135	In storye as clerkes seye.	
	They that wer here frendes byfore,	*their*
	They wepte and syked sore,	*sighed bitterly*
	Her songe was "wellawaye."	*Their*
	The knyghte and the lady hende	*gracious*
140	Toke here leve at her frende,	*from their friends*
	And forth they wente her waye.	
	For hem wepte both olde and yynge	*young*
	For that doolfull partynge,	
	Forsothe as I you seye.	

145	For they bare with hem nothynge	
	That longed to here spendynge,	*pertained*
	Nother golde nor fee,	
	But for to begge here mete	
	Where they myghte ony gete,	
150	For love of seynt charyté.	*blessed*
	Thorow two kynges londes they gan pas	
	As Cristes owenn wyll was,	
	They and here children thre.	
	Suche sorwe as they wer inne	
155	That wer wonte for to wynne,	*prosper*
	Grette dole hit was to se.	

	Sex deyes were come and gone,	*Six days*
	Mete ne drynke hadde they none	
	For honger they wepte sore,	
160	They kome by a water kene,	*swift*
	Ther over they wolde fayn have bene.	*gladly*
	Thenne was her kare the more.	*care*

His eldeste sone he toke there *he (Isumbras) took*
And over the water he hym bere
165 And sette hym by a brome. *broom-plant*
He seyde, "Leve sone, sytte her styll *Dear*
Whyle I fette thy broder the tyll *fetch; to you*
 And pley the with a blome." *flower*
The knyghte was both good and hende *gracious*
170 And over the water he ganne wende; *returned*
 His othur sone he nome. *took*
He bare hym over the water wylde;
A lyon took his othir chylde
 Are he to lond come. *Before*

175 The knyght was hende and good,
Therfore he made sory mod, *had sad thoughts*
 Forsothe as I yow say.
A lybard com and took that othir *leopard*
And bar hym evene to his brothir
180 And sone wente away.
The lady cryde and grette ful ille *wept*
And thoughte hereselven for to spylle *kill*
 On londe ther sche lay. *where*
The knyght bad the lady, "Be stylle
185 And thanke we God of His wille,"
 Thus thenne gan he say.

No wondyr though here hertes wer sore;
Bothe her chyldren loste they thore,
 Here eldere chyldren twoo.
190 Hys wyff was hym leeff and dere, *beloved; precious*
And ovyr the watyr he here bere, *bore her*
 Hys yongeste sone alsoo.
Thorwgh forest they wente dayes three
Tyl they come to Grykkyssche see, *Greek*
195 They grette and wer full woo. *wept*
As they stood upon the lande
They sawe faste come saylande
 Three hundryd schyppys and moo.

With topcastelis sett on lofte *(see note)*
200 Rychely thenne were they wroughte
 With joye and mekyl pryde. *much*
A hethene kyng was therinne
That Crystendome com to wynne, *conquer*
 To wakkyn woo ful wyde. *stir up*
205 The knyght thoughte he wolde lende *remain*

At the havene at the wodes ende, *harbor*
 A lytyl ther bysyde. *short distance away*

The knyght thoghte he wolde abyde, *wait*
Men he sawgh bothe goo and ryde,
210 Moo than he cowde nevene. *count*
The knyght sayde to the lady free,
"What maner men, dame, may these bee?"
 With ful lowde a stevene. *voice*
"We have thorwgh this forest gon,
215 Mete ne drynk hadde we non,
 Now are gon dayes sevene.
Go we aske hem off her mete,
Yif that we may ony gete,
 For the Lord off hevene."

220 To that galey gan they wynne *go*
That the Sawdon was inne, *Sultan*
 That rychely was wrought.
They askyd hym sum lyvys fode *sustenance*
For Goddes love that deyde on Rode, *the Cross*
225 That they scholde werne hem nought. *refuse*
Soone as he herde hem crye
He sayde they were come to aspye, *spy*
 "My schyp they han besought.
I comaunde yow, bete hym away!
230 They leve not upon my lay, *believe; religion*
 Be Mahoun that the bought." *Mahomet who redeemed you*

Thenne sayde a knyght to the kyng,
"Ser, this is a wondyr thyng,
 Yone pore man to see.
235 Hys lemes are longe, hys bones grete, *limbs*
Hys eyen are graye and over stepe, *bright*
 A knyght hym semes to bee.
Hys wyff is whyt so whales bon,
A fayrere sawgh I nevere non,
240 Bryght so blosme on tree.
He is a fayr man and hyghe,
A fayrere sawe I never with yye,
 A gentyl man is hee."

The Sawdon dool hym thoughte *thought it sad*
245 And bad they scholde be forth ibroughte,
 "I wole hem see with syght."
Whenne he hem saw, hym rewyd sore, *rued*
So fayre as they bothe wore,

That they ne were clothid a-ryght.

250 "Man, wylt thou leve on my lay *believe in my faith*
And doo alle thy goodes away *put aside all your gods*
 And helpe me in my fyght?
Red gold schal be thy mede;
Yyf thou be doughty man of dede *deeds*
255 I schal the make a knyght."

Stylle stood Ser Ysumbras
And sawgh an hethene man he was;
 "Sere," he sayde, "nay!
God wolde that nevere more
260 That I gayn Crystyndome wore *against; was*
 And forsake my lay. *faith*
We have thorwgh this forest gon,
Mete ne drynke ne gat we non,
 This is the sevynthe day.
265 We aske the sum lyvys fode, *ask from you sustenance*
For Hys love that deyde on Rode, *on the Cross*
 And lat us gon oure way."

The Sawdon beheeld that lady thare,
Hym thoughte an aungyl that sche ware *angel*
270 Come adoun from hevene.
"Man, I wold geve the gold and fee,
And thou that wymman wole selle me,
 More than thou can nevene. *name*
I wole the geve an hundryd pound
275 Off penyys that be hool and round *coins*
 And ryche robes sevene.
Sche schal be qwene of my lond,
And alle men bowe unto her hond
 And non withstonde her stevene." *command*

280 Ser Ysumbras sayde, "Nay!
My wyff I wole nought selle away,
 Though ye me for her sloo. *slay*
I weddyd her in Goddys lay
To holde here to myn endyng day,
285 Bothe for wele or woo."
The gold upon hys mantal they told *counted*
And to himselff they gan it folde[1]
 And took hys wyff hym froo.
And sithen on the land they hym casten *then*

[1] *They folded the cloak and gave it to him (Isumbras)*

290 And beten hym tyl hys sydys brasten *burst*
 And maden hys flesch al bloo. *blue*

 The Sawdon with hys owne hand
 Corownyd here qwene of his land
 To sende here over the see.
295 A chartre in the maner he bonde *He made a charter such that*
 Yiff sche evere come to londe
 His qwene thenne scholde sche bee.
 Whenne the woundyd man myghte stand
 He took his sone be the hande *by*
300 And forth thenne wente hee.
 Sith that the schyp was maad yare *made ready*
 With maryneres forth to fare
 With that lady free.

 Whenne the schyp was redy to goo
305 The lady cryyd and was ful woo
 And fel before the kyng.
 Sche sayde, "Sere, par charyté *for [Fr.]*
 A bone that thou woldyst graunte me *boon*
 Withouten ony dwellyng. *delay*
310 That myn hosebonde may speke with me
 Ar I passe beyonde the see, *Before*
 Alone, a privy thyng."
 Seththyn he callys hym agayn, *Then*
 Theroff the lady was ful fayn, *glad*
315 Here tokene was a ryng.

 There was joye to sen hem mete *see them meet*
 With clyppyng and with kyssyng swete *embracing*
 Whenne he to the schyp scholde goo.
 Sche sayde, "Lord, ful woo is me
320 That I ne were drownyd in the see,
 Schal we departe on twoo.
 Into the land that I am inne,
 Fonde thyselff for to wynne;
 The kyng schole we sloo.[1]
325 Thenne schole ye be kyng off that lond
 And alle men bowe unto youre hond
 And kevere yit al oure woo." *recover from*

 Mete and drynk sche dede hym geve,
 A sevene nyght that he myghte leve,

[1] *Devise a way to come into the land where I am, / And we will slay the king (Sultan)*

330 Hys lytyl sone and he.
 The lady soffte and mylde
 Kyste her lord and her chylde
 And swownyd sythis three. *swooned three times*
 They drowgh up sayl off ryche hewe; *raised; color*
335 The wynd was lowde and over hem blewe *loud*
 With that lady free.
 The knyght on the land hym sette
 And for hys wyffe sore he grette *wept*
 Whyl that he the sayl myghte see.

340 He took his sone be the hand *by*
 And wente up upon the land
 By holtes that were hore. *forests; grey*
 They sette hem doun undyr a tree,
 Neyther off hem myghte other see
345 So hadde they wept so sore.
 Mete and drynk they forth drowgh;
 Whenne the knyght hadde eete inowgh *eaten enough*
 He wepyd ful yare. *openly*
 In his mantel of scarlet red
350 Among the gold he putte his bred
 And forth with hym it bare.

 Thenne come they to an hyl ful hy *hill; steep*
 And there they thought al nyght to ly,
 They myghte no lenger dree. *endure*
355 On the morwen whenne it was day,
 An egle bar the gold away,
 The rede cloth whenne he see.
 A sory man thenne walkes hee
 And folewyd to the Grykkysche see;
360 The fowl ovyr cam flye. *came flying over*
 By that was comen an unicorne, *At that moment*
 Hys yongeste sone awey was borne —
 Swyche sorwe gan he drye. *endure*

 Offte was hym wele and woo,
365 But never so sory as he was thoo;
 He sette hym on a ston. *himself; stone*
 He sayde: "Lord, ful woo is me,
 I have lost wyff and my children three.
 Now am I lefte alone.
370 Jesu that weredest in hevene coroun *who wears*
 Wysse me the way to sum toun, *Show*
 Al amis am I gone.
 Lady of hevene, bryght and schene, *radiant*

Flour of wymmen, of hevene qwene, *Flower*
375 To the I make my mone." *lament*

As he wente be a lowe, *by a hill*
Smethy-men herde he blowe, *Blacksmiths; work the bellows*
 A grete fyre sawe he glowe.
He askyd hem mete par charyté, *them for food*
380 They bad hym swynke for "so doo wee, *work*
 We have non othir plowe." *no other plow (way to get food)*
Thenne answers the knyght agayn,
"For mete wolde I swynke fayn." *work eagerly*
 Faste he bar and drowgh. *carried; brought*
385 They goven hym mete and drynk anon
And taughten hym to bere ston;
 Thenne hadde he schame inough.

Thus they taughte hym to bere ston
Tyl the twelve monethis be comen and gon;
390 They wroughten hym ful wowgh. *made; mistake*
Be that he cowde make a fyre,
 Thenne took he mannys hyre *(see note)*
 And wroughte more than twoo. *accomplished*
Al the longe sevene yere
395 A smethis man was he there
 And yit monethis twoo.
By that he hadde hym armes dyght, *fashioned*
Al that fel for a knyght
 To batayle whenne he wolde goo.

400 Al the sevene yer long
The Sawdon werryd on Crystene lond
 And stroyede it ful wyde. *ravaged it widely*
The Crystene kynges fleygh so long *(see note); fled*
Tyl he hadde purveyyd batayle strong, *assembled a great army*
405 The Sarezynys to abyde. *meet [in battle]*
A day of batayle thenne was sette,
Crystene and hethene scholde be mete
 A lytyl ther bysyde.
In hys armes that he hadde wrought
410 On hors that coles hadde ibrought
 To batayle faste he hyde. *hastened*

Betwen twoo hyllys tho come hee,
Crystene and hethene ther he see,
 The twoo kynges hadde brought
415 Ayther batayle on a lowe; *Each one's battalions; hill*
Trumpys herde he lowd blowe

And wepne he saw on lofte. *weapons; lifted*
The knyght was hende and free *clever; noble*
And sette hym doun upon his knee. *placed himself*
420 To Jhesu he besoughte *(see note)*
To sende hym grace in the feelde,
The hethene houndes that he myghte yeld *return*
 The woo they hadde hym wroughte.

The knyght was hende and good *knightly; virtuous*
425 And styrte up with egre mood *angry manner*
 And thryys he gan hym sayn. *thrice; assay (charge)*
He rod as scharp as a flynt,
Myghte non withstonde his dynt *blow*
 Tyl his sory horse were slayn.
430 Whenne he to the erthe soughte, *went*
An eerl off the batayle hym broughte *from*
 To an hygh mountayn.
There he chaunges al his wede *armor*
And horsyd was on a good stede *steed*
435 And wente anon agayn. *went back right away*

Whenne he was armyd on that stede,
It is sene yit where hys hors yede *went*
 And schal be evere more.
As sparkele glydes of the glede *ember*
440 In that stour he made many blede *battle; bleed*
 And wroughte hem woundes sore.
He rod up unto the mountayn,
The Sawdon soone hath he slayn
 And manye that with hym wore.
445 Al that day lastyd that fyght,
Ser Ysumbras that noble knyght
 Wan the batayle thore.

Whenne the hethene kyng was islayn,
The Crystene kyng was ful fayn,
450 He gaff hym gold and fee.
"Where is now the noble knyght
That steryd hym so weel in fyght *governed himself*
 That I hym nought see?"
Knyghtes and squyers han hym sought
455 And before the kyng hym brought,
 Ful sore woundyd was he.
They askyd what was his name;
He sayde, "Sere, a smethis man.
 What wole ye doo with me?"

460 The Crystene kyng sayde than,
 "I trowe nevere that smethis man
 In werre were halff so wyght." *valiant*
 "I bydde yow geve me mete and drynk *food*
 And what that I wold afftyr thynk *whatever I think of later*
465 Tyl I have keveryd my myght." *regained my strength*
 The kyng a gret oth he sware
 As sone as he hool ware
 That he wolde dubbe hym knyght.
 In a nunnerye they hym levyd *left*
470 To hele the woundes in hys heuyd *head*
 That he took in that fyght.

 The nunnes of hym were ful fayn
 For he hadde the Sawdon slayn
 And manye hethene houndes.
475 For hys sorwe they gunne sore rewe,
 Every day they salvyd hym newe
 And stoppyd weel hys woundes. *applied salves to him*
 They goven hym meetes and drynkes lythe *gave; soothing*
 And heleden hys woundes also swythe *quickly*
480 In a lytyl stounde. *time*
 He bethoughte hym fol yore *readily*
 That he wolde dwelle ther no more
 Thenne that he were sounde. *healthy*

 He took hys leve withouten les *delay*
485 And thankyd fayre the pryores *prioress*
 And the nunnes hende. *gracious*
 He purveyyd hym bothe scryp and pyke *bag; staff*
 And made hym a palmer lyke *pilgrim*
 Redy for to wende.
490 The ryghte wey thenne took he
 Tyl he come to the Grykkyssche see
 As God Hymself hym sente.
 A schyp fond he redy thare
 On to Acres for to fare,
495 And thedyr faste he wente.

 Whenne he was in Acres lente, *arrived*
 With wery bones up he wente
 And in to the cyté yede. *went*
 Sevene yer was he palmer thore
500 In hungyr and in thurst ful sore
 In book as men rede.
 As he yede upon the day,
 Ryght so upon the nyght he lay

 In hys pore wede. *clothes*

505 Off hys paynes thoughte hym nought ille,

 Goddes hestes to fulfylle *wishes*

 For hys ovyrdon dede. *egregious*

 Al the cyté he has thorwgh gon,

 Mete ne drynk ne gat he non

510 Ne hous to herberwe inne. *lodge*

 Besyde the burgh of Jerusalem *fortress*

 He sette hym by a welle-strem,

 Sore wepande for hys synne. *Sorely weeping*

 And as he sat, aboute mydnyght,

515 Ther come an aungyl fayr and bryght

 And broughte hym bred and wyn.

 He sayde, "Palmer, weel thou bee,

 The Kyng off hevene gretes wel the,

 Forgeven is synne thyn.

520 Reste the weel Sere Ysumbras,

 Forgeven is thy trespas

 With tungge I say sertayn.

 The gretes weel oure hevene Kyng

 And geves the Hys blessyng

525 And byddes the turne agayn." *you*

 The knyght was hende and free *gentle*

 And settes hym doun upon hys kne

 And wepte sore for fayne. *joy*

 But he hadde no bete won, *Unless; better fortune*

530 He wyste nevere whedyr to gon, *knew*

 But evere to walken in payne.

 Al a land he yede thorwgh *went*

 Tyl he come to a ryche burgh;

 A fayr castel ther stoode.

535 He herde telle ther dwellyd a qwene

 That was bothe bryght and schene, *radiant; splendid*

 And gret wurd off her yode. *her reputation spread*

 Ilke day sche gaff at her gate *Every*

 To pore men off every state *state*

540 Florynys ryche and goode. *Florins*

 "Weel wer me myghte I on gete, *one*

 Therwith I myghte bye my mete

 And come to lyvys fode."

 Whenne he come to the castel gate,

545 Pore men gold to take

 Fond he many on thore. *many a one there*

Every man hadde a floreyn, *coin*
Sere Ysumbras was ful feyn
 For hym hungryd sore.
550 Pore men that myghte nought goo *walk*
Schee took in fyffty and moo,
 Whylke that febeleste wore. *Those who were most feeble*
In they tooken Ser Ysumbras
That a pore palmer was,
555 For hym they rewen sore. *had great pity*

The ryche qwene in halle was set,
Knyghtes her servyd to hond and feet
 In ryche robys off palle. *fine cloth*
In the floor a cloth was layde, *carpet*
560 "The pore palmer," the styward sayde,
 "Schal sytte above yow alle."
Meete and drynk forth they brought,
He sat stylle and eet ryght nought *ate nothing*
 But lokyd aboute the halle.
565 So mekyl he sawgh of game and gle, *amusements*
Swyche merthes he was wunt to see, *accustomed*
 The teres he leet doun falle.

Stylle he sat and eet ryght nought,
The qwene wundryd in her thought,
570 To a knyght gan sche say:
"Tak a chayer and a quysschene, lat see, *cushion (see note)*
And lat the palmere sytte be me *by*
 That he me telle may
Off manye aventures that he has sene
575 In dyverse landes there he has bene *where*
 Be manye a wylde way."
Soone ther was a chayer sset
And the qwene therinne isett,
 He tolde the qwene off hys lay. *story*

580 Goode tales the qwene he tolde,
The qwene askyd whethir he wold
 Have ony other mete.
Ryche meetes forth they broughte, *delicacies*
The qwene wonderyd in here thoughte
585 Why he wolde nought eete.
"For my lordes soule I wole the geve —
Or for his love yiff that he leve — [1]

[1] *For my lord's soul, or for his love if he is alive, I will always give you clothes and food*

Riche cloth and meete,
A chaumbyr fayr and free
590 And a knave to serve thee
Withinne the castel gete."

Now dwelles the palmere there
Tyl he were hool and fere *able to go*
And servede in the halle.
595 He was fayr man and hygh,
Alle lovede hym that hym sygh, *saw*
Ful redy he was on to calle.
For hym they deden a turnement bede *command*
And horseden hym on a sory stede
600 And yit he conqueryd alle.
Sykyrly as I yow say, *truly*
Many a Sareyyn he slowgh that day
Undyr the castel walle.

Whenne Sere Ysumbras was in feelde,
605 Was non so doughty undir scheelde
That durste hym mete on stede. *horseback*
Sum knyght he gaff swyche a clout *blow*
That bothe hys eyen styrten out *eyes burst*
And manye he made to blede.
610 He caste the Sareyynys in dyke and slak *ditch; ravine*
And barst hem bothe nekke and bak, *broke*
And manye fledde for drede.
The ryche qwene sat and lowgh *laughed*
And sayde, "My palmere is good inowgh,
615 He is wurthy to fede."

Thenne fel it upon a day
The knyght wente hym for to play
As it was er hys kynde. *formerly; nature*
A fowles nest he fond on hygh, *bird's*
620 A red cloth thereinne he sygh
Wayvande with the wynde.
To the nest he gan wynne, *he went*
Hys owne mantyl he fond therinne,
The gold there gan he fynde.
625 Whenne he sawgh the rede gold
That hys wyff was fore sold,
Thenne hadde he sorowe in mynde.

The gold to hys chaumbyr he bar
And undyr hys bed he putte it thar
630 And wente wepande away.

Whenne he on the gold gan see
He thoughte on hys wyff and on hys chyldren thre,
 Hys song was "weylaway!"
Wer he nevere so blythe off mood
635 Whenne he out off hys chaumbyr yood, *went*
 He wepte siththen al day. *afterwards*
So longe levede he that lyf
Thorwgh the court it was ful ryff, *well known*
 To the qwene they gan it say.

640 Thenne it befel upon a day
The knyght wente hym to play, *took leisure time*
 Hys sorewe for to mene. *bemoan*
Squyers brak up the chaumbyr dore *forced open*
And seygh the gold in the flore, *saw*
645 They schewyd it to the qwene.
Whenne sche seygh the gold with syght
Thenne swownyd that lady bryght,
 For sche it er hadde sene. *formerly*
Sche kyssyd it and sayde, "Allas,
650 This was my lordys, Sere Ysumbras,
 My lord was wunt to bene."

 (see note)
To the knyghtes sche it tolde
Hou sche for that monay was solde,
 "My lord was beten therfore.
655 Whenne ye may the palmer see
Byddes hym come and speke with me,
 Therto me longes sore."
The palmere come in to the halle,
For counsayl sche gan hym calle
660 And askyd hym ryght thore,
"Where thou this gold wan?
Was thou evere gentyl man?"
 Hys care was more and more.

With careful herte and drery cher *dejected countenance*
665 He gaff the qwene an answere,
 On hys knees he hym sette.
The fyrste tale that he here tolde,
"Therefore, madame, my wyff was solde, *For that*
 Myselff bar manye buffette.
670 Three chyldryn I have lorn, *lost*
My mantyl was awey iborne
 And in a nest I it fette." *found*
Thenne knelyd the lady fayr of face

And thankyd God of His grace
675 That they togedere wer mette.
 (see note)

There was joye to sen hem mete
With laykyng and with kyssyng swete *loving behavior*
 In armes for to folde.
Aythir off hem was ful fayn, *Each; glad*
680 No lenger thenne cowde they layn: *remain silent*
 To knyghtes they it tolde.
A ryche brydale dede they bede, *wedding feast; command*
Ryche and pore thedyr yede, *went*
 Welcome who so wolde.
685 They corownyd Ser Ysumbras ryght
And made hym kyng, that noble knyght,
 For he was stout and bolde.

Then was he kyng, Ser Ysumbras,
Off more welthe thenne evere he was
690 And keveryd out off care. *recovered from*
Hys Crystyndom he gan to kythe *make known*
And comaundyd crystenyd to be swythe[1]
 Tho that hethene ware.
The hethene were at on asent, *in agreement*
695 Whoso to hys parlement went,
 To brenne and make hym bare: *burn; destitute*
"And yiff we may hymselven hent *catch*
To brenne hym or to make hym schent *disgraced*
 And alle tho off Crystys lare." *belief*

700 A day off batayle ther was sette
The Crystene and the hethene to be mette,
 Sere Ysumbras to slo. *slay*
Aftyr Sareyynys gunne they sende,
There they wente fer and hende;
705 There come hethene kynges twoo.
Sere Ysumbras made hym yare *prepared himself*
To the batayle for to fare,
 With hym wente no moo.
Whenne he was horsyd on a stede
710 Hys men fayleden hym at nede,
 Hys folk wenten hym froo.

Sere Ysumbras was bold and kene
And took hys leve at hys qwene *from*

[1] *And commanded those that were heathen to be christened quickly*

 And syghed wondyr sore.
715 He sayde, "Madame, have good day,
 Sekyrly as I yow say *Truly*
 For now and ever more."

 "Helpe me, Sere, that I were dyght *dressed*
 In armes as it were a knyght,
720 I wole with yow fare.
 Yif God wolde us grace sende
 That we myghte togedere ende
 Thenne don were al my care."

 Soone was the lady dyght
725 In armes as it were a knyght,
 He gaff here spere and scheelde.
 Agayne thirty thousand Sareynys and mo
 Ther come no moo but they twoo
 Whenne they metten in feelde.
730 Ryght as they scholden have slayn bee,
 Ther come rydynge knyghtes three
 On bestes that were wylde;
 On a lyberd and an unycorn
 And on a lyoun he rod beforn,
735 That was her eldeste chylde.

 The chyldryn ferden as they were wode, *went about; crazy (see note)*
 They slowen al that beforn hem stode,
 Gret joye it was to see.
 They slowen hethene kyngys twoo
740 And othere Sarayynys manye moo,
 Twenty thousand and three.
 Sere Ysumbras prayde hem thare
 That they wolden with hym fare
 Al nyght with hym to be.
745 They answerde hym with wurdes hende, *gracious words*
 "The grace off God us hedyr sende. *sent*
 Thyn owne chyldren be we."

 A noble burgh ther was besyde; *town (see note)*
 Sere Ysumbras thedyr gan ryde,
750 Hys sones he gan thedyr lede. *lead*
 In a chaumbyr fayr and bryght
 Here clothyng was ful redy dyght,
 They chaungyd al here wede.
 Off nothyng was hem wane *lacking*
755 Neyther of wylde, neyther of tame, *domesticated (meats)*
 Those doughty men off dede.

Thenne three londes gunne they wynne *did they conquer*
And crystenyd alle that was therinne,
 In romaunse as men rede.

760 Thenne was the kyng Ser Ysumbras
Off more welthe thenne evere he was,
 Thre londes hadde he thare.
Everylkon he gaf a land *Each one*
And corownyd hem with hys owne hand,
765 Whedyr so they wolden fare.
They levyd and deyde in good entente,
Unto hevene here soules wente
 Whenne that they dede ware. *dead*
Jhesu Cryst, hevene Kyng,
770 Geve us ay Hys blessyng *always*
 And schylde us from care. *protect*

 NOTES TO *SIR ISUMBRAS*

In the text initial *ff* is transcribed as *F*. Terminal *-ff* I have left as in the manuscript, though usually modern transcription would be *-f* as in *off* for *of*.

Before 1 The text is preceded by an incipit: *Hic incipit de milite Ysumbras.*

1–18 Though the manuscripts all vary in their introductory stanzas, the Cotton manuscript includes a longer depiction of Isumbras' prosperity, with greater emphasis on his courtesy.

> God that made bothe erthe and hevenne
> And all this worlde in deyes sevenn,
> That is full of myghthe,
> Sende us alle his blessynge,
> Lasse and more, olde and yynge,
> And kepe us day and nyghte.
> I wyll you tell of a knyghte
> That dowghty was in eche a fyghte, *every*
> In towne and eke in felde; *also*
> Ther durste no man his dynte abyde, *blows sustain*
> Ne no man ageyn hym ryde,
> With spere ne with schelde.
>
> A man he was ryche ynowghe
> Of oxen to drawe in his plowghe
> And stedes also in stalle;
> He was bothe curteys and hende, *diligent*
> Every man was his frende
> And loved he was with all.
> A curteys man and hende he was;
> His name was kalled Syr Isumbras,
> Bothe curteys and fre, *noble*
> His gentylnesse nor his curtesye
> There kowthe no man hit discrye;
> A ffull good man was he.

3, 6 These lines are supplied from the Thornton manuscript. They do not appear in the Gonville-Caius text.

8 *hardy.* MS: *handy.* Broh's emendation.

9 This line is written in the margin of the manuscript, as are other tag lines on the first folio.

10	*Ysumbras.* The first "element" of this name seems to derive from the Germanic *isen* 'iron' and, according to Purdie, "continental records reveal a great variety of early medieval names containing this evocative element" ("Generic Identity," p. 119).
15	*fair.* The first letter is obscured by deterioration of the manuscript, and the fact that this is written in the margin.
19–21	Fowler has examined the significance of clothing and nakedness in *Sir Isumbras*, and states that "as these features of the narrative recur, they accumulate into the topos of investiture." In this opening passage, Isumbras is "established as a paragon of wealth and 'gentylnesse', in part by his habit of giving clothing to his followers" ("Romance Hypothetical," p. 100).
21	*and.* Broh's emendation. Parts of the line are not legible in the manuscript.
32–33	MS is scarcely legible. Broh and Schleich agree on this reading, which is based, in part, on the Cotton MS.
33	*names sevene.* Jewish tradition offers several versions of the Deity's seven names, generally agreeing on Adonai, Eloheim, El, and Yahwey Jehova. Others are Ely Saboth, Alpha, Omega, Messian, Pastor, and Agnus. They were to be spoken and written with care, for their expression evoked mystic powers.
35–172	These lines are supplied from the Cotton manuscript. A folio (fol. 97) has been cut from the Gonville-Caius text.
41	Birds are conventional messengers, though less common in romance. The Holy Ghost traditionally is depicted as a dove. A stag is the messenger in the Eustace legend.
64–102	Fowler ("Romance Hypothetical," p. 101) rightly notes the allusions to Job found in this part of the tale:

> Job-like, Isumbras suffers the loss of his animals, retainers, buildings and riches. His devastation is visually expressed by a 'a dolfull syghte' [line 97] that is as central to the reader's understanding of the tale as it is traumatic to the hero . . . Stripped of their social status, the members of his family stand before him in their original animal bodies. The phrase 'naked as they were borne' alludes to Job 1.21, where Job patiently compares his loss of his children to his state of nakedness at birth and death. This image of lack of clothing resonates as a kind of limit case, a bottom line of human existence. It figures the human body without its social inflections, without dominion of any kind.

100	In the Middle Ages, it was not uncommon to sleep naked.
133–34	Knights departing on Crusade "took the cross," that is, wore red crosses on their surcoats as a sign of their vow to fight for God. In a similar fashion, pilgrims wore badges distinctive of their destinations sewn to their sleeves. A cross indicated a journey to Jerusalem. That Isumbras carves the sign into his flesh demonstrates his extraordinary spiritual zeal, marking his identification as a penitent pilgrim, the first position in the "chain of *social persons* through which Isumbras moves in the course of the plot" (Fowler, "Romance Hypothetical," p. 101).

135 *In storye as clerkes seye.* A romance formula often used to focus attention on the strange, mythic inevitabilities of romance narrative. Compare "in romaunse as men rede," line 759, a line that recurs frequently in Breton Lays found in these same manuscripts and in *Octavian* lines 15, 282, 631, 1182, and 1806. See also line 501 for a further variation on the formula, or *Octavian*, line 1039.

157–62 The Thornton and Advocates' manuscripts include a full stanza here:

> Yitt in a wode thay were gone wylle,
> Towne ne myghte thay none wyne tille
> Als wery als thay were.
> Bot whene thre dayes till ende was gane,
> Mete ne drynke ne had thay nane.
> Thay weped for hungre sore.
> No thynge sawe thay that come of corne
> Bot the floures of the thorne
> Upone those holtes hore.
> Thay entirde than to a water kene;
> The bankes were full ferre bytene,
> And watirs breme als bare. (Lincoln)

157–62 Purdie points out several connections between *Sir Isumbras* and the Old French *Guillaume D'Angleterre.* She argues that because these correlative passages cannot be found in the legend of St. Eustace, *Sir Isumbras* and *Guillaume* have a more specific relationship than one defined simply by their association with the saint's legend and, consequently, the "Man Tried by Fate" grouping. Regarding this particular passage, she links the starving of Isumbras' family to a passage in *Guillaume* where "the royal couple [is] so hungry that . . . the wife threatens to eat one of their baby sons until Guillaume shocks her out of it by offering to cut out some of his own flesh for her" ("Generic Identity," p. 121). See notes for line 315 and lines 356–57 for other passages similar to *Guillaume* as mentioned by Purdie.

168 *pley the* is an emendation based on the Thornton reading (line 176), and suggested by Broh. The Cotton text reads *pleyde*, which is less coherent. Mills gives this as *pley de* with "thee" as a gloss.

182 In the Thornton and Advocates' texts, Isumbras, too, almost kills himself for grief.

194 *Grykkysche see.* The eastern Mediterranean, separating the Christian world from the Muslim world or the West from Jerusalem (see *Octavian*, lines 407 and 569; *Sir Eglamour*, lines 893 and 1063; *Castle of Perseverance*, line 173; and *Richard the Lionhearted*, line 1270) or separating Greece from Troy (see Lydgate's *Troy Book*, line 8017, or the Harley MS *Siege of Troy*, lines 166–71).

199 Topcastles were platforms with battlements at the tops of ships' masts from which missiles could be fired.

203–09 Deterioration of the manuscript here obscures the lettering at the beginning of these lines. My reading follows Broh and Schleich. In line 204, *wakkyn*, Broh reads *walle*.

217 *her*. MS: *hes*. Broh's emendation.

230 *not*. MS: *nt*. Broh's emendation.

 lay. Fowler highlights the "lexical polyvalence" of this word in Middle English, stating that its meanings included the following: law, principle, religion, faith, belief, system of government, system of law enforcement, justice, kingdom, practice, way of life, and custom ("Romance Hypothetical," p. 116).

231 The Sultan's puzzling expression is perhaps due to the combination of two separate lines. The Cotton text gives the second tag line of the stanza as *And with His blode us bowghte* (line 234), and the final tag line as *Of hym [the Sultan] . . . they shulde have noghte* (line 240). Thornton reads *And made this worlde of noghte* (line 248) and *Loke that ye gyffe hym noghte* (line 254). However, there is a tradition, exemplified in the Charlemagne romances, of portraying Muslim worship in Christian forms. It is conceivable that, given this context, the scribe may have noticed nothing incongruous in a Saracen believing he had been "bought" (saved) by Mohammed; certainly the line is formulaic with a Christian referent. Broh points out that the use of "bought" here forms a parallel with the Sultan's attempts to buy Isumbras' services and his wife (lines 271 ff.).

236 *over* may be a mistake for *ever* (see Broh), but this cannot be confirmed by reference to other manuscript readings, since all vary.

240–43 Here deterioration of the manuscript obscures the lines. My reading follows Broh and Schleich with minor variation in lines 240 and 241.

250–55 In effect, the Sultan offers him three new social positions (that of a Muslim, a legal subject of the Sultan, and a knight in the Sultan's retinue) in return for Isumbras making an oath of fealty, one that directly conflicts with his initial vow in lines 52–54 (Fowler, "Romance Hypothetical," p. 107).

272 Perhaps the plot toys loosely with a biblical analogue here, where Abram gives Pharoah Sarah for which they get safety but Pharoah gets plagues. See Genesis 12:10–20; also Genesis 20:1–8 and 26:1–11.

280–85 This reiteration of the wedding vow seeks to justify Isumbras' eventual revenge and conquering of Saracen lands. As Fowler ("Romance Hypothetical," p. 111) states:

 The vow contrasts a Christian ideal of consent with the heathen king's wicked violation of that ideal in three spheres: the political (expressed by his plan to conquer unconsenting Christian territories), the religious (expressed by his attempt to force Isumbras to convert), and the sexual (expressed by the raptus).

288 The abduction by the Sultan of the queen has been linked by Fowler ("Romance Hypothetical," p. 108) with the topos of *raptus*:

 a criminal act that, according to medieval lawyers, covers actions we would now describe as ranging from abduction to rape. Raptus is the mirror-opposite of lawful marriage, because, in canon law if not always in practice, marriage

consisted of an exchange of vows that performs the consent of two qualified persons; raptus, of course, is defined as proceeding by force rather than by consent.

291 All the later manuscripts include a stanza:

> The littill childe one lande was sett
> And sawe how mene his fadir bett,
> He wepid and was full waa.
> The lady grete and gafe hir ill,
> Unnethes thay myght halde hir still
> That ne scho hirselve walde slaa.
> Hir armes scho sprede and lowde gane crye
> And ofte scho cryed one oure lady,
> "Sall we departe in two?
> Allas, for sall I never blythe be,
> My weddede lorde sall I never see.
> Now wakyns all my woo." (Lincoln)

307 *par charyté*. Schleich's emendation. The lettering of the Gonville-Caius manuscript is obscured. Broh reads *perchaunce*, which is less idiomatic.

315 Purdie connects this line to a passage from *Guillaume D'Angleterre* by pointing out that in the Old French tale a ring token also plays a prominent role: "Guillaume's wife recognizes him years later by a ring, while Isumbras' wife manages to give him a ring before she is abducted. In one version of the text, this ring reappears to identify him to her later on" ("Generic Identity," p. 121).

353 *thought* makes better sense than the manuscript's reading, *nought* (perhaps a scribal error brought on by the proximity of *nyght*). Cotton (line 361) reads *thowghte*.

376–97 This reference to ironworking, and the author's fairly specific knowledge of the trade, have suggested to some that the poem was composed near Norfolk, a center for that industry. See Trounce, "English Tail-Rhyme Romances," p. 37.

378 This line has been obliterated in the Gonville-Caius manuscript. It is here supplied from the Cotton text. Broh's emendation.

392 Isumbras is no longer an apprentice and hires himself out at journeyman wages. His ability to build and maintain a good fire would have been valued in a smithy.

395–99 According to Fowler, Isumbras' position as a smith is a pivotal point in his journey back to noble status: "He forges armour as if he were reconstituting the social person of the knight he once was: he rebuilds his social body as he builds the armour" ("Romance Hypothetical," p. 102).

403 The plural *kynges* does not agree with the singular pronoun in the following line. The Thornton manuscript refers to kings throughout the passage, the Cotton refers to one.

417 The manuscript reads *wepne*, but the plural provides a smoother reading, and it occurs in the Cotton manuscript. Thornton refers to *swerdes*.

420–24 The Advocates' manuscript contains lines which make the prayer one for
 vengeance:

> Ther he saw rydand in felde
> Mony semely under schelde
> That knyths were hym thought.
> "Lord, thou leve me myght in feld
> The hethen sowden that I myth yelde
> This wo that he me wrogth.
> For and I myght ons with hym mete
> Syche a stroke I schuld hym reche,
> That ys dede chuldder be bogth.

436–47 The Advocates' manuscript includes a greatly expanded and more heroic ac-
 count of the battle (33 lines), which lasts three days. Isumbras is not wounded,
 nor his horse slain; rather, he kills a heathen king and seizes his horse. More is
 made of the killing of the Sultan.

465 *my* is repeated in the manuscript.

469 Isumbras is healed by nuns, but other romance heroes in similar circumstances
 are usually healed by courtly ladies.

494 Acre, now in northwest Israel, was a major port and seat of a Crusader kingdom
 which fell in 1291.

571 *lat see*. This is a filler phrase (tag), usually having the sense "let us/me see," "I'll
 show you."

597–99 Ashmole, Advocates', and Thornton manuscripts include the following details:

> When knyghtis went to pute the stane
> Twelve fo[t]e befor theym everychon
> He putte it as a balle;
> Therefor envye at hym thei hade
> They justyd at hym with strokis sadde,
> And he overcam them all. (Advocates')

 The cause of the tournament, then, is the knights' jealousy because of their
 defeat. The Cotton manuscript says all envy him for his high status. The Ash-
 mole text includes a longer description of the combat.

603 *Sareyyn*. Fowler draws on the expansive *OED* entry on 'Saracen' to point out that
 the word had a range of meanings in Middle English, one that included "Arab,
 Turk, Muslim, non-Christian, pagan, unbeliever, or infidel" and was "inherited by
 medieval Europe from the Roman Empire's designation for the nomadic Arab
 peoples that troubled its Middle Eastern boundaries" ("Romance Hypothetical,"
 p. 98).

627 The manuscript reading *sore* is perhaps a misspelling of *sorowe*, which appears
 in the Cotton text (line 645) and to which I have emended the reading here.

639 In the Cotton text, the knights think Isumbras may be a thief:

> This palmere hath done somme traytorere
> Of your golde or your fee
> By nyghte or by daye.

652 Cotton includes the lines:

> "Jhesu Criste, hevenne kynge,
> Sende me somme tokenynge
> Of my trewe fere,
> That I myghte wyte somme gladnes
> Of my lorde Syr Isumbras
> In what londe that he were."

659 *For* has been emended following Broh. The letters *or* have been obliterated in
 the manuscript.

676 The Cotton manuscript includes a passage not found in other texts, which de-
 scribes the reunion of the hero and his wife through the recognition of rings.
 This is a conventional motif in the reunion episode.

> "Say me, palmere, or thou go,
> Was ther any token betwene you two
> Whenne ye departed atwynne?"
> The palmere answered thus:
> "A rynge was broken betwyx us,
> That no man shulde it kenne."
> The lady toke up a grete sykynge
> And seyde, "Lette me se that rynge,
> If that thou trewe be."
> "Loo, madame, have it here,
> I have born it this fourtene yere,
> I shewde hit non but the."
> She toke forth a purse so clene,
> The halle shone therof bydene,
> So wele it was iwrowghte.
> That othur party thereinne was
> Nowe was this a wonthur kace,
> So mony londis as he hadde sowghte.
> She layde togydur the partyes tweyne;
> Hole it wax, the sothe to seyne,
> Ryghte amonge hem alle.
> "Blessed be God of His swete grace,
> Nowe have I my lord, syr Isumbras,
> Here all in myn halle."
>
> The lady that was so fayre of face,
> Swonedde thryse in that place,
> For fayne she hadde her lorde bolde.

The Thornton, Advocates', and Ashmole manuscripts present the whole reunion
scene in three stanzas.

676–90 This recognition scene "embodies the triumph of unity of person and the long-waited final accession of Isumbras to lordship: he is at that moment simultaneously and suddenly a knight, a husband, and a king" (Fowler, "Romance Hypothetical," p. 104).

692 The speech in Advocates' is harsher:

> And cummandded that yche baron bolde
> Ryche and pore, yong and olde,
> That thei Cryston schull be.
> And all that wold not see
> He badde that men schuld them sloo
> That no thyng for them schuld goo
> Neder golde nor fee.

698 The last three letters in *schent* have been obliterated, and are supplied following the Cotton text. The Cambridge manuscript's more southerly dialect uses *sch* spellings. Cotton uses *sh*.

736 In the Advocates', Ashmole, and Thornton texts, the sons appear in angelic garb, led by an angel:

> In an angell wede were thei clade,
> And an angell them to batell badde,
> That semely was to se. (Advocates')

741 Powell ("Models of Religious Peace," pp. 122–23) spends considerable time examining the difference in the number of dead Muslims across the various versions of this tale:

> In some of the manuscripts . . . Isumbras and his small band kill twenty thousand and three of the soldiers they are facing, about two-thirds of them, while in other manuscripts, they kill thirty thousand and three, all or essentially all of them.
> The difference between 20,003 and 30,003 might be dismissed as evidence of a simple scribal error. . . . But rather than a meaningless variant, the discrepancy might instead be a sign of a genuine scribal disagreement, too, considering that the figure of 20,003 leaves ten thousand Muslims standing, alive and apparently unconverted, when the poem ends. At the least, even if all we hope to accomplish is the restoration of an original reading, the variant forces us to ask: for a medieval audience, does a happy ending require the annihilation of a religious enemy? In a poem that is pervasively aware of the permanence of religious conflict, such a question about heathen survival seems likely to have been of great ideological significance.

745 In most other manuscripts, an angel tells the sons what to say.

748 Ashmole, Advocates', and Thornton manuscripts contain the following stanza emphasizing Isumbras' piety and the reunion of the family:

> Ofte was Syr Ysambrace wele and woo
> But never yitt als he was tho,

> One knees than he hym sett.
> He grett and sayde with mylde stevene, *wept*
> "Thankede be the heghte kyng of hevene
> My bale thane hase he bett."
> Sir Ysambrace and that lady free
> Kyssed all thare childir three,
> Ilkane for joye thay grett.
> Mare joye myghte never no mane see
> Thane men myghte one thame see
> In armes whene thay were mett. (Lincoln)

755 Dishes of wild game and domesticated animals were served, presumably at a banquet.

After 772 The lines *Explicit Ser Ysumbras. Incipit Vita de Katerine virginis* follow in the Gonville-Caius manuscript.

❦ INTRODUCTION TO *OCTAVIAN*

Though this romance is always known as *Octavian*, and Octavian is mentioned in catalogues of romance heroes, the title seems something of a misnomer. The story begins with the Roman Emperor Octavian and his calumniated queen, and relates her separation from their twin sons, one of whom is also named Octavian. However, the tale of the separated family gives way to the career of the other son, Florent. His exploits as a youth, his prowess in battle, and his wooing of the sultan's daughter offer possibilities for social comedy and exotic adventure that make this romance distinctive among Middle English treatments of the formulaic plot.

The story of Octavian was popular throughout late medieval Europe; texts in many languages survive from Italy to Scandinavia. All derive from a French couplet romance composed towards the middle of the thirteenth century by someone who knew Paris and wrote in the Picardian dialect. In fashioning the narrative, the writer employed incidents and motifs common in legend, romance, and *chanson de geste*. The sultan, his daughter, his giant champion, and the Saracen attack on Paris all have parallels in stories of Charlemagne. The treacherous mother-in-law appears in legends of Constance; the children carried off by animals and raised by foster parents are found in legends of St. Eustace.

The only surviving copy of the Old French romance was made by an Anglo-Norman scribe at the beginning of the fourteenth century. By the middle of that century, two English versions of the romance had appeared, one composed in the northeast Midlands, perhaps Yorkshire, the other in the southeast near Essex. The English redactors worked independently but followed the same principles in handling their source. They considerably abbreviated the story as told in French, reducing the narrative from 5700 lines to 1800 by simplifying the treatment of the love story, shortening passages of introspection and analysis of emotion, and omitting details and episodes not essential to the plot. This condensation highlights the variety of incident and quickens the pace of action. Such modifications are typical of those made by other authors who composed Middle English romances from French sources, recasting the material for a new audience.

There are significant differences between the southern and northern versions: the former is composed in an unusual six-line stanza (rhyming *aaabab*); the latter employs the common twelve-line tail-rhyme stanza. The southern has a looser, more paratactic style of narration and relies on oral address to announce transitions between episodes. It follows the French version's alternation in narrating the separation of mother and sons, while Northern *Octavian* has a more linear sequence. Southern *Octavian* embroiders upon the exploits of Clement and the sultan's flying horse, and the final scene includes the empress' lengthy recapitulation of her story. The northern version is presented in this edition, since it is in tail-rhyme, and its rendition of the story is, on the whole, more effective. It seems to have been more widespread as it survives in more copies, including a print by Wynkyn de Worde.

The plot is set in motion by infertility and the desire for an heir. Octavian's empress, seeking divine favor, suggests that they build an abbey, and soon conceives twin boys. At their birth, Octavian's mother tells him they were fathered by the cook's helper. Octavian kills him, and later accuses the empress of treason. Condemned to burn by advice of her own unwitting father, the empress begs her husband to have the children baptized; the pitiful spectacle moves him to relent, and he has his wife and children exiled. In the wilderness, an ape seizes one child, a lioness the other, but the empress, voyaging to the Holy Land, is reunited with this son. The lioness will not be parted from him and so accompanies them to Jerusalem; there the empress attracts the attention of the king, who recognizes her and installs her in the entourage of his queen. The king has the boy christened Octavian, and when he comes of age, knights him.

At this point, about one-third of the way through the romance, the story turns to the child seized by the ape. A knight attacks the ape and takes the boy; outlaws attack the knight and sell the boy to a Parisian pilgrim, Clement, who christens him Florent and raises him as his own. But the child's noble character soon asserts itself in contrast to his foster father's bourgeois values; Clement's wife defends the boy, suggesting he is of superior blood.

Meanwhile, France has been attacked by Saracens. Many Christian rulers, including the Emperor Octavian, come to help Dagobert, the French king. The sultan's giant, Arageous, challenges Dagobert, in return for the hand of the sultan's daughter, Marsabelle. Florent determines to fight the giant. In a mock-heroic arming scene he dons Clement's rusty gear, then vanquishes the enemy and beheads him, carrying his trophy to Marsabelle in ironic fulfillment of the giant's own promise. He then abducts her. She is subsequently returned to her father, but plans with her confidante to meet Florent again. In Paris, the victor is joyously received by the Christian leaders and Dagobert appoints a day for his knighting. Clement is invited to the feast, where his bourgeois values are once again in evidence. The Emperor Octavian wonders that Florent could be the son of such a man and prompts Clement to reveal his story, whereupon Octavian recognizes the youth as his own son.

There follows a series of combats and clandestine meetings of the lovers. Marsabelle agrees to become Christian and tells Florent he may overcome her father by taking his marvelous steed. Clement is able to accomplish this task through trickery and disguise. In the next battle things go badly for the Christians — Florent, Dagobert, and Emperor Octavian are imprisoned. However, word of their duress comes to Jerusalem, where young Octavian undertakes to aid his father and right his mother's case. Accompanied by the empress and the faithful lioness, he journeys to France, slaughters the Saracens, and releases the prisoners. At the feast following the victory the family is reunited. Marsabelle and Florent wed; the emperor's mother, condemned for treachery, commits suicide. Finally, after appropriate celebration, the family returns to Rome.

Octavian is a family romance: it begins with the story of a calumniated wife and separated twins, and the focus on family is maintained in the episodes with Clement. The villain of the piece, duly punished at the end, is the jealous mother-in-law. Though adultery, illegitimacy, and infanticide threaten family stability, other family taboos associated with such romances, for example, incest or patricide, do not appear. Nurture is a particularly important theme in *Octavian*'s treatment of the family. It is first developed in the episodes where the boys are carried away by animals. The lioness is looking for food for her cubs when she finds Octavian, and much is made of her suckling the infant and her tender, playful treatment of him. Clement procures a wet nurse to accompany Florent to Paris, and his wife loves the boy as her own child, protecting him from her husband's wrath. Clement is a loving,

and, finally, supportive foster father. Like Bernard, the adoptive father in *Tryamour*, Clement arms his son and shouts encouragement during his battles, rallying him to victory over the giant.

The family romance gets a pious treatment. The French version presents the emperor as a penitent father in search of the family he has wronged (like the heroes of *Isumbras* and the St. Eustace legend), and emphasizes the redemptive value of his suffering. Though this emphasis is lacking in the English versions, the northern composer elaborates the piety of the calumniated wife, keeping her steadily in focus through the first part of the story. Only in the northern *Octavian* does she propose the building of an abbey, pray for the baptism of her infants, and meekly accept her fate without asserting her innocence. Later she accepts the separation of her family as punishment for her sins and dedicates her life to serving God in the Holy Land. Once the story turns to Florent, it loses some of its pious perspective. Though the opponents are enemies of the faith, the narration of the conflict features the prowess of the hero, not religion. The Christian forces are even ineffective against the forces of heathendom until Florent arrives; later all the leaders are captured by the sultan.[1] The composers passed over an opportunity for pious emphasis in the story of the Saracen princess, showing no particular interest in her conversion. The later parts of the romance focus on social, not spiritual, matters.

Its treatment of social class distinguishes *Octavian* from other similar Middle English romances. Clement is a *velayne*, a person of the lower classes, but here the word is also used in the sense of *bourgeois*, a townsman. His predominant characteristic is a concern for money — his "florins whole and round," as a frequent tag line puts it. He bargains with the robbers when he buys Florent and seems to have named the boy after the coins for which he is exchanged. In some versions of the story, Clement sends Florent to become a moneychanger. Invited to Florent's knighting, Clement worries that he will have to pay for the feast. He seizes the nobles' cloaks as surety for their share of the cost, demonstrating his total incomprehension of that fundamental noble virtue, *largesse*. Then, to everyone's amusement, he insists on paying for his and Florent's dinners. As the narrator observes, "He wend alle had bene marchandyse, / The pryde [splendor] that he sawe thore" (lines 1251–52). Florent, on the other hand, is unconcerned with money. It is merely the means by which he is able to procure things of real (i.e., chivalric) value, which are essentially priceless and of worth according to the worthiness of their possessor. When Clement sends him with two oxen to learn the butcher's trade, Florent exchanges them for a falcon only to be beaten by Clement, who sees no value in the noble bird. Florent never bargains; he even insists on paying forty pounds for a warhorse though the seller asks only thirty.[2] Eventually Clement accepts the superiority of courtly values by admitting that the boy has made appropriate use of his goods. The money for the horse was well spent, since Florent rides him to fight the giant and save the city.

Stereotypical bourgeois characters like Clement are not common in Middle English romance. An instructive parallel is Grim, the fisherman who is Havelok's foster father. The point being made about innate nobility is the same in both romances, and in both there is class humor; but Grim is not burlesqued, and manners are not an issue. Grim goes on to

[1] In these episodes, the northern composer has expanded a brief mention of an encounter in the French *Octavian* and omitted the penitent father treatment whereby only Florent and his father are captured, and the emperor interprets this as penance for his sins against his wife.

[2] In Southern *Octavian* only, Florent haggles with the horse's owner, which is very out of character.

become a leading citizen and his sons are ennobled and made advisers to their foster brother the king. The treatment of the bourgeois in *Octavian* is a function of its French source, which makes even more of Clement's rejecting the assumptions of chivalry. The figure of Clement would have had its own special resonances to readers in the commercial regions of Picardy and the Ile de France; upper-class Englishmen in the era of the Peasant's Revolt might have seen him in the context of their own time's social unrest.[3] Though his antics at court cause Florent great shame, Clement is generally treated sympathetically, and he does carry off the chivalric exploit of winning the sultan's horse. The emperor makes Clement a handsome settlement for life, but *Octavian* is not a fantasy of social advancement; the composer's use of humor in relating Clement's behavior emphasizes the gap between noble and bourgeois.

The humor with which conflicting class values are presented is another distinguishing feature of this romance. To some extent, the capacity for humor, ironic understatement, and epic boast is inherent in noble character. A romance hero is expected to exhibit a certain high-spiritedness. There are many intentionally funny scenes in *Octavian*, and a range of comedy from slapstick to subtle irony. Nor is the humor merely an embellishment; often it is employed to direct the audience's response to the class-determined values of Clement and Florent. Humor arises from the incongruity of behavior and context: first the relatively gentle humor of Florent's courtly behavior in bourgeois surroundings, as when unperturbed he demonstrates the proper arrangement of the falcon's feathers to the exasperated Clement, then the more critical treatment of Clement's behavior at court, where the audience is encouraged to join the feasting nobles in their derisive laughter at his expense. Earlier, when the knights mock Florent in his makeshift armor, we do not identify with them but recognize the literal truth of their ironic wit — despite appearances, he is a "nobylle knyghte / The geaunt for to habyde" (lines 993–94).

Florent's career is a demonstration of the proposition that nobility of character is dependent on noble lineage. The youth is constitutionally unfit to become a butcher's apprentice: he instinctively understands the care of chivalric animals and insists on arming himself and challenging the giant, though the other citizens run in fright. In fact, both twin boys' inherent nobility is apparent from birth: the knight and the robbers who seize Florent are struck by his fairness, and the lioness spares young Octavian because she recognizes him for a king's son. While unaware of their relationship, the emperor and Florent feel a natural attraction for each other, as do father and son in *Tryamour*.[4]

Florent's chivalrous nature is further exemplified in his courtship of Marsabelle. Theirs is a courtly love, especially by the standards of Middle English romance: it is sudden, consuming, private, conducted in secret with the aid of a confidante. But the love interest in *Octavian* is not especially linked to class; the lovers differ in religion, not status, so the fantasy of social advancement through marriage is not evoked. Rather, love seems to be of interest for its own sake, and for the exotic overtones of the Saracen princess. Marsabelle demonstrates the forwardness and penchant for scheming against authority often attributed to Saracen princesses, for example Josian in *Bevis of Hampton*, and Floripas in *The Sultan of Babylon* and *Ferumbras*.

[3] Simons, "Northern *Octavian*," p. 108.

[4] The natural affinity is more striking in the southern and French versions, where father and son do not recognize each other until the end of the romance.

All the composers of the Octavian romances faced the same challenge: maintaining a consistent focus while presenting a multiplicity of characters and incidents. A successful combination of family romance, pious legend, social farce, love story, and epic was not easy to achieve. Scenes of combat are not particularly embellished; the action is often vague when compared to the deeds of arms recounted in other romances such as *Tryamour* or *Eglamour*. The diversity of themes and directions results in a certain incoherence, which is reflected in assessments of the romance. Some scholars read *Octavian* as a pious tale, while others stress its political themes.[5] Actually, the composers seem to have aimed to fulfill as many generic expectations as possible. No doubt its variety and the appeal of its familiar plot account for the popularity of *Octavian* and its influence on such later romances as *Erle of Toulous* and *Torrent of Portengale*, among others.

The northern version exists in two manuscripts and a fragment of a print by Wynkyn de Worde. The Thornton manuscript is the older, closer to the Old French poem, and presents the fuller version of the narrative. The other text, Cambridge University Ff. 2.38, omits passages from the episodes of the giant slaying, Florent's knighting, and Clement at the feast. The scribe/editor seems to have wanted to shorten the poem. Otherwise, the two texts closely resemble each other (allowing for the usual formulaic variation). Rhyme schemes of stanzas almost always agree. McSparran says the texts are related by written, not oral, transmission.[6] The Thornton text is the basis for this edition, but as the folio following 102 is missing and half of folio 108 has been torn away, the missing lines have been supplied from the Cambridge text.

The dialect of the Thornton text, copied by Robert Thornton of Yorkshire, is more northern than that of the Cambridge. We find such northern features as the *-ir* plural in *brethir*, the *th* pronoun forms of *they/them/their*, and the feminine singular pronoun *scho*. *S* rather than *sh* appears in such words as *sall* (shall). The present participle ending is *-and(e)*. Thornton's idiosyncratic spelling produces some unusual forms, like the doubled consonants of *wonndir*, *twentty*, etc., and the indiscriminate use of *ie/ye* and *ie/ey*, for example, "wife" (*wife*, *wiefe*, *wyefe*) and "this" (*this*, *thies*, *theis*).

MANUSCRIPTS AND PRINTS

Indexed as item 1918 in Boffey and Edwards, eds., *New Index of Middle English Verse*:

- Lincoln, Lincoln Cathedral Library Thornton MS 91 (1430–40), fols. 98v–109r. [Northern version; base-text.]
- London, British Library MS Cotton Caligula A.ii (1446–60), fols. 22v–35r. [Southern version.]
- Cambridge, Cambridge University Library MS Ff. 2.38 (c. 1450), fols. 90r–101v. [Southern version.]

- San Marino, Huntington Library 14615. London: Wynkyn de Worde, 1504–06 (*STC* 18779), incomplete. [Northern version.]

[5] For examples of the former see Barron, *English Medieval Romance*, p. 204, and Mehl, *Middle English Romances*, p. 114. For examples of the latter see Ramsey, *Chivalric Romances*, p. 186, and Simons, "Northern *Octavian*," p. 106.

[6] McSparran, *Octovian Imperator*, p. 18.

 OCTAVIAN

1 Mekyll and littill, olde and yynge,	*Great; young*
Herkyns all to my talkynge	*Listen*
Of whaym I will yow kythe.	*tell*
Jhesu fadir of heven kynge,	
5 Gyff us all thy dere blyssynge	
And make us glade and blythe.	
For full sothe sawis I will yow synge,	*true sayings*
Off whaym the worde full wyde gan sprynge,[1]	
And ye will a stownde me lythe.	*If; while; listen to me*
10 In the bukes of Rome als it es tolde	*as; is*
How byfelle amange oure eldyrs olde,	
Full ofte and fele sythe.	*Very; many times*
Somtym byffell ane aventure,	*adventure*
In Rome ther was ane Emperoure,	
15 Als men in romance rede.	
He was a man of grete favoure	
And levede in joye and grete honoure	
And doghety was of dede.	*valiant*
In tornament nor in no fyghte	
20 In the werlde ther ne was a better knyghte,	
No worthier undir wede.	*in clothes*
Octovyane was his name thrughowte;	*widely known*
Everylke man hade of hym dowte	*Every; fear*
When he was armede one stede.	*on horseback*
25 Ane Emprice he hade to wyffe,	
One of fayreste that was one lyffe,	
Thus thies clerkes sayne us so;	
Seven yeres had thay samen bene	*together been*
With joy and gamen tham bytwene,	*games*
30 And other myrthis moo;	*more*
The seven yere were comen and gone,	
Bot child togedir had thay none	

[1] *Of whom the word began to spread very widely*

 Getyn bytwene tham two,
 That after tham thair land moghte welde, *govern*
35 When that thay drewe till elde: *approached old age*
 And forthi tham in hert tham was full woo.

 And als the Emperoure satt appon a daye,
 In his chambir hym to playe
 With his lady bryghte,
40 He byhelde hir faire lyre, *face*
 Was whyte so blossome on the brere, *briar*
 That semly was of syghte. *That was pleasing to behold*
 A sorow than to his herte ther ranne
 Forthi that thay childir hade nanne *Because*
45 Thaire landis to rewle one ryghte. *by rights of inheritance*
 And by his lady so als he satte,
 For sorowe his chekes wexe all wate, *became wet*
 That was so hende a knyghte. *accomplished*

 Bot when the lady that gan aspye, *began to notice*
50 All chaunged than hir bryghte blyee *face*
 And scho syghede full sore. *she sighed*
 Scho felle hir lorde one knees agayne, *She fell on her knees before her lord*
 And of his sorow scho gan hym frayne, *inquire*
 And of hs mekyll care.
55 "Sir," scho sais, "if it were your will
 Youre concelle for to schewe me till *thoughts; to*
 And of your lyffes fare, *And how your life fares*
 Ye wote I ame youre werldes fere, *know; earthly mate*
 Opyn your herte unto me here,
60 Youre comforthe may be the mare." *more*

 Than in his armes he gan hir folde *embraced her*
 And all his sorow he to hir tolde
 And all his hertis wonde. *wound*
 "Now hafe we seven yere sammen bene *together*
65 And hafe no chylde us bytwene,
 For fay we sall hythen fownde, *fated to die; hence go*
 And I ne wote how this land sall fare *don't know; shall*
 Bot lyfe in werre and in kare *But [shall] exist; war*
 When we are broghte to grownde. *buried*
70 Therefore I hafe so mekyll thoghte *great*
 That when I am to bedde broghte
 I slepe bot littill stownde." *a short time*

 And than answerde that lady bryghte,
 "Sir I kan rede yow full ryghte, *advise*
75 Gyffe yow nothynge ill. *If; don't take it wrong*

A ryche abbaye schall ye do make *have made*
For oure swete lady sake, *lady's (i.e., Mary's)*
 And landis gyffe theretill, *give*
And scho will pray hir Son so fayre
80 That we may samen gete an ayere, *together; heir*
 This land to welde with skyll." *rule wisely*
An abbaye than he gerte wyrke so *had built*
And sone he gatt knave childire two, *begat male children*
 Als it was Goddis will.

85 With childe thane yode that lady thore; *went; there*
Full grete scho wexe with paynnes sore, *grew; pains*
 That was so faire and free. *noble (generous)*
Till the tym felle that it was soo,
The lady hade knave childir two
90 That semly weren to see.
Tythande come to the Emperoure *Tidings*
There he laye in his ryche towre; *Where*
 A full glade man was hee.
Two maydynes hym the bodworde broghte — *message*
95 Withowttyn gyftes yede thay noghte: *They didn't leave without gifts*
 Aythire hadde townnes three. *To each he gave*

The Emperoure rosse with mylde mode
And till his chambir he hym yode *to; went*
 And thankes God His sande. *for what He sent*
100 Erly are the daye gan sprynge, *Early before*
He did a pryste his messe to synge; *made; priest; mass*
 His modir thore he fande. *found*
"Sone," scho said, "I am full blythe
That the Empryse sall haf hyre lyfe *didn't die in childbirth*
105 And lyffe with us in lande, *live*
Bot mekyll sorowe dose it me
That Rome sall wrange ayerde bee *inherited*
 And in uncouthe hande." *unknown*

"Modir," he sayse, "why saye ye soo?
110 Haffe I noghte knave-childir two?
 I thanke it Goddes will."
"Nay certis" scho said, "sone myn,
Wete thou wele thay are noghte thyn, *Understand*
 And that lykes me full ill. *pleases*
115 For thou myghte no childir have, *Since*
Scho hase takyn thy kokes knave; *cook's boy*
 I will it prove thurgh skyll." *cleverness*
A sorowe there to his herte gan goo

That wordis moghte he speke no moo
120 But yod awaye full still. *went*

Till his chapelle forthe he yode; *To; went*
Full sory at his messe he stode
 Als man that was in kare.
His modir iwhils garte calle a knave *meanwhile had called*
125 And highte hym grete gyftis to hafe, *promised*
 A thowsande pownde or mare.
To the chambir bothe thay tuk the waye
There the Empryce in childbed laye; *Where*
 All slepede that were there,
130 For scho had wakyd ryghte longe
In paynes and in thoghte full strange
 Or scho delyvered ware. *Before*

Than said that lady to that knave,
"Hye the faste, the golde to hafe; *Hasten*
135 Thou schall be rewarde this nyghte.
Haste the tyte with all thi myghte, *you quickly*
Prevely that thou were dyghte *Secretly; prepared*
 And that thou were unclede. *undressed*
Softely by hir thou in crepe
140 That scho ne wakyn of hir slepe,
 For full seke es scho bystadde." *sick; beset*
Whatte for lufe and whatt for drede, *love (loyalty)*
Into the ladyes beedd he yede; *went*
 He dyd als scho hym badd. *ordered*
145 Bot ever he droghe hym ferre awaye *drew; farther*
For the rechese that scho in laye, *riches*
 Full sore than was he drade. *afraid*

The Emperours modir away yode than *went*
And till hir son full tite scho wan *quickly; went*
150 There he att his messe stode. *Where*
"Son," scho saide, "thou trowed noghte me; *believed*
Come forthe, thou sall the sothe now see." *truth*
 With hir to chambir he yode.
Bot when the Emperoure sawe that syghte,
155 For sorowe no worde speke he ne myghte,
 For he wexe nerhande wode. *almost insane*
A scharpe baselarde owte he droghe; *dagger*
That giltles knave there he sloghe —
 Alle was byblede with blode. *covered*

160 Ay lay that lady faste and slepee *As*
A dolefull swevenynge gan scho mete; *vision; dream*

Scho was a wofull wyghte. *creature*
Hir thoghte scho was in wyldyrnes, *It seemed to her*
In thornes and in thyknes, *in a dense grove*
165 That scho myghte hafe no syghte.
And ther come flyande over the strande *flying; shore*
A dragon all full bryghte birnande, *brightly burning*
 That all schone of that lyghte.
In his palmes alle byrnand so *claws*
170 Up he tuke hir childir two
 And away he tuke his flyghte.

Therewith the lady bygan to wake,
A dolefull gronyng gan scho make
 And scho syghede full sare.
175 The Emperour to the knave wente;
The hede up by the hare he hente *head; hair; seized*
 And caste it till hir thare.
The lady blyschede up in the bedde; *started*
Scho saw the clothes all byblede — *bloody*
180 Full mekyll was hir care. *great*
Scho bygan to skryke and crye *shriek*
And sythen in swonynge for to ly; *then; fainting*
 Hirselfe scho wolde forfare. *destroy*

Wordis of this were spoken no mo
185 To that lady to the kirke solde go, *Until; church should*
 Als the lawe was in that lede. *among those people*
The Emperoure made a full riche feste
Of kynges and dukes that were honeste,
 Of many and dyverse stede. *place*
190 The kynge of Calabre, allas, *Calabria*
That the lady fadir was, *lady's*
 Thedir than gan he bede. *summon*
Alle were thay sampnede appon a daye *assembled*
With grete solace and mekill playe; *pleasure*
195 To the kyrke that lady yede. *went*

And there duellyn the kynges samen *remained; together*
With joy and myrthe and mekill gamen
 At that mawngery, *feast*
With gud myrthis tham emange, *among*
200 Harpes, fethils and full faire songe, *fiddles*
 Cytoles and sawtrye, *Citoles; psaltery*
Till the sevenyghte was gone,
With alkyn welthis in that wone *With all kinds of wealth in that dwelling*
 Of myrthis and mynstralsye.
205 Was never so riche a gedirynge *gathering*

That hadd so sary a partynge, *sorry*
 I sall yow tell for why.

Grete dole forsothe it es to telle, *in truth*
Oppon the haghten daye byfell; *eighth*
210 Herkyns and ye may here. *Listen; hear*
The Emperoure to the chambir yode,
All the lordes abowte hym stode
 With full mery chere.
The Emperoure said, "I undirstande
215 Swylke an awnter fell in this lande *Such; adventure*
 By a lady to yere *this year*
That was overtaken with swylk a treson. *discovered; such*
I aske juggement of this with reson *judgment*
 Of hir whate worthy were."

220 When the Emperoure his tale hade tolde,
The kyng of Calabire answere wolde,
 He ne wyste whate it bement. *didn't know*
He said: "It es worthi for hir sake,
Withowtten the ceté a fyre to make *Outside; city*
225 With rightwyse juggement,
And when the fyre es byrnand faste,
Hir and hir childir in it to caste,
 Till thay to the dede be bryntte." *death; burnt*
The Emperoure answeres to hym sone, *soon*
230 "Thyn awen dogheter hase it done,
 I holde to thyn assent."

There was dole and grete peté; *sorrow; pity*
A fyre thay made withowtten the ceté, *outside*
 With brondes byrnande bryghte. *coals*
235 To the fyre thay ledde that lady thare;
Two sqwyers hir childir bare,
 That semly weren of syghte.
In a kirtyll of sckarlett rede *gown*
Into the fyre to take hir dede *death*
240 All redy was scho dyghte. *prepared*
The kynge of Calabire made evyll chere, *grim countenance*
He ne myghte for sorowe stande hir nere.
 Bothe wepede kynge and knyghte. *wept*

The lady than, the sothe to telle,
245 Byfore hir lorde one knees scho felle
 And bothe hir handes uphelde.
Scho sayde, "My lorde, for Jhesu sake,
Graunt me ane orysoune to make *one prayer*

Till Hym that alle sall wellde, *rule*
250 And then of me ye do youre wyll,
The dede that I am ordeynede till *death; condemned to*
 Therto I will me yelde."
The Emperoure graunted hir righte so,
Ilke a man than was full woo *Every*
255 That were that day in the felde.

Than the lady hir one knes there sette,
Till Jhesu Cryste full sore scho grette; *To; called out*
 No wondir thoghe hir ware wo.
"Now Lorde," scho sayd, "of hevens blysse,
260 This day thou me rede and wysse, *counsel; advise*
 And heven qwene also. *heaven's*
Mary, mayden and modir free,
My prayere make I to the
 For my childir two:
265 Als thou lete tham be borne of me *allowed*
Helpe that thay crystoned may be, *christened*
 Or that thay to the dede goo." *Before; death*

Than lordis that abowte hyr ware
And laydes felle in swonyng thore, *fainting there*
270 And knyghttes stode wepande.
The Emperoure stode by hyr full nere;
The teris trykylde one his lyre *face*
 That wele nere ne myghte he stande.
Than spake he wordis of gret peté
275 And sayde, "Thi dede will I noghte see, *death*
 With herte nor yitt with hande."
The Emperoure gafe hire leve to goo
And take with hir hir childir two,
 And flemed hir of his lande. *banished her from*

280 The Emperoure gafe hir fowrty pownde *gave*
Of florence, that were riche and rownde, *florins*
 In romance als we rede.
And he bytaghte hir knyghtes two *entrusted her to*
And bad that thay solde with hir goo *commanded; should*
285 Owt of his lande to lede.
Two sqwyers hir childir bare
In stede ther thay were never are, *places where; before*
 And intill uncouthe thede. *into; strange terrain*
When scho was flemyd that was so gent, *banished; gentle*
290 Ilke a lorde to hys lande es went, *Each*
 For sorow thaire hertes gan blede.

When this lady was in a wyldirnes
That full thyke of wylde bestes bysett was,
 And all wylsom it semed to syghte. *deserted*
295 Thay hir bytaghte hir childir two, *handed over to her*
Gafe hir hir golde and bad hir go;
 A stye ther laye full ryghte. *path*
They bade hir holde the hye strete, *follow; highway*
For drede with whilde bestes to mete,
300 That mekill weren of myghte;
And agayne thay went with sory mode, *back*
And allone that lady, forthe scho yode,
 Als a full wafull wyghte. *woeful person*

Scho hade so wepede ther byforne
305 That scho the ryghte way hase sone forlorne, *lost*
 So mekill was hir thoghte. *great*
And into a wode, was ferly thykke, *marvelously*
There dales weren depe and cleves wykke; *cliffs wicked*
 The ryghte waye fonde scho noghte. *way*
310 In a greve undir ane hill *grove*
Scho found a welle full faire and schille, *spring; lovely; loud (babbling)*
 And ane herbere therby was wroghte. *arbor*
With faire trees it was bysette,
The lady sett hir down and grette, *wept*
315 For ferrere scho ne moghte. *further; might not go*

Bot by the welle scho sett hir down;
Scho gret and cryede with sory sown, *grieved*
 For scho was lefte allone.
"Now Lorde," scho said, "if it be Thi will,
320 In this wode late me nott spylle *die*
 For full will I am of wone. *I am utterly without shelter*
Mary mayden, qwene of heven,
I pray the herkyn to my steven *voice*
 And mend my carefull mone. *sorrowful lament*
325 So full I am of pyn and wo *pain*
That thre dayes es gon and mo,
 That mete ne ete I none." *food; ate*

And by that scho had hir childir dyghte, *made ready*
By that than wexe it even myrk nyghte *dark*
330 Als scho satt by the welle.
So in that herbere down scho laye *lodging*
Till it was lyghte on the tother day, *next*
 That fowlles herde scho than synge and yelle. *chirp*
Thare come an ape to seke hir pray; *its prey*
335 Hir one childe scho bare awaye

Up heghe appon ane hyll. *high*
What wondir was yif hir were wo *if she*
When hir child was fro hir so?
 In swonynge doun scho felle.

340 And in all the sorow that scho in was,
Ryghte so com rynnande a lyones *running a lioness*
 Of wode als scho wolde wede. *In a rage as if she would go crazy*
In swonynnge als the lady laye,
Hyr other childe scho bare awaye, *second child it bore*
345 Hir whelpes with to feede.
Whate wonndir was thofe hyr were wo, *though she*
Awaye were borne hir childir two;
 In swoghe scho lay for drede. *faint*
Bot for it was a kynge sone iwysse, *Except since; certainly*
350 The lyones moghte do it no mys, *harm*
 Bot forthe therwith scho yede. *went*

There come a fewle full faire of flyghte, *flying creature*
A gryffone, sayse the buke, he hyghte, *it was called*
 Over those holtes so hare. *woods; gloomy*
355 The fewle than was so mekill of myghte,
That esyly myghte he bere a knyghte
 Alle armed thofe he ware. *though*
The lyones with the childe tuke he,
And intill ane ile of the see *island; sea*
360 The gryffone bothe tham bare.
The child slepid in the lyones mouthe,
Of wele ne wo it ne kouthe, *good or bad fortune; knew nothing*
 Bot God kepid it fro kare.

And whane the lyones gatt fote on lande,
365 Full styfly than gan scho up stande, *fiercely*
 Als beste bothe stronge and whilde. *As beast*
The gryffone thurgh Goddis grace scho sloghe, *slew*
And of that fewle scho ete ynoghe
 And layde hir by that childe.
370 The childe sowkyde the lyones, *suckled*
Als it Goddis will was,
 When it the pappes felide. *nipples felt*
The lyones gan it wake *protect*
And lufe it for hir whelpes sake *loved*
375 And was therwith full mylde.

With hir feet scho made a dene, *den*
That lyttill childe in broghte scho then
 And kepede hym day and nyghte.

And ay, when hir hungirde sore, *always; she (the lioness)*
380 Scho yode and ete of the gryffone more,
 That are was mekill of myghte. *formerly; great*
 And thus, als it was Goddis will,
 The lyones byleves thore styll *remains*
 With that barne so bryghte. *child*
385 The lady that was leved allone, *left*
 To Jhesu Criste scho made hir mone
 Als a full wofull wyghte.

 Scho sais, "Jhesu, kyng of alle,
 With carefulle herte to the I calle,
390 That thou be my socoure.
 Als I was kyngis dogheter and qwene
 And Emprice of Rome hase bene
 And many a riche towre.
 And thorowe the lessynges es one me wroghte *lies that are contrived about me*
395 Till mekill sorow thus am I broghte,
 And owte of myn honoure.
 This werldes blysse hafe I forlorne, *lost*
 And my two childir er fro me borne; *are; taken*
 This lyfe may I noghte dowre! *endure*

400 "This sorowe, Lorde, that I am in,
 Full wele I wote, es for my syn;
 Welcome be alle Thi sande. *punishment*
 To the werlde will I me never gyffe, *never give myself*
 Bot serve The, Lorde, whills I may lyfe,
405 Into the Holy Londe."
 And over an hille the waye scho name *took*
 And to the Grekkes se scho came
 And welke appon the strande. *walked; shore*
 And byfore hir an haven scho seghe *saw*
410 And a ceté with towris full heghe; *high*
 A redy waye ther scho fand.

 Whan the lady com than to that town,
 A schipe scho fond all redy bowne *prepared*
 With pylgremes for to fare.
415 Scho badd the schipmen golde and fee *offered*
 In that schipp that scho moghte be,
 If that thaire willes it were.
 A bote thay sente appone the flode
 To the lady right ther scho stode,
420 A wyghte man in hir bare. *An able; carried*
 And by the maste thay badde hir sytt, *asked her to*

There myghte no man hir sorowe wete *know*
 And ay scho wepede sare. *But continually*

The schippe come sayland by an ile syde,
425 The mayster badd that thay sold byde, *should pause*
 "For fresche water hafe we nane."
Bysyde tham was a roche on hye,
A welle streme thare thay see
 Come rynnande over a stone.
430 Two men to the lande thay sent,
Heghe upe ovir that roche thay went; *rock*
 The welle thay found anone. *then*
The lyones laye in hir dene
And was full blythe of tho two men, *glad*
435 And full son scho hade tham slayne.

So lange one ankir gan thay ryde,
Thies two men for to habyde, *wait*
 Till none was of the daye. *noon*
Than gan twelve men tham dyghte *arm*
440 With helme and with hawberke bryghte, *helmet; coat of mail*
 And till the lande wente thay.
The lyones fonde thay in hir dene,
A knave childe laye sowkand hir then
 And gan with the lyones to playe. *began*
445 Umwhile the childe sowkede hir pappe, *Sometimes*
Umwhile gan thay kysse and clappe; *embrace*
 For drede thay fledde awaye. *they (the men)*

Thay tolde the wondir that thay seghe,
And that thay fonde on the roche on heghe *high*
450 A lyones in hir den.
A knave childe ther in laye,
Therewith the lyones gan hir playe,
 And dede were bothe thaire men.
Than spake that lady so mylde,
455 "Mercy, syrris, that es my childe —
 One land ye late me rynn." *go*
A bote thay sett appon the flode,
The lady unto the lande ther yode,
 Full sore wepide thay then.

460 When scho com on that roche on heghe,
Scho ran ywhils that scho myght dreghe *ran as fast as she could*
 With full sory mode.
The lyones thurgh Goddis grace,
When scho sawe the lady face,

465 Full debonorly up sche stode. *meekly*
 Thurgh the myghte of Mary mylde
 Scho sufferd that lady to tak hir childe *permitted*
 And scho forthe with hir yode; *went*
 Bot when the schippmen the lyones seghe,
470 The land durste thay noghte com neghe; *dared; near*
 For drede thay were nere wode. *fear; crazed*

 Sum hent an ore and som a sprete, *seized; pole*
 The wylde lyones for to mete,
 And thaire chippe for to werre. *ship; protect*
475 The lady intill thair chippe thay hente; *ship; took*
 Thritty fote after the lyones sprent — *leapt*
 Durste no man in hir bere. *obstruct her*
 There was than bot lyttill glee,
 For many lepped into the see,
480 So ferde of hir thay were; *afraid*
 Bot by the lady downe scho laye
 And with the childe bygan to playe
 And to no man wolde scho dere. *do harm*

 They droghe up saile of riche hewe, *hue*
485 The wynd tham owte of haven blewe
 Over that wan streme. *dark*
 The fyrste lande than that thay seghe,
 Was a ceté with towres full heghe
 That hyghte Jerusalem. *was called*
490 Als blythe were thay than of that syghte
 Als es the fowlles, when it es lighte,
 Of the dayes gleme. *dawn*
 When it was ebbe and no flode, *ebb tide; high tide*
 The lady to the lande than yode,
495 Into that riche rewme. *realm*

 Over all the ceté wyde and longe
 Of that lady the worde than spronge,
 That thore one lande was lente, *come*
 And how scho hade a lyones
500 Broghte owte of wyldirnes.
 The kyng after hir sente;
 He bad scho solde lett for no thynge *should stop*
 And the lyones with hir brynge.
 To the castelle es scho went.
505 When scho byfore the kynge ther come,
 He kende hir for the Emprice of Rome *recognized*
 And by the hande he hir hente. *took*

The kyng than frayned of hir fare; *asked*
Scho tolde hym of hir mekill care *sorrow*
510 And of hir grete unryghte. *injustice*
He garte hir duelle with the qwene stille, *caused her to*
Scho hadd maydyns redy to will *to (do her) will*
 To serve hir bothe daye and nyghte.
The childe that was so faire and fre,
515 The kyng did it crystened for to be.
 Octovyane it highte.
When the childe was of elde *age*
That he couthe ryde and armes welde, *knew how to; wield*
 The kyng dubbede hym to knyghte.

520 The lyones that was so wilde,
Belefte with the lady and the childe; *Remained*
 Hir comforthe was the more.
The lady byleved with the qwene *remained*
With joye and blysse tham bytwene,
525 To covyre hir of hir care. *recover from*
Ilke man hir plesyde day and nyghte *Everybody; pleased*
To make hir glade with alle thair myghte,
 Unto hir better were. *Until she*
In Jerusalem thus gan scho duelle;
530 Of hir other childe now will I telle,
 That the ape away bare.

Now comes the ape that was wilde
Thurgh the forest with the childe
 Over the holttis so hare. *wood; gray (dark)*
535 Als the ape come over a strete, *path*
With a knyghte so gan scho mete,
 Als scho the childe bare.
Thore faghte the knyght wondirly longe
Agayne the ape styffe and stronge,
540 His swerde so brake he there.
The ape leved the childe and away ran, *left*
The knyght the child son up wan *soon caught up with the child*
 And with it forthe gan fare. *did go*

Forthe with the child the knyght went than,
545 In the wode mett he owtlawes tene, *ten*
 That mekill weryn of myghte. *great were*
Yitt was never the knyghte so wo,
For his swerde was brokyn in two,
 That he myghte nothyng fyghte.
550 If all the knyghte were kene and thro, *Although the knight was fierce and bold*
Those owtlawes wan the child hym fro,

That was so swete a wyghte. *person*
The knyghte was wondid, forsothe to saye,
Unnethes his horse bare hym awaye, *with difficulty*
555 So dulefully was he dyghte. *grievously; struck*

Those outlawes sett tham on a grene,
The child thay laide tham bytwene,
 And it faste on tham loghe. *vigorously; laughed*
The mayster owtlawe spake then,
560 "Grete schame it were for hardy men,
 If thay a childe sloghe. *should slay*
I rede we bere it here besyde *advise*
To the se with mekill pride,
 And do we it no woghe; *woe*
565 It es comyn of gentill blode;
We sall hym selle for mekill gude, *great profit*
 For golde and sylver enoghe."

Two owtlawes than made tham yare, *ready*
To the Grekkes se thay it bare;
570 Thay couthe the way full ryghte.
It was no man that it seghe *saw*
That thay ne wepid with thaire eghe
 So faire it was of syghte.
A burgesse of Pareche com than nere *citizen; Paris*
575 Had bene a palmere seven yere; *pilgrim*
 Clement the Velayne he hyghte. *Villein; was called*
"Sirris," he said, "will ye this child selle,
The golde will I for hym telle, *count out*
 Florence bothe brode and bryghte." *Florins*

580 For fourty pound hym selle thay wolde.
He said, "Full lange may ye hym halde, *keep him*
Are ye hym so selle may. *Before*
 Gode men," he said, "be my hode, *by my hood*
I trowe ye kan ful littill gude, *understand little about merchandising*
585 Swilke wordis for to saye!
 Golde and silver es me bot nede, *do I lack*
Bot twentty pownd I will yow bede *offer*
And mak yow redy paye."
 The childe thay unto Clement yolde, *gave*
590 And twentty pownde he tham tolde *he counted out for them*
And went forthe one his waye.

Clement hase the childe boghte,
A payneyere did he to be wroghte, *basket he had made*
 The childe in forthe to lede. *carry*

595	A noresche gatt he hym also, *nurse*
	Into Fraunce with hym to go,
	That yong childe for to fede.
	Home he tuke the way ful ryghte
	And hastede hym with all his myghte,
600	And unto Paresche he yede.
	The burgesche of Paresche wer ful fayne, *citizens; happy*
	Full many went Clement agayne; *toward*
	A slavyne was his wede. *pilgrim's mantle; clothing*

	Thay haylsest Clement and kyssed hym alle *embraced*
605	And broghte hym till his awen haulle. *to; own manor*
	His wyfe was glade and blythe.
	Scho hym fraynede the ryght dome *asked him for a true report*
	How he to the childe come; *How he came by the child*
	He tolde hir also swythe: *quickly*
610	"In the Holy Lond I hym gatt, *got*
	And thore I wold hym noghte lett, *leave*
	The sothe I will the kythe." *make known to you*
	His wyfe ansuerde with herte mylde,
	"He sall be myn awen childe."
615	Scho kyste hym ful ofte sythe. *many times*

	Clement saide to his wyfe tho,
	"Sen the childe es getyn so
	In the hethen thede,
	And now es it to this land broghte,
620	I pray the, dame, that thou greve the noghte,
	And riche sall be thi mede." *reward*
	"Sir," scho said with wordis free,
	"Full welecom es it unto me.
	Full faire sall I hym fede
625	And yeme hym with oure awen child, *keep*
	To that he come of helde, *Until; age*
	And clothe tham in one wede." *the same clothing*

	Clement was therof full blythe,
	He garte crysten the child ful swythe; *had the child christened*
630	It was not duellid that nyghte. *delayed*
	And als it es in romance tolde,
	The right name that thay it callde,
	Florent the child hyghte. *was called*
	And when the child was seven yere olde
635	He was bothe wysse, faire, and bolde,
	The man that redis righte.
	Alle the rewme wyde and longe *realm*

Worde of the childe spronge,
 So was he faire to syghte.

640 Ever the burgesse and his wyfe
 Loffed the childe als thaire lyfe, *Loved*
 With tham he was full dere. *To them*
 When he was tuelve yere olde and more,
 He sett his owun son to the lore[1]
645 To be a chawndelere. *candlemaker*
 And Florent bytaughte he oxen two *placed in charge of*
 And bad hym over the bryge go *bridge*
 Unto a bouchere, *butcher*
 To lere his crafte for to do.
650 Als hym was never of kynd therto, *But he was by nature unsuited*
 To use swylke mystere. *To follow that trade*

 Als Florent over the brygge gan go,
 Dryvand on his oxen two,
 A semely syghte sawe he:
655 A sqwyere bare, als I yow telle,
 A gentill fawcon for to selle, *falcon*
 That semly was to see.
 Florent to the sqwyere yede
 And bothe his oxen he gan hym bede *offered*
660 For that fowle so fre.
 The sqwyere therof was full glade,
 He tuke the oxen als he hym bade,
 Florent was blythe in ble. *countenance*

 The squyer therof was full gladd
665 When he tho oxen taken had
 And hyed owt of syght. *hurried*
 And Florent to fle was full fayne — *flee [also] was eager*
 He wende he wolde have had hys hawk agayne *He [Florent]; he [the squire]*
 And ranne wyth all hys myght.
670 Home he toke the ryght way
 To Clements hows as hyt lay, *house*
 And yn he wente full ryght.
 He fedde the hawke whyll he wolde,
 And sythen he can hys fedurs folde *Then he began; feathers preen*
675 As the squyer had hym teyght. *taught*

 Clement came yn full sone;
 "Thefe, where haste thou my oxen done, *Thief*

[1] *He (Clement) sent his own son to learn the trade*

That Y the begyfte?" *gave you*
Grete dele myght men see thore; *distress*
680 Clement bete the chylde sore,
That was so swete a wyght.
"Wyth odur mete shalt thou not leve *other food*
But that thys glede wyll the yeve, *bird of prey; give*
Neythur day ne nyght."
685 As sore beton as the chylde stode,
Yyt he to the fawcon yode,
Hys fedurs for to ryght. *groom*

The chylde thoght wondur thore *thought it strange*
That Clement bete hym so sore,
690 And mekely he can pray.
"Syr," he seyde, "for Crystys ore, *mercy*
Leve and bete me no more, *Cease*
But ye wyste well why. *Unless; knew*
Wolde ye stonde now and beholde
695 How feyre he can hys fedurs folde,
And how lovely they lye,
Ye wolde pray God wyth all your mode *heart*
That ye had solde halfe your gode, *goods*
Soche anodur to bye."

700 The burgeys wyfe besyde stode,
Sore sche rewyd yn hur mode *grieved; soul*
And seyde, "Syr, thyn ore. *mercy*
For Mary love, that maydyn mylde, *Mary's*
Have mercy on owre feyre chylde
705 And bete hym no more.
Let hym be at home and serve us two,
And let owre odur sonys go
Eche day to lore. *learn [a trade]*
Soche grace may God for the chylde have wroght,
710 To a bettur man he may be broght *He may become a better man*
Than he a bocher were!" *Than [if]*

Aftur all thys tyme befelle
Clement forty pownde can telle *did count*
Into a pawtenere. *purse*
715 Clement toke hyt chylde Florent
And to the brygge he hym sente,
Hys brothur hyt to bere.
As the chylde thorow the cyté of Parys yede, *went*
He sye where stode a feyre stede, *saw*
720 Was stronge yn eche werre. *every battle*
The stede was whyte as any mylke,

The brydyll reynys were of sylke, *reins*
 The molettys, gylte they were. *bosses*

Florent to the stede can gone;
725 So feyre an hors sye he never none *saw*
 Made of flesche and felle. *skin*
Of wordys the chylde was wondur bolde
And askyd whedur he schoulde be solde,
 The penyes he wolde hym telle. *pennies*
730 The man hym lovyd for thirty pownde, *valued at*
Eche peny hole and sownde,
 No lesse he wolde hym selle.
Florent seyde, "To lytull hyt were, *Too*
But never the less thou schalt have more."
735 Forty pownde he can hym telle. *he counted out*

The merchaund therof was full blythe
For to take the money swythe, *quickly*
 And hastyd hym away.
Chylde Florent lepe up to ryde,
740 To Clementys hows wyth grete pryde
 He toke the ryght way.
The chylde soght noon odur stalle,
But sett hys stede yn the halle
 And gave hym corne and haye. *grain*
745 And sethyn he can hym kembe and dyght *comb; groom*
That every heer lay aryght *[So] that*
 And nevyr oon wronge lay.

Clement comyth yn full sone:
"Thefe," he seyde, "what haste thou done?
750 What haste thou hedur broght?"
"Mercy, fadur, for Goddys peté
Wyth the money that ye toke me, *entrusted to me*
 Thys horse have y boght."
The burges wyfe felle on kne thore, *there*
755 "Syr, mercy," sche seyde, "for Crystys ore, *mercy*
 Owre feyre chylde bete ye noght. *beat*
Ye may see, and ye undurstode,
That he had never kynde of thy blode *kinship*
 That he these werkys hath wroght."

760 Aftur thys hyt was not longe,
In Fraunce felle a werre stronge, *war*
 An hundred thousande were there ylente. *arrived*
Wyth schyldys brode and helmys bryght, *shields*
Men that redy were to fyght,

765 Thorowowt the londe they went.
They broke castels stronge and bolde,
Ther myght no hye wallys them holde, *withstand*
 Ryche townys they brente.
All the kyngys, ferre and nere,
770 Of odur londys that Crysten were,
 Aftur were they sente.

Octavyon, the Emperour of Rome,
To Parys sone he come
 Wyth many a mody knyght. *spirited*
775 And othur kynges kene wyth crowne,
All they were to batell bowne *made ready*
 Wyth helmys and hawberkys bryght.
In Parys a monyth the oost lay, *host*
For they had takyn a day
780 Wyth the Sowdon moche of myght.
The Sowdon wyth hym a gyaunt broght;
The realme of Fraunce durste noght *dared*
 Agenste hym to fyght.

The Sowdon had a doghtur bryght,
785 Marsabelle that maydyn hyght, *was called*
 Sche was bothe feyre and fre;
The feyrest thynge alyve that was
In crystendome or hethynnes, *heathen lands*
 And semelyest of syght.
790 To the kynge of Fraunce the maydyn sende
To lye at Mountmertrous there nerehonde, *Montmartre*
 From Parys mylys thre.
At Mountmertrous besyde Borogh Larayn, *Borough of the Queen*
That stondyth over the banke of Sayne, *across*
795 For aventours wolde sche see. *combats*

The kyng of Fraunce the maydyn hyght, *was called*
As he was trewe kyng and knyght,
 And swere hur be hys fay *faith*
That she must savely come therto;
800 Ther schulde no man hur mysdo *mistreat*
 Neythur be nyght ne day.
The mayde therof was full blythe;
To the castell sche went swythe
 And seven nyghtes there sche lay.
805 For sche thoght joye and pryde

To see the Crystyn knyghtes ryde,
 On fylde them for to play.

 *(see note)*

 "Merveylle therof thynkes mee,
 If thou and alle thi men will blyn, *cease to fight*
810 I will undirtake to wynn
 Paresche, that stronge ceté;
 Bot Mersabele than weedde I will."
 Sayd the Sowdanne, "I halde thertill
 With thi, that it so bee." *Provided that*

815 Arageous, appon that same daye *(the giant's name)*
 To the Mount Martyn ther the lady laye, *Montmartre*
 The waye he tuke full ryghte.
 And hir hade lever dede to hafe bene *rather dead*
 Than hym in hir chambir to hafe sene,
820 So fulle he was of syghte. *ugly (foul); to look upon*
 He sayse, "Leman, kysse me belyve, *Beloved; quickly*
 Thy lorde me hase the graunte to wyefe,
 And Paresche I hafe hym hyghte. *promised*
 And I hete the witterly *promise you truly*
825 The kynges hevede of Fraunce, certanely, *head*
 Tomorowe or it be nyghte." *before*

 The mayden sayse with mylde mode *gentle manner*
 To the geaunte, ther he stode,
 And gaffe hym this answere:
830 "The kynges hevede if thou me brynge,
 Than sall thou hafe thyne askynge,
 For full lefe to me it were." *pleasing*
 Thane armede the geaunt hym ful wele
 Bothe in iryn and in stele,
835 With helme and schelde and spere.
 It was twenty fote and twoo
 Bytwyxe his crown and his too, *toe*
 There myghte none horse hym bere.

 The geaunte tuke the ryghte waye
840 Unto Paresche that ilke daye,
 With hym wente no moo.
 He lenede hym over the towne walle, *leaned*
 And thus he spake the folke withalle
 Wordis kene and throo. *bold; fierce*
845 He badde thay solde send owte a knyghte
 That myghte hym fynde his fill of fyghte,

Ore he that londe wolde overgoo. *overrun*
Therin solde he nother leve one lyffe, *alive*
Beste ne man, childe ne wyffe,
850 That he ne sold tham bryne and sloo. *burn; slay*

Than all the folke of that ceté
Rane the geaunte for to see,
 At the bretage thare he stode. *barricade*
Bot als ferre als thay myghte hym se or ken, *as soon as*
855 Faste awaywarde gan thay ryn; *run*
 For ferde thay were nere wode. *fear; nearly insane*
There wente owte armede knyghtes fyve
And sayd thay wolde aventure thair lyfe; *risk*
 The geaunt thoghte it gode.
860 Full hastyly he hase tham slayne.
Skapede never one qwykke agayne, *Escaped; alive*
 That owte unto hym yode. *went*

When he had slayne the knyghtes fyve,
Agayne to the walles gan he dryve
865 And over the bretage gan lye. *barricade; lie*
"Kynge Dagaberde of Fraunce," he sayde,
"Come thiselfe and fyghte abrayde *fight out in the open*
 For thi curtasye!
For I will with none other fyghte:
870 Thi hevede I hafe my leman highte; *head; to my lover promised*
 Scho salle me kysse with thi. *on that account*
And if thou ne will noghte do so,
Alle this ceté I will overgo; *overrun*
 Als dogges than sall thay dy!" *As*

875 Grette dole it was than for to see
The sorowe that was in that ceté,
 Bothe with olde and yonge.
For ther was nother kynge ne knyghte
That with that geaunt than durste fyghte, *dared*
880 He was so foulle a thynge.
And ay iwhills Arageous with his staffe *always meanwhile*
Many a grete bofete he gaffe *buffet*
 And the walles downe gan he dynge. *batter*
And than gane alle the pepille crye
885 Unto God and to mylde Marye
 With sorowe and grete wepynge.

Florent than askede his fadir Clement
Whate alle that spetous noyes than ment, *pitiful noise*
And whedir the folke so faste ren. *whither; ran*

890 Clement saide: "My dere sone,
 A geaunte to the walles es wonne, *come*
 Hase slayne fyve of oure men.
 Oure kynges hede hase he highte *promised*
 The Sowdan dogheter that es so bryghte, *lovely*
895 For scho solde kysse hym then.
 There es no man dare with hym fyghte;
 Forthi my dere sone, hase he tyghte *ordained*
 This ceté to breke and brynne." *destroy and burn*

 "Now fadir," he sayde, "I hafe a stede,
900 Wanttes me no thynge bot wede — *I only lack armor*
 Nowe helpes that I were dyghte. *prepared*
 A, lorde, why ever thus many men hym drede?
 Me thynke I myghte do alle his nede
 And I were armed ryghte." *If*
905 Sayse Clement, "And thou therof speke, *If*
 I trow I sall thyn hede breke,
 For had thou of hym a syghte,
 For all this ceté nolde thou habyde, *you would not abide*
 Bot faste awaywarde wold thou ryde,
910 He es so fowle a wyghte!" *evil a being*
 "A, fadir," he said, "takes to none ille,
 For with the geaunt fighte I wille,
 To luke, if I dare byde. *try; endure*
 And bot I titter armede be, *more quickly*
915 I sall noghte lett, so mote I the, *desist; thrive*
 That I ne salle to hym ryde." *Until I have ridden against him*
 Clement saide, "Sen thou willt fare, *Since*
 I hafe armoures swylke as thay are;
 I sall tham lene the this tyde, *lend to you; time*
920 Bot this seven yere sawe thay no sonne." *sun*
 "Fadir," he sayd, "alle es wonne!
 Ne gyffe I noghte a chide." *I'll stop complaining*

 "Bot Fadir," he sayde, "I yow praye,
 That we ne make no more delaye
925 Bot tyte that I ware dyghte; *quickly; armed*
 For I wolde noghte for this ceté
 That another man before me
 Undirtuke that fyghte."
 "Nay, nay," saise Clement, "I undirtake *guarantee*
930 That ther will none swylke maystres make,[1]
 Nother kynge ne knyghte.

[1] *That no one will attempt such feats of mastery*

Bot God sone sende the grace wirchipe to wyn *honor*
And late me never hafe perelle therin, *danger*
　　To the dede if thou be dyghte." *death; prepared*

935 For sorowe Clement herte nere braste *nearly broke*
When he one hym an actone caste; *padded jacket*
　　The childe was bolde and kene.
Ane hawberke abowne lete he falle, *coat of mail on top*
Full rysty weren the mayles alle, *rusty*
940 　　And alle his atyre bydene. *indeed*
Clement broghte forthe schelde and spere
That were unsemly for to were, *wear*
　　Soyty and alle unclene. *Sooty; dirty*
A swerd he broghte the child byforne,
945 That seven yere byfore had not bene borne
　　Ne drawen, and that was sene. *apparent*

Clement drewe the swerd, bot owte it nolde; *would not*
Gladwyn his wyfe sold the schawebereke holde, *scabbard*
　　And bothe righte faste thay drewe.
950 And when the swerde owte glente, *came*
Bothe unto the erthe thay went —
　　Than was ther gamen ynoghe.
Clement felle to the bynke so faste *bench*
That mouthe and nose al tobraste,
955 　　And Florente stode and loghe. *laughed*
Grete gamen it es to telle
How thay bothe to the erthe felle,
　　And Clement laye in swoghe. *lay unconscious*

Child Florent in his unfaire wede, *ugly apparel*
960 Whane he was armede on his stede,
　　His swerde with hym he bere. *bore*
His aventayle and his bacenete, *(see note)*
His helme appon his heved was sett, *head*
　　And bothe full soyty were. *sooty*
965 Bothe two, Clement and his wyfe,
Luffede the childe als thaire lyfe;
　　For hym thay wepede sore.
To Jhesu Criste full faste thay bede, *prayed*
"Lene hym grace, wele for to spede!" *Give*
970 　　Thay myghte do hym no more. *could do no more for him*

For his atyre that was unbryghte, *Because of; tarnished*
Hym byhelde bothe kyng and knyghte,
　　And mekill wondir tham thoghte. *great; it seemed to them*
Many a skornefulle worde he hent *received*

975	Als he thrughe the ceté went,	
	Bot therof gafe he noghte.	*he didn't care*
	Than gane the folke to the walles goo	
	To see the batelle bytwyx tham two	
	When thay were samen broghte.	
980	His fadir Clement, full sory was he,	
	To that he wyste whether mayster solde be,[1]	
	And glade ne was he noghte.	

	Florent come to the gates full sone	
	And bade the portere swythe undone	
985	And open the gates wyde.	
	All that abowte the gates stode,	
	Loughe so faste thay were nere wode,	*Laughed so hard*
	And skornede hym that tyde.	
	Ilk a man sayde to his fere,	*Each; companion*
990	"Here commes a doghety bachelere,	*young knight*
	Hym semes full wele to ryde;	
	Men may see by hys brene bryghte	*shining corselet*
	That he es a nobylle knyghte	
	The geaunt for to habyde!"	*encounter*

995	Bot than the geaunt upryghte gan stande	
	And tuke his burdone in his hande,	*club*
	That was of stele unryde.	*strong*
	And to the childe he smote so	
	That his schelde brake in two	
1000	And felle one aythire syde.	
	Than was the childe never so wo	
	Als when his schelde was in two,	
	Bot more he thoghte to byde.	
	And to the geaunt he smote so sore	
1005	That his righte arme flowe of thore;	*flew off*
	The blode stremyde than full wyde.	

	Than Clement appon the walles stode	
	And full blythe he wex than in his mode	*became*
	And gan amend his chere	*cheered up*
1010	And said, "Son, I hafe herde, I wene,	
	Thi nobill dynt that es so kene;	*blow; fierce*
	With me thou arte full dere.	*To*
	Now thynke me righte in my mode	
	That thou hase wele bysett oure gude,	*provided for*
1015	Swylke lawes for to lere."	*practices; learn*

[1] *Until he knew which of the two would be victorious*

Childe Florent in his unfaire wede
Spronge als sparke dose of glede, *does from a burning coal*
 The sothe I will yow saye, *truth*
And rode hym forthe with egre mode *eager*
1020 To the geaunt, righte ther he stode —
 Was thore no childes playe!
The geaunt smote to the childe so *noble youth*
That childe and horse to the grownde gan go,
 The stede one knes laye.
1025 Than cryede Clement with sory mode
And said, "Sone, be of comforthe gude
 And venge the, if thou maye."

And als ill als the childe ferde, *fared*
When he the speche of Clement herde,
1030 His herte bygan to bolde. *strengthen*
Boldly his swerde up he laghte *drew*
And to the geaunt a stroke he raughte *wroght*
 That all his blode gan colde. *grew cold*
The childe hym hitt one the schuldir bone
1035 That to the pappe the swerde gan gone,
 And the geaunt to the grounde gan folde. *fall*
And thus it felle thorow Goddes grace, *it came about*
He slewe the geaunt in that place,
 In bukes als it es tolde.

1040 The kynges appon the walles stode;
When the geaunt to the grounde yode, *fell*
 The folke, full blythe thay were.
Alle the folke at the childe loughe,
How he the geaunt hede of droghe *giant's; pulled off*
1045 When he hade smetyn hym thore.
The childe leppe up appon his stede
And rode awaye wele gude spede;
 With tham spekes he no more.
The childe toke the ryghte waye
1050 To the castelle ther the mayden laye, *where; maiden*
 And the hede with hym he bare. *head*

When he come to the mayden haulle, *maiden's*
He founde the burdes coverde alle *boards (tables)*
 And tham bowne to the mete. *ready for dinner*
1055 The mayden that was mylde of mode,
In a surkott in hyr haulle scho stode
 And redy was to hir sette. *at her seat*
"Damesele," said Florent, "faire and free,
Wele now gretis thi leman the *lover*

1060	Of that he the byhete.	*With what he had promised you*
	Lo, here an hevede I hafe the broghte —	*head*
	The kynges of Fraunce ne es it noghte,	
	For it were full evylle to gete."	*difficult*

	That mayden brighte als golden bey,	*ornament*
1065	When scho the geaunt heved sey,	
	Full wele scho it kende,	*recognized*
	And sayde, "He was ay trewe of his hete —	*promise*
	When he the kynges hevede myght not get,	
	His owen he hase me sende."	
1070	"Damesele," he sayde, "faire and bryghte,	
	Now wolde I hafe that, that ye hym highte."	*promised*
	And over his sadylle he lende.	*leaned*
	Full ofte sythes he kyssede that maye	*times*
	And hent hir upe and wolde awaye,	*took*
1075	Bot thay alle the brigges did fende.	*Although all the bridges were defended*

	Crye and noyse rose in thate towne,	
	And sone thay ware to the batelle bowne —	
	Full many an hardy knyghte.	
	With speres longe and swerdes brounne.	*polished*
1080	And Florent lete the mayden downe	
	And made hym bowne to fyghte.	*ready*
	Hyre surkotte sleve he rofe of then	*Her; tore off*
	And sayde, "By this ye sall me kene	*know*
	When ye se me by syghte."	
1085	Swylke lufe wexe bytwix tham two,	*Such*
	That lady grett, so was hir wo,	*grieved*
	That he ne wyn hir myghte.	

	Childe Florent in his unfaire wede,	
	Full many a Sarezene made he to blede,	
1090	The sothe I will yow saye.	*truth*
	Many a hethyn man in a stownde	*short time*
	He made to lygge appon the grownde —	
	Was ther no childes playe.	
	When Florent thoghte that he wold founde	*depart*
1095	Withowtten other weme or wounde,	*either hurt*
	To Paresche he tuke the waye	
	The hethyn men were so adrede,	
	To Cleremont with the may thay flede,	*maiden*
	There the Sowdanne laye.	

1100	And in hir fadir paveleone	*father's tent*
	Thore lyghttede the mayden down	*alighted*
	And knelede appon hir knee.	

Than was the Sowdane wondir blythe
And to his dogheter went he swythe
1105 And kyssed hir sythes thre. *times*
He sett hir downe appon the dese *dais*
That full riche was, withowttyn lese, *without lying (i.e., truly)*
 With grete solempnyté
Scho tolde hir fadir and wilde nott layne, *would not be silent*
1110 How Arageous the geaunt was slayne.
A fulle sorye man was he.

Scho saide: "Leve fadir, thyne ore, *Dear*
At the Mont Martyn late me lye no more,
 So nere Christen men to bene.
1115 In swylke ane aventure I was this daye,
A rebawde me hade nere borne awaye *rascal*
 Fro alle myn knyghttes kene.
Thore was no man of hethen londe
That myghte a dynt stonde of his honde, *blow sustain from*
1120 That he ne fellede tham bydene.
Als ofte als I appon hym thynke,
I may nother ete nor drynke,
 So full I ame of tene." *distress*

Bot when the Sowdane this tythande herde, *news heard*
1125 He bote his lippes and schoke his berde, *bit; shook*
 That grymly was to see, *dreadful*
And swore with hedouse contenance *hideous*
That he sulde hange the kynge of Frauncce
 And bryne alle Cristyanté, *burn*
1130 And that he sulde nother leve one lyve *alive*
Man, beste, childe no wyfe,
 With eghene that he myghte see. *eyes*
"Dougheter," he said, "go to thi chambir
And luke thou make full glade chere;
1135 Thow salle wele vengede be."

Full richely was hir chambir sprede
And thedir in was that lady lede
 With birdis that scho broghte. *ladies*
One softe seges was hir sete, *On; seats*
1140 Bot myghte scho nother drynke ne ete,
 So mekill scho was in thoghte *deep*
Sumtyme one his faire chere, *expression*
And one his coloure, and one his lyre; *face*
 Scho myghte forgete hym noghte.
1145 Full stylle scho saide with hert sore,

"Allas! that I ne with my lemane wore *beloved were*
 Whedir he wolde me hafe broghte." *Wherever*

One hir bede righte als scho laye *bed*
Scho callede unto hir a maye *maiden*
1150 Full prevaly and stylle. *secretly; quietly*
That mayden highte Olyvayne *was named*
That was full faire of blode and bane *fair in appearance (blood and bone)*
 And moste wiste of hir wille. *understood; desire*
Scho saide, "Olyve, in prevaté *secret*
1155 My concelle I will schewe to the
 That greves me full ille,
For one a childe es alle my thoghte *young man*
That me to Paresche wolde hafe broghte,
 And I ne maye come hym tille!" *If*

1160 Olyve hir answers tho *then*
And sais, "Lady, sen ye will so, *since*
 Ne drede yow for no wyghte, *person*
For I sall helpe yow that I may,
Bothe by nyghte and by day,
1165 That he wynn yow myghte.
Yitt may swylke aventure be *such*
At youre wille ye may hym see
 Or this daye fowrtene nyghte, *Before; fourteen*
At the Monte Martyne I wolde ye were,
1170 There salle ye somewhat of hym here *hear*
 Whether he be sqwyere or knyghte."

The Cristyn men than were full blythe
When thay sawe Florent on lyfe; *alive*
 Thay wende he hade bene lorne. *thought; lost (killed)*
1175 And when he come nere the ceté
Agayne hym wente kynges thre, *Towards*
 And the Emperoure rode byforne.
And to the palayse the childe was broghte,
Full riche atyre thay for hym soghte *attire*
1180 Of golde and sylver schene. *bright*
Men callede hym Florent of Paresche,
For thus in romance tolde it es,
 Thoghe he ther were noghte borne. *wasn't born there*

And Clement, for the childes sake,
1185 Full faire to courte thay gan take
 And gaffe hym full riche wede.
One softe seges was he sett *seats*
Amonge grete lordes at the mete *feast*

	And servede of many riche brede.	*food*
1190	The childe was sett with grete honowre	
	Bytwixe the kynge and the Emperoure,	
	His mete thay gan hym schrede.	*cut up (carved)*
	He was so curtayse and so bolde	
	That alle hym lovede, yonge and olde,	
1195	For his doghety dede.	

	Noghte longe after, als I yow saye,	
	The childe solde be knyghte that other daye;	*next day*
	No lenger wolde thay habyde.	*delay*
	His atyre of golde was wroghte,	
1200	Byfore the Emperoure the childe was broghte,	
	A kyng one aythir syde.	
	The kyng of Fraunce byfore hym yode	*went*
	With mynstralles full many and gode	
	And lede hym up with pryde.	
1205	Clement to the mynstralles gan go	
	And gafe some a stroke and some two;	
	There durste noghte one habyde.	

	Clement so sorye was that daye	
	For alle thaire costes that he solde paye,	
1210	That he gane wepe wele sore.	
	And whills the kynges dauwnsede in the halle	*danced*
	Clement tuke thaire mantills alle	*cloaks*
	And to his howse tham bare.	
	Than the kynges gan thaire mantills myse	
1215	And ilke man askede after his,	
	Where thay bycomen were.	
	Than swore Clement, "By Goddes daye,	
	For youre mete moste ye paye	*must*
	Or ye gete tham no more."	

1220	Thereatt all the kynges loghe,	*laughed*
	There was joye and gamen ynoghe	
	Amonges tham in the haulle.	
	The kynge of Fraunce with hert ful fayne	
	Said, "Clement, brynge the mantils agayne,	
1225	For I sall paye for alle."	
	Clement thoreof was full blythe	
	And home he rane als so swythe	
	To his owen haulle;	
	And to the palays he mantils bare	
1230	And bade tham take tham alle thare	
	And downe he lette tham falle.	

	The burdes were sett and coverd alle, Childe Florent was broghte into the haulle With full mekill presse.	
1235	The childe was sett with gret honowre Bytwixe the kyng and the Emperoure, Sothe withowtten lese. The Emperoure gan the childe byholde; He was so curtayse and so bolde,	
1240	Bot he ne wiste what he was.	*knew*
	And ever he thoghte in his mode	*If; heart*
	The childe was comen of gentill blode. Hym thoghte righte, als it was.	
	When the folke all had eten	
1245	Clement hade noghte forgetyn, His purse he openede thore.	
	Thritty florence forthe keste he	*cast*
	And said, "Hafe here for my son and me, I may paye for no more."	
1250	Clement was curtaise and wyse,	
	He wend alle had bene marchandyse,	*thought; merchandise (for sale)*
	The pryde that he sawe thore.	*splendor*
	At Clement loghe the knyghtes alle,	*laughed*
	So did the kynges in the haulle,	
1255	Childe Florent schamede full sore.	*was ashamed*
	Than spekes the Emperoure anone ryghte To Florent, that was faire and bryghte, Wordis full wondir stille And said, "Yonge knyghte, telle thou me,	
1260	If yone man thyn owen fadir be." The childe answerde hym till, "Sir, lufe hade I never hym too,	
	Als I solde to my fadir doo,	*should*
	Never in herte ne wille;	
1265	Bot of alle the men that ever sawe I,	
	Moste lufes myn herte yowe sekirly.	*truly*
	Syr, takes it to none ille."	*Sir, take no offense*
	The Emperoure did calle Clement thore And made hym come and sytt hym nere	
1270	Oppon the heghe dese.	*high dais*
	He bade hym telle the righte dome,	*explanation*
	How he to the childe come,	*came by the child*
	Sothe withowtten lese.	*Truth; lies*
	"Sir," he said, "this childe was taken in a foreste	
1275	Fro a lady with a wylde beste	

In ane grete wildirnes;
And I hym boghte for thritty pownde,
Everylke peny bothe hole and rownde, *Every; whole*
 And sayde myn owen he was."

1280 Than was the Emperoure joyefull and blythe,
Of his tales for to lythe, *hear*
 And thanked God almyghte.
The Emperoure felle one knes als swythe
And kyssede the childe full fele sythe, *many times*
1285 Thoghe he ne wiste whate he highte, *was named*
For full wele he trowede, withowtten lese, *believed*
His owen sone that he was.
 Alle gamnes, bothe kyng and knyghte. *rejoice*
The childes name was chaungede with dome, *duly*
1290 Thay callede hym than Florent of Rome
 Als it was full gude ryghte.

The Emperoure was so blythe of chere
That the teris trekelide one his lyre. *face*
 He made than full grete care
1295 And said, "Allas, my faire wyfe,
The beste lady that was one lyfe,
 Salle I hir see no mare?
Me ware lever than alle the golde *It would be dearer to me than*
That ever was appon Cristyn molde, *ground*
1300 Wyste I one lyve scho ware!" *[If] I knew she were alive*
The Emperoure gafe Clement welthis fele *many*
To lyfe in reches and in wele, *riches; bounty*
 Aye nowe for evermore. *Always*

Als Florent one an nyghte in bede laye, *As*
1305 He thoghte one Marsabele that faire maye,
 And full mekill he was in kare.
The childe had nother riste ne ro *rest nor peace*
For thoghte how he myghte com hir to,
 And whate that hym beste ware.
1310 The childe thoghte for the mayden sake *maiden's*
A message that he wolde make
 And to the Sowdane fare.
And sone the childe did sadill his stede
And armede hym in full riche wede,
1315 A braunche of olyve he bare.

For that was that tym messangere lawe[1]
A brawnche of olyve for to schewe
 And it in hand to bere.
For the ordynance than was so, *decree*
1320 Messangers solde savely come and go *safely*
 And no man solde tham dere. *should; harm*
The childe takes the heghe waye
To Cleremont thare the Sowdan laye
 With alle his grete here; *army*
1325 And at the haulle dore he reyngened his stede
And one fote in he yede,
 Messangere als he were.

Than spekes the childe with hardy mode,
Byfore the Sowdane there he stode,
1330 Als man of mekill myghte:
"The kynge of Fraunce me hedir sende
And byddis the owte of his lande wende, *orders you out*
 For thou werreys agayne the righte; *war against justice*
Or he wille brynge agayne the
1335 Twentty thowsande tolde by thre *multiplied*
 With helmes and hawberkes bryghte.
And ilke a knyghte sall thritty sqwyers hafe,
And ilke a sqwyere a foteknave *foot-soldier*
 Worthe an heythen knyghte." *Worthy to be*

1340 Than the Sowdane bygane to speke,
Als he satt at his riche mete
 Amonge his knyghttes kene:
"The kynge of Fraunce welecome sall be;
Ever agayne on I sall brynge thre, *against one [of the king's men]*
1345 Weite he withowtten wene, *Wait; doubt*
That als fayne bene for to fyghte *eager*
Als fowle es of dayes lyghte, *bird; dawn*
 To schewe thaire scheldes schene. *bright shields*
To prove tomorowe, by my laye, *law (faith)*
1350 I kepe to take no langere daye; *intend*
 Than salle the sothe be sene!"

Than spekes that may with mylde mode *maiden*
To faire Florent thare he stode,
 That was so swete a wyghte:
1355 "Messenger, I wolde the frayne *ask you*
Whether he es knyghte or swayne, *person of servile rank*

[1] *For it was at that time the law of messengers*

That es so mekill of myghte

That hase my fadir geaunt slayne *father's*

And wolde hafe ravesched me fra Borow Lerayne *carried me off from*

1360 And slewe ther many a knyghte."

Alle thoghe scho nevenede hym with ille, *referred to him in anger*

Fulle mekill was it than hir wille,

Of hym to hafe a syghte.

"Lady," he sayse, "he es nother lesse ne more,

1365 Than it I my selfe wore.

Sythe ye will of hym frayne, *ask*

Ye sall hym knawe thurgh alle the here, *army*

Youre sleve he wille hafe on his spere

In the batelle al playne." *visible*

1370 Withowtten any more worde

Ilke man stirte upe fro the borde *table*

With swerdes and knyves drawen;

For alle thay wiste wele by than, *knew*

That he it was, that ilke man *same*

1375 That hade the geaunt slayne.

Than Florent sawe no better bote *remedy*

Bot nedely hym tydes to fighte one fote[1]

Agayne the Sarazenes alle;

And ever he hitt tham amange

1380 Where he sawe the gretteste thrange; *throng*

Full many he did to falle. *made fall*

Sum by the armes he nome *took*

That the schuldir with hym come,

The prowdeste in the haulle;

1385 And some he swilke a boxe lent *blow gave*

That the heved fro the body went,

Als it were a foteballe.

And when his swerde broken was,

A meteforme he gatt par cas *bench; by chance*

1390 And therewith he gan hym were; *defend*

And to the grounde sone garte he go *caused*

Ten score and somdele mo *somewhat more*

That heythen knyghtes were.

Florent made a waye ful gode

1395 To his stede righte ther he stode,

There myghte no man hym dere. *harm*

And home he takes the righte waye

[1] *But of necessity it happens that he must fight on foot*

Unto Parische als it laye,
　　Thurgheowte the heythen here. *army*

1400　Than were the Crysten folke full blythe
　　When thay sawe Florent one lyve;
　　　　Thay wende he lorne hade bene. *thought; lost*
　　And whenne he come nere the ceté,
　　Agayne hym went kynges thre, *Towards*
1405　　　The Emperoure rode bytwene. *in the middle*
　　Alle the folke pressede hym to se.
　　Ilke a man fraynede, "Whilke es he?" *Each; asked*
　　　　Als thay hym never hade sene. *As if*
　　Unto the palese he was ledde;
1410　He tolde tham alle how he had spede
　　　　Amonge the Sarazens kene.

　　"Lordynges," he saide, "lukes ye be yare *ready*
　　Unto the batelle for to fare,
　　　　And redy for to ryde.
1415　Tomorowe moste it nede be sene
　　Who es hardy man and kene,
　　　　No lengere ne may we byde."
　　The folke sayde that thay were blythe
　　To wende to that batelle swythe —
1420　　　In herte es noghte to hide. *It is not to be concealed*
　　A riche clothe one the borde was sprede
　　To make the childe bothe blythe and glade,
　　　　A kyng one aythir syde.

　　One the morowe when the daye was lyghte,
1425　The folke tham to the batelle dyghte, *for; prepared*
　　　　Alle that wapen moghte welde. *wield*
　　There men myghte se many a wyghte
　　With helmes schene and hawberke bryghte,
　　　　With spere and als with schelde.
1430　With trompes and with mekill pryde *trumpets; much*
　　Full boldly owt of borowe thay ryde *town*
　　　　Unto a full brode felde.
　　The felde was bothe longe and brode,
　　Thore bothe the partyes one habode,
1435　　　And aythere other byhelde. *on waited*

　　Marsabele, that mayden fre,
　　Was broghte that batelle for to see,
　　　　To the Mont Martyne appon Seyne.
　　Florent hir sleve did on his spere *fixed*
1440　For in the batelle he wolde it bere,

And forthe he rode in the playne
For that men solde wele se than
That he it was, that ilke man *that very man*
 That haved the geaunt slayne, *had*
1445 And also for that mayden free
Was broghte that batelle for to see;
 There of scho was full fayne. *glad*

Than was there mekill sorow and syte, *distress*
When the batells bygan to smytte *forces*
1450 With many a grymly wonde.
Fro morow that the daye was lyghte *morning*
To it was even and dirke nyghte, *Until; evening; dark*
 Or owthir partye wolde fownde. *depart*
Florent gan ever amonges ryde
1455 And made thore many a sory syde *sore*
 That ore was hale and sownde. *previously*
So many folke thore to the dede yode *death went*
That stedis wode in the blode *horses waded*
 That stremyd one the grounde. *flowed*

1460 Thore men myghte see helmes bare
And hevedis that full faire waree *were*
 Full lawe to the grownde than lyghte. *low; alight*
The Cristen men bycome so thyn *sparse*
That the felde myghte thay noghte wyn,
1465 Alle cryede, bothe kyng and knyghte.
Than Florent smote with herte so gude,
His swerde thurghe thaire helmes wode, *went*
 So mekyll he was of myghte. *great*
Thurghe Goddes grace and Florent thore
1470 The Cristen men the better wore
 That ilke daye in the fyghte.

The parties ere withdrawen awaye *are*
And taken there es another daye *designated*
 That the batelle sulde be. *should*
1475 Florent rode to Borow Lerayne
Besyde the water banke of Sayne,
 For aventurs wolde he see.
The mayden whitt als lely floure *lily*
Laye in a kirnelle of a towre, *embrasure*
1480 Was ferly faire and fre. *wondrously*
Florent scho sawe on the felde fare; *go*
By hir sleve that he bare
 Scho knewe wele that it was he.

Then spekes that may with mylde mode *gentle heart*
1485 To Olyve that byfore hir stode
 That wyste hir prevaté, *Who knew; secret thoughts*
 And saide, "Howe were it beste to do,
 A worde that I myghte speke hym to?
 Iwysse, than wele were me." *Indeed*
1490 Scho saide, "Lady, we one two *alone*
 By the rever banke sall go,
 That he may us see.
 If he yow lufe with hert gude,
 He lettes no thyng for the flode; *delays not at all on account of the water*
1495 A full gude horse haves he." *has*

 Forthe than went theis maydenes two,
 Owte of the castelle gan thay goo
 By the revere syde.
 When Florent sawe that swete wyghte *creature*
1500 He sprent als any fowle of flyghte, *leapt up*
 No lenger then wolde he byde.
 His horse he was full wondir gude
 And bare hym smertly over the flode, *quickly*
 Hymselffe couthe full wele ryde.
1505 It was grete joye to se tham mete
 With haulsynge and with kyssynge swete — *embracing*
 In herte es noghte to hyde.

 "Lady," he sayde, "full wele es mee,
 A worde that I may speke with the,
1510 So bryghte ert thou of hewe. *complexion*
 In alle this werlde es non so free *noble*
 Forwhi that thow wolde cristenede be *If only*
 And sythen of herte be trewe." *then*
 "Sir, if that thou myghte me wyn,
1515 I wolde forsake all my kyn,
 Als I them never knewe. *As if*
 Sythen thou wolde wedde me to wyfe *Since*
 I wolde lyve in Cristen lyfe;
 My joye solde ever be newe."

1520 "Lady," he sayde, "withowtten fayle,
 Howe were than thi beste consaile, *advice*
 That I the wynn myghte?"
 "Sertes, ye me never wyn ne maye *Surely*
 Bot if it were that ilke daye
1525 That ye hafe tane to fyghte, *arranged*
 That ye wolde send up by the flode
 Men that bene styffe and gude,

	And a schippe that wele were dyghte,	*fitted out*
	And ywhills the folke weren at thaire dede,	*deeds*
1530	That thay me myghte awaye lede	
	Into youre ceté full ryghte.	

	"My fadir has a nobille stede,	
	In the werlde es none so gude at nede	
	In tornament no in fyghte.	*nor*
1535	In his hevede he hase an horne,	*head*
	Es schapen als an unycorne	*unicorn*
	That selcouthe es of syghte.	*marvelous*
	Sir, if you myghte that stede now wyn,	
	There were no man in heythen kynn	
1540	Agayne the that stande myghte."	
	Florent kyssede that faire maye	
	And sayd, "Lady, hafe gud daye	
	And holde that thou hase highte."	*keep your promises*

	Florent hase his stede nomen	*taken*
1545	And over that water es he comen,	
	To Paresche he tuke the waye.	
	He wolde neythir stynte ne blyn	*stop nor cease*
	Bot home to Clement gan he wyn,	*did he go*
	His awntirs for to saye;	*adventures; explain*
1550	And tolde hym of that gude stede	
	That nobille was in ilke a nede,	*such a circumstance*
	And of that faire maye.	
	And he said, "Sone, be doghety man of dede,	*Son*
	And certes thou sall hafe that stede	
	Tomorowe, gyff that I maye."	*if*

1555	One the morne when the day was lyghte,	
	Clement gan hymselven dyghte	*prepare*
	Lyke an unfrely fere	*ugly companion*
	And went into the heythen oste	*heathen host*
	Thore the presse was althermoste,	*Where; crowd; greatest*
1560	A Sarazene als he were.	
	And to the paveleone he gan wynn	*go*
	There the Sowdan hymselfe was in.	
	Full brymly he gan bere	*boldly; shout*
	And askede tham sum of thaire mete.	*food*
1565	Full wele he couthe thaire speche speke;	*knew how; language to speak*
	The Sowdane hymselfe gan here.	*hear*

	Grete dole the Sowdane of hym thoghte,	
	And sone he was byfore hym broghte	
	And with hym gan he speke.	

1570	He saide he was a Sarazene stronge	
	And in his oste hade bene full longe	*army*
	And hade grete fawte of mete.	*lack*
	"Sir, there es no man in heythen thede	*land*
	That better kane ryde and kepe a stede	
1575	Or other horsses grete."	
	The Sowdane saide that ilke tyde,	*time*
	"If that thou wele a stede kan ryde,	
	With me thou sall be lette."	*allowed [to stay]*

	Thay horsede Clement one a stede,	
1580	He spronge als any sparke one glede	
	Appone a full faire felde.	
	Alle that stode on ilk a syde	*every*
	Hade joye to se Clement ryde	
	Byfore the Sowdans telde.	*tent*
1585	And when he hade reden courses thre	*ridden*
	Alle had joye that hym gan see,	
	The Sowdan hym behelde.	
	Clement lyghtede down full sone	
	And one a better horse was done;	*set*
1590	Full faire he gan hym welde.	*control*

	Grete joye the Sowdan of hym thoghte	
	And badde his owen stede solde be broghte	
	And Clement one hym solde ryde.	
	And when Clement was on that stede	
1595	He rode awaye wele gud spede —	
	No lengare he wold habyde.	*remain*
	And when he was redy for to fownde,	*set out*
	"Fare wele," he said, "heythen honde,	*dog*
	For thou hase loste thi pryde."	*prized possession*
1600	Clement tuke hym the heghe waye	
	Unto Paresche als it laye,	
	Full blythe he was that tydee.	*time*

	"Florent," he said, "whore art thou?	
	That I the highte, I hafe here nowe,	*What I promised you*
1605	I hafe the broghte the stede."	
	Florent was full blythe that daye,	
	And saide, "Fadir, if that I maye,	
	I salle the yelde thi mede.	*give; reward*
	Bot to the Emperoure of Rome	
1610	The stede I wolde were present sone;	*presented*
	To the the palesse ye hym lede.	
	For ever me thynke in my mode,	

That I ame comen of his blode,
 So proudly if I moghte spede."

1615 Than to the palays the stede was ledde,
The knyghttes were than alle full glade,
 One hym for to see.
The Emperour byfore tham stode
And resceyvede hym with mylde mode,
1620 So wondir faire was hee.
Florent spake with grete honour
To his lorde the Emperour,
 "Sir, this stede gyffe I the."
Alle that evir abowte him stode
1625 Sayde he was comen of gentull blode,
 It moghte nevir othirwis be.

Aftur thys the day was nomyn *set*
That the batell on schulde comyn
 Agenste the Sarsyns to fyght.
1630 Wyth trompes and wyth moche pryde *pomp*
Boldely owte of borogh they ryde
 Als men of mekill myght.
Florent thoghte on the feyre maye,
To the batelle wente he not that day
1635 A schipe sone he hath hym dyght.
Fro Mont Martrons there the lady lay
To Paresche he broght hur away,
 Wist nother kynge ne knyght. *Knew*

That while was moche sorowe yn fyght
1640 When the batell began to smyght
 With many a grymme gare; *sword*
Fro morowe that hyt was daylyght
To it even was and myrke of nyght,
 Wyth wondes wondur sore.
1645 And for that Florent was not there
The heythen folke the bettur were;
 The batelle thay venquyscht thore. *won there*
Or Florent was to the felde comyn, *Before*
The Emperoure and the kynge were ynomyn *captured*
1650 And the Crysten kynges all that were.

Than Florent smote with herte so gode
And rode thurgh tham als he were wode,
 Of witt als he wolde wede. *As though he would lose his mind*
Thore was no Sarazene of myghte ne mayne
1655 That myght with strenghe stande hym agayne,

Whills that he hade his stede.
Than was of Florent dole ynoghe,
How thay his stede undir hym sloghe *slew*
 And he to the gronde than yode.
1660 Sir Florent was taken in that fyghte —
 Bothe the Emperoure, kynge and knyghte,
 Bownden thay gan thaym lede.

 The Sarsyns buskyd them wyth pryde *hastened*
 Into ther own londys to ryde;
1665 They wolde no lenger dwelle.
 Takyn they had Syr Florawns,
 The Emperour and the kyng of Fraunce
 Wyth woundys wondur fele. *many*
 Othur Crystyn kyngys moo, *more*
1670 Dewkys, erlys and barons also,
 That arste were bolde and swelle. *previously; arrogant*
 And ladd them wyth yron stronge *iron fetters*
 Hur fete undur the hors wombe, *Their feet; stomach*
 Grete dele hyt ys to telle.

1675 Wyde the worde sprange of thys chawnce,
 How the Sowdon was yn Fraunce,
 To warre agenste the ryght.
 In Jerusalem men can hyt here, *heard it*
 How the Emperour of Rome was there
1680 Wyth many an hardy knyght.
 Than spekyth Octavyon, the yyng, *young*
 Full feyre to hys lorde, the kyng,
 As chylde of moche myght,
 "Lorde, yf hyt were yowre wylle,
1685 I wolde wynde my fadur tylle
 And helpe hym yn that fyght." *go to*

 Than spekyth the kyng of moche myght
 Full fayre unto that yong knyght,
 Sore hys herte can blede,
1690 "Sone, thou schalt take my knyghtes fele *many*
 Of my londe that thou wylle wele *choose*
 That styffe are on stede, *powerful*
 Into Fraunce wyth the to ryde,
 Wyth hors and armys be thy syde,
1695 To helpe the at nede.
 When thou some doghtynes haste done,
 Then may thou shewe thyn errande soone, *reveal*
 The bettur may thou spede." *succeed*

He bad hys modur make hur yare, *ready*
1700 Into Fraunce wyth hym to fare,
He wolde no lenger byde.
Wyth hur she ladd the lyenas, *lioness*
That sche broght owt of wyldurnes,
Rennyng be hur syde. *by*
1705 There men myght see many a knyght
With helmys and wyth hawberkys bryght
Forthe ynto the strete.
Forthe they went on a day,
The hethyn ooste on the way
1710 All they can them meete.

By the baners that they bare,
They knewe that they hethyn ware
And stylle they can abyde.
They dyght them wyth brenyes bryght *fitted themselves; chain mail*
1715 And made them redy for to fyght;
Ageyn them can they ryde.
They hewe the flesche fro the bone, *cut*
Soche metyng was never none *meeting (i.e., battle)*
Wyth sorow on ylke syde.
1720 Octavyon the yong knyght,
Thorow the grace of God almyght,
Full faste he fellyd ther pryde.

The lyenas that was so wyght,
When she sawe the yong knyght
1725 Into the batell fownde,
Sche folowed hym wyth all hur myght
And faste fellyd the folke yn fyght;
Many sche made onsownde. *injured*
Grete stedys downe sche drowe
1730 And many hethen men sche slowe
Wythynne a lytull stownde. *short time*
Thorow God that ys of myghts gode,
The Crysten men the bettur stode —
The hethyn were broght to grownde.

1735 The Crysten prysoners were full fayne
When the Sarsyns were yslayne,
And cryed, "Lorde, thyn ore!" *mercy*
He ne stynt ne he ne blanne *neither stopped nor ceased*
To the prysoners tyll that he wanne,
1740 To wete, what they were. *know*
The Emperour, wythowt lees,
That hys own fadur was,

 Bowndon fownde he there. *Bound*
 The kyng of Fraunce and odur moo, *others as well*
1745 Dewkys, erlys and barons also,
 Were woundyd wondur sore.

 Hys fadur was the furste man,
 That he of bondys to lowse began, *loose*
 Ye wete, wythowten lees;
1750 And he lowsyd hys brodur Floraunce
 Or he dud the kynge of Fraunce,
 Yyt he wyste not what he was.
 Be that hys men were to hym comyn,
 Soon they were fro yrons nomyn, *taken*
1755 The pryncys prowde yn prees. *valiant in battle*
 Whan he had done that noble dede,
 The bettur he oght for to spede
 To make hys modur pees. *peace (reconciliation)*

 A ryche cyté was besyde
1760 Boldely thedur can they ryde
 To a castell swythe.
 Ryche metys were thore dyghte,
 Kyngys, dewkys, erlys and knyghte,
 All were gladd and blythe.
1765 Syth came Octavyon the yong with grete honoure
 And knelyd before the Emperoure.
 Hys errande for to kythe. *make known*
 That ylke tale that he thore tolde,
 Ryche and pore, yong and olde,
1770 Glade thay were to lythe. *listen*

 He seyde, "Lorde, in this lande I hafe the soghte,
 My modir I hafe with me broghte,
 I come to make hir pese."
 The Emperoure was never so blythe,
1775 Als for to kysse the childe full swythe,
 And for his sone hym chese. *chose*
 "Lorde, for a lesesynge that was stronge, *lie; outrageous*
 Scho was flemede owt of londe. *exiled*
 I prove that it was lese." *a lie*
1780 For joye that he his wiefe gan se, *wife did*
 Seven sythes swonede he *swooned*
 Byfore the heghe dese. *dais*

 Faire Florent than was full blythe,
 Of that tydandes for to lythe, *listen*
1785 His modir for to see.

"Lorde," scho said, "for alle the noye that me was wroghte, *trouble*
Thyn on childe I hafe the broghte *own*
 And yemede hym evir with me. *protected*
Thyn othir sone in a foreste
1790 Was taken with a wilde beste; *by*
 He was bothe faire and fre.
Alle, I wote, es Goddes grace,
I knowe hym by his faire face:
 That yone yong knyghte es he!"

1795 Than was thore full mekill gamen,
With halsynge and with kyssyngez samen *hugging; as well*
 Into the chambir thay yode.
And full grete joye there was also
At the metyng of the brethir two,
1800 That doghety weren of dede.
A riche feste the Emperour mad thare
Of lordes, that were ferre and nere, *[from] far*
 And of many a londes lede. *people*
This tale whoso telles ryghte,
1805 The feste lastede a fourtenyghte, *fortnight*
In romance thus we rede.

Marsabele that faire maye
Was after sent, the sothe to saye,
 To Paresche righte thore scho was.
1810 Cristenede scho was on a Sonondaye *Sunday*
With joye and gamen and mekill playe;
 Florent to wyefe hir chese. *chose*
Swylke a brydale als was thore, *wedding*
In that ceté was nevir ore, *before*
1815 Ye wiete withowtten lese. *know; lie*
Child Florent thore hir gan wedde,
And into Rome was scho ledde
 With prynces prowde in prese.

And then byfelle appon a daye,
1820 The Emperoure bygan for to saye
 And tolde alle how it was.
And alle than gafe juggement,
That his modir sulde be brynte *burnt*
 In a belle of brasse. *cauldron*
1825 Als sonne als scho therof herde telle,
In swonynge to the gronde scho felle,
 Hir hare of scho gan rase. *she tore out*
For schame that scho was proved false,

In two scho cutte hir owen halse *neck*
1830 With a longe anelase. *dagger*

 And therat alle the kynges loghe, *laughed*
 There was joye and gamen ynowghe;
 Alle tuke thaire leve that tyde.
 With trowmpes and with lowde songe *trumpets*
1835 Ilke a man wente to his owun londe
 With joye and mekill pryde.
 With gamen and joye and grete honoure
 To Rome than wente the Emperoure,
 His lady by his syde
1840 And his two sonnes also
 And with tham many one mo,
 Home than gan thay ryde.

 And thus endis Octovean,
 That in his tym was a doghety man,
1845 With the grace of Mary free,
 Now, Jhesu lorde, of heven kynge,
 Thou gyffe us alle thi dere blyssynge.
 Amen, amen, par charyté! Amen.

NOTES TO *OCTAVIAN*

Before 1 The text is preceded by an incipit: *Here bygynnes the Romance off Octovyane.*

1 The line begins with a large rubricated *M*.

10 Romances conventionally cite "books of Rome" as their source (see *Eglamour*, *Emaré*) to suggest the story's authenticity. Here it is appropriate since Rome is the emperor's capital city.

15 The reference to romance reading is in contrast to the oral presentation of the first stanza; both are conventional. See note to *Isumbras*, line 135.

21 *No worthier undir wede.* Literally, in clothes; an idiom meaning roughly, "no worthier person alive."

32 Southern *Octavian* alone does not suggest barrenness; there the unmarried emperor is urged by his barons to take a wife so that he may have an heir. He does and twin sons are born.

66 *fay* (doomed to die) is infrequent in Middle English, surviving longest in Scotland (see *Octovian*, ed. McSparran, p. 182).

76 The building of an abbey to win the intercession of the Virgin is found only in Northern *Octavian*. (It is unnecessary in Southern; see note to line 32 above.) The building of abbeys to earn spiritual rewards occurs in other romances and the endowment of ecclesiastical foundations was a common practice in the Middle Ages (see, e.g., *Sir Gawain and the Carl of Carlyle* and *Sir Gowther*). Here it is a functional analogue of the pilgrimage undertaken by Tryamour's barren father.

 The empress' association with the Virgin Mary, initiated here, continues throughout the romance. She enlists Mary's help once again less than two hundred lines later when she is sentenced to death by burning (lines 259–64), and it is through the "myghte of Mary mylde" that she is able to regain one of her sons from the lioness. According to Salter, this persistent association with the Virgin establishes the empress as both the "personification of loving, patient, and self-sacrificing motherhood," and the antithesis of her inexplicably evil mother-in-law ("'Born to Thraldom and Penance,'" p. 49).

95 The giving of gifts to bearers of good news was traditional; these rewards of three towns to each messenger were generous.

124 ff. The episode of the supposed lover is derived from the Crescentia story (see *Erle of Tolous*).

172–84 In the Cambridge text the empress remains asleep during this scene.

185 Churching was a purification ritual for women after the birth of a child (usually forty days). Only in Northern *Octavian* is the punishment of the empress so delayed.

217 Adultery with the wife of one's lord was classified as an act of treason, according to medieval English law.

223 The role of the empress' father here is suggestive of the cruel father found in other romances of calumniated queens. There the father intends to punish his daughter; here his condemnation of her is unwitting, and later he laments her ordeal (line 241).

244–55 Only the first three triplets appear in the corresponding Cambridge stanza, where they follow an introductory triplet that does not appear in Thornton.

273 *nere ne myghte*. MS: *nere myghte*. McSparran's emendation.

281 Florins were issued in Florence and circulated widely from the mid-thirteenth century. Edward III introduced a florin to England in 1343. Broh says a florin was worth six shillings, eight pence (*Sir Isumbras*, p. 111). Extrapolating from his calculations, a florin would have been worth roughly two hundred dollars in modern money.

303 *wafull*. MS: illegible. McSparran's emendation.

349 The belief that a lion will not harm those of royal blood is traditional. E.g., it occurs in *Bevis of Hampton* and in Spenser's *Faerie Queen*, Book 1. The motif of the child carried off by a lion is found in the later romance *Torrent of Portengale*. Lost children suckled by wild animals are not uncommon in European legend, the story of Romulus and Remus being perhaps the best-known example. The English romance *Chevalere Assigne*, a version of the swan-knight legend, features a nurturing hind. Such episodes in the lives of culture heroes harken back to more primitive explorations of concepts of nature and culture, animal and human.

353 In the Old French *Octavian*, the child is carried off by a dragon. This seems to be one of the first references to a griffin carrying off a child. Later it appears in *Eglamour* and *Torrent*.

407 See *Sir Isumbras*, ed. Broh, p. 111 (note to line 359).

411 This line has been moved from after line 405 where it appears in the manuscript, following McSparran's emendation.

476 Another faithful lioness appears in the ballad *Sir Aldinger*. The faithful lion in *Yvain* is better known, and, like the lioness, fights beside its master, though its faithfulness is earned by an act of kindness.

| 511 | In Southern *Octavian* her circumstances are humbler; she supports herself by needlework, as does the heroine in *Emaré*. |

| 515 | Apparently the emperor did not follow his queen's request to christen the children before burning them (see lines 266 ff.), but rather, in his pity, just banished them all without a christening. Second christenings were strictly forbidden in the fourteenth century; thus the christening of the one child here and the other in line 629 should not be perceived as second christenings. |

| 532 | The line begins with a large rubricated *N*, marking the turn of the story to the career of the other twin, Florent. |

| 575 | A badge in the shape of a palm was often worn by those who had been on pilgrimage to Jerusalem. |

| 606 | Clement's wife is named Gladwyn in line 948. She is nameless in other versions, but in the French *Octavian* Clement's son is named Gladwains. Her gladness here thus befits her. |

| 627 | In the Thornton manuscript, this line follows line 625. In moving the line, I follow McSparran's emendation. |

| 645 | *chawndelere.* That is, chandler, i.e., candlemaker, but the Cambridge text has *chaungere.* In the French *Octavian*, Clement's son is to become a money-changer, while Florent is sent to be a butcher. In Southern *Octavian* only, Clement himself is a butcher. |

| 664–807 | Only the first line of the stanza remains in the Thornton manuscript where a leaf is missing after folio 102, so 147 or possibly 159 lines have been lost (*Octavian*, ed. McSparran, p. 11). The missing passage is supplied from the Cambridge text. However, the Thornton text resumes in a stanza to which none in Cambridge or the French *Octavian* corresponds, relating the giant's interview with the sultan. (Line 664 in the Thornton manuscript reads: *The squyer therof was full gladd.*) |

| 675 | In the Cambridge manuscript *hym* is repeated. |

| 760 | This line begins with a large letter *A*, marking the conclusion of the *enfance* of Florent and the beginning of the episode of the war with the sultan. |

| 793 | *Borogh Larayn* corresponds to Bourg-la-reine in the Parisian *arrondissement* of Sceaux (Mills, *Six Middle English Romances*, p. 203). The reference to this locale is unique to Northern *Octavian*. |

| 807a | Mills, following Cambridge Ff. 2.38, provides a transition from what is missing in Thornton that smooths over the gap: |

> The gyauntys name was Aragonour;
> He lovyd that maydyn par amour,
> That was so feyre and free;
> And sche had levyr drawyn bene
> Than yn hur chaumber hym to sene:
> So fowle a wyght was he! (lines 805–10)

808 The Thornton text resumes at this point. The sultan has promised Marsabelle to the giant, should he win the battle, and the giant eagerly accepts the challenge to single-handed combat.

816 *Mount Martyn*. The Cambridge text reads throughout *Mount Mertrous* which corresponds to the French *Octavian*'s topographically accurate reference to Montmartre.

863–86 These two stanzas are not present in the Cambridge manuscript, omitting the giant's bargain of Dagobert's head for Marsabelle's hand.

866 Dagobert was king of the Franks in the early seventh century.

867 *abrayde*. Mills treats as two words, *a brayde*, and glosses the phrase as "a bout," rather than as an adverbial form of *abraiden*, "abroad," "out of the house," or "out in the open." A third possibility might be an adverbial form of *abreiden*, meaning "violently" (*Six Middle English Romances*, p. 204).

899 Here begins a series of stanzas of dialogue notable for their use of repetition and formal structure of statement and reply.

908 *nolde*. MS: *wolde*. McSparran's emendation; the context requires a negative.

911–34 These two stanzas are not present in Cambridge. Their omission would seem to be due to the composer's desire to shorten the narrative.

935 ff. This follows the French *Octavian* closely, preserving its mock-heroic tone (see *Octovian*, ed. McSparran, p. 194). The knight setting out in inferior, borrowed armor is conventional, especially in chivalric *enfances* (see *Sir Perceval of Galles*).

936 An *actone* was a padded jacket worn under the hauberk (coat of mail).

945 *seven yere*. MS: *seven*. Emendation by McSparran and Sarrazin following the Cambridge text.

962 The *aventayle* is the chain-mail neckpiece of a suit of armor. A *bacenete* is a type of helmet.

1007–15 Thornton's nine-line stanza lacks three lines present in the Cambridge MS and the Old French *Octavian*:

> Jhesu that syttyth yn trynyté
> Blesse the fadur that gate the
> And the modur that the dud bere

1058 ff. The ironic detail of Florent's presentation of the giant's head does not appear in the Old French *Octavian* or the southern English version. There the head is presented to the French king and publicly displayed.

1064 The word *brighte* is written at the end of the line and marked for insertion after *als*. The sense demands that it be read before *als* or that a second *als* be added after it.

1072	Florent is apparently still on horseback, having ridden into the hall.
1098	Clermont is a town north of Paris. The reference to this locale is unique to Northern *Octavian*.
1123	Marsabelle's seemingly negative attitude toward Florent is a little puzzling. In the French *Octavian* she is at first favorably disposed to the giant and only admits her feelings for Florent after much soul-searching. Here she seems to put up a front to hide her feelings from her father.
1125	*He bote*. MS: *He*. Emendation by McSparran and Sarrazin, following the Cambridge text.
1146	*that I ne*. MS: *that ne*. McSparran emends the line: *Allas, þat ne with my lemane [I] wore*.
1172	A large rubricated capital *T* at the beginning of this stanza marks the fourth division: the episode of the knighting of Florent.
1175–1231	These lines are omitted in the Cambridge text, diminishing Clement's role and the social comedy.
1192	The king and the emperor cut his meat to honor him. It was an honor to serve and carve for those of higher rank. Even great nobles coveted appointment to such ritualized service.
1206	Clement's beating the minstrels is especially uncourtly, not to mention unmotivated. Romance heroes are more often characterized by their patronage of minstrels; this bourgeois "hero" seems more concerned with cutting costs.
1280	Only in Northern *Octavian* does the recognition of father and son come here. In the French and southern versions it comes at the end in the family reunion scene, as is usual in Eustace/Constance/Crescentia-type narratives. Northern *Octavian*'s separation of the recognitions gives rise to inconsistencies in lines 1613 and 1625. Octavian's recognition of Florent as his son is best explained by the fact that in the French *Octavian* the father is penitent.
1295	The Emperor's lament for his lost wife is more consistent with his character in the French *Octavian*, where he has (somehow) realized her innocence and gone in search of her.
1316	The hero disguised in the enemy's camp, and his narrow escape, is a conventional episode in epic romances. See *King Alexander* and Gawain's bold foray into Lucius' camp in *The Alliterative Morte Arthure*.
1332	Florent here uses the singular pronoun *the* rather than the royal *ye* in addressing the sultan, indicating his inferiority. See also line 1599.
1373	Cambridge reverses the order of lines 1370–73 and 1373–75, giving a superior reading. There the sultan's men first recognize Florent, then seize their weapons and attack him.

1387 This gruesome head/football simile may be conventional; see *Sir Gawain and the Green Knight*, where members of Arthur's court fend off the Green Knight's rolling head with their feet.

1420 *herte*. MS: *herde*. McSparran's emendation. See line 1507 for another occurrence of this formula.

1436–71 The weak verse here and the vagueness of the events may be due to a departure from the French *Octavian*. Only the northern version develops this encounter into a major battle. The treatment serves to demonstrate Florent's prowess, but permits the other Christians to seem ineffective by contrast.

1448 I have emended the manuscript reading *in* to *and*. *Syte* (distress, grief) is a rare Northern form. The formula used here, *sorow and syte*, occurs in Old Norse (see *Octovian*, ed. McSparran, p. 197).

1506 *haulsynge*. Literally, "necking."

1532 The father of Josian, Saracen princess of *Bevis of Hampton*, also has a magic horse. In spite of Marsabelle's suggestion, the steed is not particularly instrumental in the defeat of the sultan.

1564–65 These lines are inverted in the Cambridge manuscript.

1580 This description of Clement's superior horsemanship repeats a simile used in line 1017 to describe Florent: "Sprong als sparke dose of glede." As Wright notes, "This new skill is grossly inconsistent with Clement's usual role as a rebuttal to chivalry, and illustrates the infirmity of the fabliau-romance partition" in Northern *Octavian* because Clement's successful manipulation of the sultan depends on actual prowess and not "the pure workings of guile" ("Fabliau Ethos," p. 493). Both the Old French and southern versions of *Octavian* exemplify a more traditional fabliau ethos in which Clement is the honored champion.

1612–13 As in lines 1624–26, Florent's parentage seems to be unknown here, an inconsistency created by the northern composer's rearrangement of the recognition scenes. See note to line 1280.

1621–1770 These lines are mutilated in the Thornton manuscript, where half of folio 108 is missing. The first parts of lines 1621–52 and almost all of lines 1651–62 remain on folio 108 recto, column A, but column B and column A on the verso are missing. The ends of lines 1740–73 are present on 108 verso in column B. In the text, the missing and mutilated passages have been supplied from the Cambridge manuscript. These lines agree substantially with what remains in the Thornton manuscript.

1627 A large capital *A* begins the line, marking the final battle and the reunion episode where the other twin, Octavian, again appears.

1714 *brenyes*. MS: *bremus*. McSparran's emendation.

1774–79 Cambridge reverses the order of these two three-line units and gives the
 better reading since Octavian's defense of the mother is continuous, fol-
 lowed by his father's reaction.

1785 The Cambridge manuscript includes three lines not present in the Thornton
 text:

> Than spekyth the lady of honowre
> To hur lorde the emperour
> Wordys of grete pyte.

 These seem to be original, since they provide an important transition and
 the Thornton stanza is short.

1823 Death by burning was the usual punishment for women convicted of treason.
 McSparran cites the statutes of Edward III (*Octavian*, p. 199).

1824 *[B]elle*, meaning cauldron, is a local Yorkshire term; it always appears with
 reference to burning (see *Octovian*, ed. McSparran, p. 199).

1828–33 Wright suggests that this disturbing use of laughter in a romance that other-
 wise fails to preserve most of the fabliau humor found in both the Old French
 and Southern versions of *Octavian* "can only be interepreted as a signifier of
 social and moral opprobirum" ("Fabliau Ethos," p. 492).

1844 The Cambridge text here concludes briefly:

> Jhesu lorde, hevyn kynge
> Graunt us all thy blessyng
> And yn hevyn to abyde.

 ## INTRODUCTION TO *SIR EGLAMOUR OF ARTOIS*

Sir Eglamour of Artois tells a familiar story of lovers separated by a disapproving father, their vicissitudes, and their eventual marriage in a triumph of faithful love. Despite its French locale, the poem seems to be of English origin; it has no known French analogues or antecedents. The romance was probably produced around 1350 somewhere in the northeast Midlands, perhaps in Yorkshire. To judge from the number of surviving manuscripts (six) and prints (four), it was widely known and well liked. The story's appeal is further attested by references to *Eglamour* in writings from the Middle Ages and Renaissance and the existence of other romances which show its influence: *Emaré*, *Sir Torrent of Portengale*, and *The Squire of Low Degree*. The narrative was dramatized, for a London chronicle records that a play of *Eglamour and Degrebelle* was performed at St. Albans in 1444. The story circulated in ballads and one episode found in the romance may still live in Kentucky ballad tradition as "Bangum and the Boar."

No doubt *Eglamour*'s audiences would have been attracted to its formula plot, which is a vehicle for the exploration of such concerns as family and social conflict, codes of conduct, and moral values. The romance is carefully structured, the action highly unified, the narration lively. The story threatens taboos such as illegitimacy, incest, and patricide while concluding with a wish-fulfillment fantasy of love and social success. The wronged lovers are natural objects of sympathy while the treacherous father makes a suitably evil villain. Though *Eglamour* has not been much esteemed by scholars, it has its virtues and repays close scrutiny.

The hero, a knight in the service of the earl of Artois, loves his lord's daughter, Cristabelle. Though he is of lesser rank, she is receptive to his marriage suit. The earl assents and proposes a series of tests through which Eglamour can win Cristabelle and all of Artois; however, it soon becomes evident that he intends the knight to die in his attempts. The tasks to win the bride are those customary to mythic heroes: the slaying of a deer, a boar, giants, and, finally, a dragon. In the course of these adventures, Eglamour saves the princess Organata who promises to wait fifteen years for him. The first two tasks accomplished, Eglamour returns to Artois; when he departs to complete his third task, Cristabelle is pregnant.

At this point, the focus shifts to Cristabelle and the legend of the calumniated queen; however, she is not falsely accused. When a son, Degrebelle, is born to her, the earl sets mother and child adrift. A griffin carries Degrebelle to Israel where he is raised by the king as his son and heir; Cristabelle washes ashore in Egypt, whose king, her uncle, takes her in. When Eglamour returns to Artois and discovers the earl's treachery, he seizes power and undertakes a pilgrimage to the Holy Land where he remains for fifteen years. Then, as the kings of Egypt and Israel arrange the marriage of their wards, the family is reunited by a series of tournaments in which son and father both win the hand of Cristabelle. Degrebelle's identity is recognized before the marriage to his mother is consummated. Eglamour is identified as he claims Cristabelle for his wife. Degrebelle marries Organata and both couples

return to Artois where the fleeing earl falls to his death, leaving the lovers to rule happily to their lives' ends.

In this tale of love triumphant there is never any doubt as to the characters' moral valences. Eglamour and Cristabelle are sustained by heavenly aid for which they often give thanks; the wicked earl is destroyed through divine providence. The Middle English romances rarely feature heroines and heroes who bear a child out of wedlock (but see *Sir Degaré*) and generally condemn premarital sex (*Amis and Amiloun*); *Eglamour* conforms to this morality by establishing the orthodoxy of the lovers' union. Their love is not secret and the earl has assented to their betrothal; the consummation of their union and Eglamour's gift of a ring to Cristabelle ("Yyf God send the a chylde," line 705) even constituted a valid marriage according to canon law. The lovers' guilt is diminished in contrast to the treachery and cruelty of the earl. He breaks his pledge to Eglamour, schemes to have the knight destroyed, and only grudgingly allows him respite to heal his wounds. Further, the earl attempts to kill his daughter and grandson, the latter without benefit of baptism. His cowardice makes him even more despicable and literally causes his downfall, for he retreats to his tower and, when Eglamour returns, tumbles to his death.

The story is given further moral and structural cohesion since the tests Eglamour undergoes form a graduated series developed in a parallel manner. Each combat is more difficult and lasts longer than the preceding one, and in each his opponents are more deserving of destruction. Eglamour easily slays the hart in the giant Arrok's dolorous forest and dispatches him after a day of battle. The boar is further away, in Sidon, and as Eglamour approaches, he finds the dismembered bodies of the beast's earlier opponents. The boar kills the knight's horse and requires three days to subdue, but his eradication is a great boon to the country which he had ravaged. In a further combat, undertaken of his own chivalrous volition, Eglamour defeats the boar's giant owner who has been demanding the king's daughter, Organata. After these trials, the knight requires a month's recuperation. The dragon of Rome is Eglamour's most formidable opponent — the most unnatural and destructive of all. The serpent has ravaged a whole city, the very center of Christendom. In this battle, not only is Eglamour's horse slain, but he himself is wounded, which Edmund Reiss suggests is punishment for his sin.[1] The wound requires a year of healing in the care of the Roman emperor's daughter.

The narrative exhibits parallelism and balance throughout. The structure is binary: the first movement brings the couple together, culminating in their betrothal and the conception of Degrebelle; in the second movement the lovers are separated from each other and their child, tested, then reunited. The plot is developed by doubling and tripling typeepisodes: tournaments, combats, adoptions, departures, returns, recognitions. The doubled exile and return plot occurs frequently in Middle English romances. *King Horn* and *Havelok the Dane* are early exemplars of the type, but the formulas are handled differently in *Eglamour* and in the romances it influenced. In the earlier romances, the heroes are orphaned, exiled princes who win noble brides in the process of recovering their patrimonies. These narratives develop themes of kingship and right rule; the conflicts are national in scope. *Eglamour*, however, uses the separation and return formula to explore conflicts within families. Problems of incest, patricide, and clandestine marriage are featured in these works. As Lee Ramsey has observed, in these romances family is very important, but relations

[1] Reiss, "Romance," p. 126.

among family members are not close; indeed, the major threats to the family come from within.[2] The possessive, treacherous father of *Eglamour* comes from a tradition of jealous, even incestuous fathers, as, for example, in *Emaré* or *Apollonius of Tyre*. Degrebelle's narrowly avoided incestuous union with his mother is much remarked by the narrator and the characters and reminds one of a similar episode in *Sir Degaré*. Actual patricide is avoided in *Eglamour* since the earl is killed by divine providence, but in other similar romances, such as *Torrent of Portengale*, the wronged suitor vindicates himself by killing the father. An earlier opportunity for patricide occurs when father and son joust incognito for the hand of Cristabelle, but they fight to a draw and the father prevails with humor over his son's braggadocio.

The family conflicts arise because the parents and children can not agree on the choice of a spouse. *Eglamour* posits contradictory models of marriage — marriage for love's sake and marriage for status' sake. The agendas of patriarchy and patrilineage require the latter, and it was accepted practice among gentry and nobility in the fourteenth century. Marriage for love's sake, or companionate marriage, gives greater autonomy to women. Cristabelle goes further, defying her father and conventional morality by consummating her relationship with Eglamour before they are formally married. The romance threatens the authority of parents and lords and affirms the authority of love for its own sake, yet this love renews the family and reestablishes social order, validating the very structures it once seemed to threaten.

In addition to conflicting models of marriage, *Eglamour* incorporates contradictory notions of social status. The choice of a spouse is important because Cristabelle is an heiress; with her goes Artois. She is thus in an ambiguous position. She is a liability to her family since the patrimony will pass to her husband. However, she is an opportunity for other families who would marry into that patrimony. Though he is preeminent among the earl's men and of gentle birth, Eglamour is a "knyght of lyttyll land" (line 64), not at all the peer of the emperors and kings who vie for Cristabelle's hand, nor of the earl. *Eglamour* offers the hope of upward mobility to worthy men of lower status while simultaneously suggesting that, in the words of Susan Wittig, "worth and birth are synonymous" and that "only a gentleman can be a gentle man."[3] Thus *Eglamour* takes up the debate on *gentilesse* which claimed the attention of other writers of the period, most notably Chaucer. The relationship of personal worth to lineage and social status was a fundamental concern to the gentry who made up a large portion of the romances' audience. Historians show them to have been devoted to family aggrandizement and social advancement, particularly through marriage. In the romance, the attention given to chivalric matters — polite conversation, the lady's gifts of weapons and hunting animals, descriptions of heraldic devices, arms, and feasts — further develops the theme of social status. Even the minstrel-style narration may assert the story's claim to gentle status since minstrels were still retained in aristocratic households where they had traditionally composed narratives of their patrons' chivalric activities.

Eglamour achieves its happy ending without resolving the dilemmas of patrilineage which cause disequilibrium in family and society. Circumstances allow the characters to avoid the dilemmas: the heiress bears only sons, who will keep the patrimony in the family; the son is adopted by a ruler who has no other heirs and accepts an arranged marriage to marry an heiress, so he is supported independently of his patrimony; Eglamour does not have to share Artois or give up control as the earl did. It has been said that the appeal of popular romance

[2] Ramsey, *Chivalric Romances*, p. 158.

[3] Wittig, *Stylistic and Narrative Structures*, p. 189.

stems from its ability to simultaneously create tension by questioning received values and offer reassurance by affirming them. *Eglamour* makes the most of this aesthetic.

Texts of *Eglamour* survive in four medieval and two Renaissance manuscripts. The earliest, Egerton, contains only the first 160 lines of the romance. Three fifteenth-century volumes preserve complete texts which present two slightly different versions of the narrative. The romances in MS Cotton Caligula A.2 and MS Cambridge Ff. 2.38 contain material not present in the text in the Thornton manuscript, and tend to agree with each other in varying from Thornton and Egerton. Most notably, the Cotton and Cambridge texts contain narratorial intrusions dividing the narrative into three fitts and describing the hero's arms and the vanquished dragon, as well as a lengthier treatment of the reunion scene. These may be later modifications to an earlier version preserved in the Egerton and Thornton manuscripts. The Cotton text is the basis for this edition since it preserves the fullest form of the narrative.

As it is a Northern poem, *Eglamour* exhibits characteristic dialectal features. The most pervasive is the *a/o* isogloss, still found in Scots dialect; that is, *a* appears where more southerly dialects, and Modern English, would have *o*: *bald-bold, mare-more*. The present participle ending is *-ande* rather than *-ing*. The third-person singular feminine pronoun is *scho*. More southerly Midland forms appear in the third-person plural pronouns which begin with *h* rather than *th* (*hem*=them, *here*=their). The neuter pronoun "it" also begins with *h* (*hyt*).

MANUSCRIPTS AND PRINTS

Indexed as item 1725 in Boffey and Edwards, eds., *New Index of Middle English Verse*:

- London, British Library MS Egerton 2862 (c. 1400), fols. 148r–179v.
- Lincoln, Lincoln Cathedral MS 91, called the Thornton MS (c. 1440), fols. 138v–147r.
- London, British Library MS Cotton Caligula A 2 (c. 1450), fols. 5b–13a. [Base-text for this edition.]
- Cambridge, Cambridge University Library MS Ff. 2.38 (c. 1460), fols. 71r–79v.
- Oxford, Bodleian Library MS Douce 261 (1564), fols. 26r–48v.
- London, British Library MS Additional 27879, called the Percy Folio (c. 1650), pp. 296–313.

- Edinburgh, National Library of Scotland. Edinburgh: Chepman and Myllar, 1508? (*STC* 7542). [Three leaves missing.]
- Cambridge, Cambridge University Library. Inc. 5.J.1.2. London: Wynkyn de Worde, c. 1530 (*STC* 7541). [A fragment.]
- Cambridge, Cambridge University Library. Syn 7.52.12. London: Richard Bankes, c. 1530. [Three fragments.]
- Oxford, Bodleian Library S. Selden d. 45(5). London: William Copland, 1548–69 (*STC* 7543).
- London, British Library C, 21.C.59. London: John Walley, 1570? (*STC* 7544).

SIR EGLAMOUR OF ARTOIS

Jhesu Crist, of heven Kyng,
Graunt us all good endyng
 And beld us in Hys bowre; *shelter; abode*
And gef hem joye that love to here *give them; hear*
5 Of eldres that before us were *predecessors*
 And lyved in grett antowre. *adventure*
I woll you tell of a knyght
That was both hardy and wyght, *valiant*
 And stronge in ylke a stowre; *every battle*
10 Of dedys of armys that he myght here
He wan degré with jurnay clere,[1]
 And in felde the floure. *[was]; flower*

In Artas he was geten and born, *Artois; begotten*
And all his eldres hym beforn. *ancestors*
15 Lestenyth, I wyll yow say.
To dede of armys he ys went,
Wyth the Erle of Artas is he lent *Artois does he reside*
 For deernes, nyght and day. *favor*
Syr Prynsamour the erle hyght, *was called*
20 Syr Eglamour men call the knyght
 That dughty was evyr and ay. *doughty; always*
And this erle hadde hym in wold; *protection*
To dedes of armes he was bold
 For to no man seyde he nay.

25 The Erle had nevyr child but on,
That was a dowghtir, white as fom, *foam*
 Hys ryche eyr schulde be. *heir*
The maydens name was Cristabell,
A feyrer thing of flesch ne fell *fairer; skin*
30 Was none in Cristyanté.
Syr Eglamour so hym bare *bore himself*
In all the worlde he loved no mare *more*

[1] *He won pre-eminence with valiant deeds (jousting)*

<div style="margin-left:auto;">

 Then that lady bryghth of blee; *Than; countenance*
 Certeynly, both day and nyght,
35 So dyd sche that nobyll knyght, *did she [love]*
 Hit was the more pyté! *it*

 The knyght was both bold and stronge
 Therfor the lady loved hym longe. *greatly*
 Lestenyth, I wyll you tell.
40 Syr Eglamour, he gart crye *had announced*
 Of dedys of armes, wyttyrly, *certainly*
 For love of Crystabell.
 Ther com lordes of fer lond *from distant*
 To aske her, I undyrstond, *ask for her (hand)*
45 With fers folke and fell. *fierce; dangerous*
 What manere man her wold have,
 So sore buffettys he hem gave
 For ever he gart them to dwelle.[1]

 Tyl hit befell upon a day,
50 The knyght to his sqwyer gan say
 In chambur ther he gan reste, *where*
 "Belamy, and thou kowdest leyne, *Friend, if you could keep a secret*
 A counsell I wold to the sayne — *tell you*
 Thou walkest both est and west." *You travel widely*
55 "Yys, sir," he seyd, "per ma fay, *by my faith*
 What so evur ye to me say
 I schall hit nevur out kast." *spread about*
 "The Erles doughtur, so God me save,
 The love of her but I hit have
60 My lyf may not long last."

 The sqwyere seyde, "So mote I the, *So may I prosper*
 Ye have tolde me your pryvyté; *secret*
 I schall you gyf answere.
 Ye ar a knyght of lytyll lond,
65 Take not to evyll, I undirstond, *Don't take it ill*
 For mykyll wolde have more. *much (see note)*
 Yif I went to that lady and told her so,
 Perauntur on skorn take hit wold scho *Perhaps she would take it scornfully*
 And lyghtly lett me fare. *treat me lightly*
70 Syr, a mon that hewyth ovyr hye *high*
 Lyghtly the chyppus fallen in his eye,
 Thus happis hyt ofte aywhare. *everywhere*

</div>

[1] *For always he made them remain (i.e., killed them)*

"Syr, bethynke the of thys thynge,
Ther wowes here emperour and kynge *woos her*
75 And dukes that ar bolde,
Erles, barouns and knyghtis also,
Yytt wyll sche none of all tho *those*
 But evur in goodnes her holde. *virtue held herself*
Sche wold never a kyng forsake
80 And a sympull knyght take,
 Butt yif your lufe wer olde. *life (love)*
I swere be God, heven kynge, *by*
Wyste her fadyr of sych a thyng *Know*
 Full dere hytt scholde be solde!" *dearly*

85 The knyght answered with wordes mylde,
"My sqwyer, sethen thou was a chylde *since*
 Thow hast ben lened with me: *attached to*
In dede of armes, in many a stowre, *battle*
Wher saw thou evur my dyshonowre?
90 Sey on, so God save the!"
"Nay, syr, be Jhesu bryghth!
Ye ar on of the noblest knyghth
 That ys knowen in Cristyanté.
In dede of armes, be God on lyve, *by the living God*
95 Ye ar counted worth othur fyve."
 "Gramarcy, syr," seyde he. *Thank you*

The knyghth sykud and seyd, "Alas!" *sighed*
Mornyng tyll his bed he gas *Mourning to; goes*
 That rychely was wroght.
100 Both his handys he cast up sone,
To Jhesu Crist he made his bone, *prayer*
 To that Lord that us bowght. *redeemed*
"The Erles dowghtur, that swete thyng,
She myght be myn at myn endyng, *death*
105 On her ys all my thoght.
That I myght wedde her to my wyfe
And sythen kepe her all my lyfe; *afterwards*
 Owt of care then were I browght."

Uppon the morn the maydyn small *gracefully formed*
110 Sche ete befor hyr fadyr in hall
 Among her berdes bryght. *lovely ladies*
All gentyllmen sembled butt he; *assembled*
The lady seyde, "For Goddes pyté, *pity*
 Wher ys Syr Eglamour, my knyghth?"
115 Hys sqwyer answered with sympull chere, *expression*
"He ys seke and deed full nere; *sick; nearly dead*

He prayes yow of a syght.
He ys kest into such care *fallen*
Butt ye hym help he wyll mysfare, *Unless; do poorly*
120 He lyves not tyll nyghth."

The Erle to his dowghtyr spake,
"Damysell," he sayde, "for Goddis sake
Herken what I schall yow say; *mark*
Aftyr mete do as the hende, *dinner; courteous*
125 To his chambur that ye wende. *go*
He hath served us many a day,
Full trewly in hys entent; *purpose*
In justyng and in turnament *joust*
He seyde us nevyr nay. *falsely*
130 In dede of armes, wher he myght here, *fight*
He wynnes the gre with jurnay clere, *victory; combat*
My worschyp evyr and ay."

Aftyr mete the lady gent
Dose her fadyr commawndement: *father's*
135 She takes leve to wende.
To the chawmbur gan sche go,
And with here toke maydens two
Ther as the knyght gon lende. *To where; did dwell*

Then seyde that lady, whyte as flowr,
140 "How fares my knyth, Sir Eglamour,
That dowghty ys aywhare?"
"Damesell, as ye may se,
Thus am I cast for love of the, *driven*
In angur and in care." *anguish*
145 The damesell seyd, "So mote I the, *So may I prosper*
And ye have any care for me *If*
My herte ys wondur sore."
"And I myght turne unto lyve, *If; return*
I wolde wedde you to my wyfe,
150 Yyf that your wyll hyt wore." *were*

The lady swere, "Be Crystus myght,
For thou art a nobyll knyghte
And comen of gentyll blode,
And evur trewe undur thy schylde
155 Thou wynnes the gre in every fylde, *prize; battleground*
Worschypfully, be the Rode. *Honorably; Cross*
I wyll avyse me of this yytt, *yet*
And at my fadyr wyll I wytt *from; know*
Yyf that his wyll be good.

160	As I am lady feyr and gent,	*graceful*
	When my fadyr and I ar at assent	
	I feyle you for no good!"	*fail; advantage*
	The knyght kepeth no more blys	*cares for*
	When he hadde gette sent of this,	*understood the meaning*
165	Butt makes full good chere.	
	He bad hys sqwyer for to gan	
	And two hundur pownde for to tan,	*take*
	To geve hyr maydens clere.	*lovely*
	"Damysels," he sayde, "so God me save,	
170	This to your mariage schall ye have	
	For ye be gyntyll and dere."	*gentle*
	She takes her leve at the knyght	
	And thonkes hym anon ryght,	
	And seyde, "Farewell, my fere!"	*mate*
175	Crystabell has taken the way	
	To hir fadir chambur, as it lay,	*father's*
	That made was of ston.	
	He sayd, "Welcom dowghtur, as white as flour,	
	How fares thy knyght, Sir Eglamour?"	
180	She answered hym anon,	
	"Grete othes he me sware	
	That he ys coverd of mykyl car,	*recovered from his great woe*
	And good comfort to hym tane.	*taken to himself*
	He tolde me and my maydens hend	*courteous*
185	That to-morn he wolde wende	*tomorrow; set out*
	Wyth his hawkes ylkane."	*each one*
	The Erle sayde, "So mote Y the,	*may I prosper*
	I schall ryde to se hem fle	*them fly*
	For comfort of the knyght!"	
190	The Erl buskys and made hym yare	*hastens; ready*
	To ryde forth to se the fare,	
	And beholde that semyly syght.	*event*
	Tyll a wrathe fyll betwen hem two,	*quarrel*
	Ore hyt nyghed the nyght thoo,	*Before the night came nigh then*
195	Yyf ye wyll lysten and lere.	*learn*
	As they rode homward by the way	
	The knyght to the Erle gan say,	
	"Good lord, wyll ye me here?"	
	"Ye," he sayde, so mote Y the,	
200	What so ever thou seyst to me	
	Hyt ys me lefe and dere;	*to me dear; precious*
	For on of the best knyghtes art thou	*one*

That in my londe lyveth now
 Owther fer or nere."
205 "Good lord, for charyté,
Cristabell, your dowghtyr fre,
 When shall she have a fere?" *mate*

The Erle sayd, "So God me save,
I knowe non that hyr schall have,
210 Sche ys so bryght of ble!"
The knyght gan the Erle pray,
"Lord, I have served the many a day:
 Wouche ye her save on me." *Vouchsafe her to me*
"Ye, syr," he sayde, "be Cristys payne,
215 Yyf thou hir wynne as I schall sayne
 Wyth dedes of armes thre,
Browke thou well my dowghtyr dere, *Possess*
And all Artas, both ferre and nere, *far*
 I holde therto," seyde he.

220 The knyght sware, "So mote I the,
At my jurnay wolde I be,
 Yyf I wyste evere where!"
The Erle sayde, "Her by weste *Here to the west*
Ther wones a gyaunt in the forest, *dwells*
225 Syche on thou sawe nevyr ere. *before*
Cypré treys growe ther fayre and longe, *Cypress trees*
Grete hertys walken hem amonge, *deer*
 The fayrest that on fote may fare.
Wend thedur and fett me on away *Go thither; fetch*
230 And then dar I savely say
 That thou haste ben thare."

"Be Jhesu!" sware the knyght than,
"Yyf he be a Cristen man *If*
 I schall hym nevyr forsake.
235 Holde wele my lady and my lond."
"Yys," sayd the Erle, "lo, her my hond."
 Hys trowthe to hym he strake. *promised*

Aftyr mete, as I you telle,
He toke lefe at Cristabell, *leave of*
240 And thus then seyde he,
"Damysell, now as a man
For thy love have I tan *undertaken*
 Dedes of armes thre."
"Syr," she sayde, "make yow gladde.
245 For hardure jurnay nevur ye hadde, *journey*

Be God, in no countré.
Or thy jurnay shall all passe *Before*
For my lofe thou may say 'Alas!'
 And I well more for the.
250 Sir knyght, to huntyng when thou fondis *set out*
I shall gefe the two grehondys; *give you; greyhounds*
 As I am trewe gentyll woman and fre.
Ther was nevyr best that on fote ran *beasts*
Butt they woll full sone hym tan, *capture*
255 So swyfte bothe they be.

"Also a good swerde I schall geve the,
Sent Pole fond it in the Grekes see, *St. Paul*
 Of egge syche knowe I none. *edge; no other*
Ther was never helme made of stele *helmet*
260 And thou have happe to hit hym wele *the [good] fortune*
 Butt hyt woll thorowgh gone." *pierce (go through)*
He sayde, "God yelde you, lady gent." *protect*
He toke his leve and forth he went;
 His weys has he tane. *taken*
265 A brode gate he helde faste *road; steadfastly*
Tyll ho come to the foreste, *he*
 Suche on sawe he nevyr nane.
Cypré treys were growen owte;
The wode was walled all abowte,
270 Well corven of ryall stone. *carved*
Forth he wente, I undurstonde,
To a brode gate ther he fonde
 And in ther ys he gone.

He blewe hys horn in that tyde; *time*
Hertys rose on yche a syde; *Deer; each*
285 A nobyll dere he chose.
Hys hondes began for to bay, *hounds*
That herde the gyaunt ther he lay *where*
 And repys hym on a rese. *aroused him from his rest*
"Me thynkes howndes that I here,
290 Some thefe ys come to stele my dere — *thief; steal*
 Hym were well bettyr sese. *It were better for him to cease*
Be hem that me gette and borne, *them who; begot*
In wers tyme blewe he never horne,
 Nor derrere bowghth he flesch!" *dearer bought; meat*

295 Arrok the gyaunt has tane the wey *taken*
To his forest gate as hyt lay;
 Hys bakke he sette thertylle. *thereto*
Be that Sir Eglamour had done the dede, *When*

	A gret hert sleyn and tane the hede,	*taken; head*
300	The prise he blewe full schyrlle.	*(see note)*
	He come ther the gyaunt was	*where*
	And sayde, "Good sir, lett me pas,	
	Yyf hit be your wylle."	
	"Nay, thef! traytour! thou art tane!	*captured*
305	My chef hert thou hast sclayne;	*slain*
	That schalt thou lyke full ylle."	

The gyaunt to the knyght ys gon
With a clubbe of yren in his honde tan, *iron*
 Full mykyll and unryde. *large; rough*
310 Grete strokes to hym he gafe;
Into the erthe flewe his staffe
 Too fote on ylke a syde. *Two*
"Thefe, traytour! What doos thou here *Thief*
In my forest to stele my dere? *deer*
315 Thefe, her schalt thou abyde!"
Syr Eglamour his swerde out drowgh *drew*
And to the gyaunt he gafe a swogh, *stroke*
 And blynded hym in that tyde. *time*

All yyf the lordan had lost his syght *Although; knave*
320 Thus he fyghtys with the knyght
 All the day full yare, *entirely*
Tyll on that othur day at prime *next; about 6:00 a.m.*
Syr Eglamour waytes his tyme *bides*
 And to the erthe hym bare.
325 He thonkis Crist that all schall welde; *control*
At the grownd downe he hym helde.
 The thefe began to rare. *roar*
Sith he meted hym, as I you say, *Afterwards; measured*
On the grownde as he lay
330 Fyfty fote and mare.
He thonked God and his knyfe *sword*
That he beraft the gyant his lyfe,
 And loved ay Goddis lore. *ever; law*

Syr Eglamour ys gon hys way
335 With the gyantes hed, as I you say,
 To a castell made of stone.
All the countré come hym agayn, *country folk; [to] him*
Siche an hed, as they seyn,
 They sawe nevur non.
340 Before the Erle he hit bare:
"Lo, lorde, I have ben thare!"
 That bere they wyttenes ylkane. *everyone*

Make we mery, so have we blysse.
For thys ys the fyrst fytte, I wys, *episode truly*
345 Of Sir Eglamour that he has tane. *undertaken*

"What," seyd the Erl, "and this poynt be don? *task*
Thow getys anothur jurnay sone:
 Buske the forth to fare! *Prepare yourself quickly*
In Sydon, that ryche countré,
350 Ther dar no man abyde ne be
 For dredyng of a bare: *boar*
Best and man, all sleys he *Beast; slays*
That he may with ye se, *eye see*
 And wondes them wondur sore. *wounds*
355 His tusschus passen a yerd longe: *tusks*
The flesch that they fasten amonge
 Hyt coveres nevyr more." *recovers*

The nobyll knyght, he seyd not nay.
Upon the morn, when yt was day,
360 Hys lefe then takes he. *leave*
Forth he wente, I undyrestonde,
A fortnyght jurnay on the londe *journey*
 And als mykyll be the see, *by sea*
Tyll agayn an evyn tyde *at evening time*
365 In a forest ther he gan ryde
 As the bore was wont to be. *Where; boar*
Tokenyng of hym sone he fond: *Signs*
Sleyn men on ylke a hond, *on all sides*
 That grymly it was to se.

370 Sir Eglamour rest hym undur an ake *oak*
Tyll on the morn that he gan wake,
 The sonne rose and schone.
Aftyr into the forest he drowgh, *drew*
Of the see he herde a swowgh *sea; rushing sound*
375 And thydur the knyght ys gon.
Bryght helmes fond he strowed wyde where
That men of armes had leved there; *abandoned*
 The wykked bore had hem sleyn.
Tyll a clyf of stone then rydes he *To*
380 And seys the bore com fro the see; *sees; sea*
 Hys morn drynke has tane. *taken*

The bor saw hym ther he stode
And whetted his tuskys as he were wode, *crazed*
 And to hym come on syde. *side*
385 Sir Eglamour wendis well to do, *thinks*

With a spere he rydys hym to
 Als fast as he myght ryde.
Yyf that he rode nevyr so faste
Hys good spere asownder brast; *burst*
390 The hed wolde not in hym hyde. *penetrate its hide*
The bore come to hym with a schowe: *shove*
Hys good stede undur hym he slowe, *slew*
 And afote the knyght moste abyde.

Tyll a bownke he sette his syde *bank*
395 At a full hye roche that tyde,
 And behylde the swyn thare.
Hys nobyll swerde he drowgh out syne *immediately*
And fyghtes with the wylde swyne
 Thre dayes and mare.
400 Tyll on the fowrth day abowt none *noon*
He thowght hys lyfe was nere done *nearly finished*
 For fyghtyng with the bore.
The knyghte can no bettur rede; *knew; council*
He stroke at the swynes hede,
405 Hys tuskes then brake he thore. *there*

He thankys Cryst that ylke stounde *very moment*
He has geve the bore dedde wounde, *deadly*
 The boke of Rome thus gan telle.
The kyng of Sydon on huntyng is gon
410 With men of armes many on;
 The bore then herde he yelle.
He comaunded a sqwyer for to fare:
"Sum man ys fyghtyng with the bare
 I trow full well he dwelle."
415 A sqwyer rydes to a clyfe of stone
And sygh a knyght lyyng hym on *sees*
 With swerd scharpe and felle. *dangerous*

The sqwyer hoves and beholdes them two; *halts*
Agayn to the kyng then wold he go
420 And seyde, "Lorde, the bore ys sleyn!"
"Seynt Mari!" seyd the kyng, "Hou may that be?"
"Yys, syr, a knyght on hym I se,
 Be God, he has ben hys bane. *By; conqueror*
He beris of gold a well fayr syght: *bears (a shield) of gold a very fair sight*
425 A stede of asar, and a knyght *steed; azure*
 All armed for to gon.
The crest on his hed hit ys
A lady of golde in hyr ryches;
 Hys sperys of sabull ylkon." *spears; sable (black)*

430 The kyng swore, "So mot I the! *may I prosper*
 Tho gentyll armes wyll I se." *Those*
 And thethur he takes the way.
 Be that hadde Syr Eglamour
 Ovyrcomyn that styf stowre, *fierce struggle*
435 And ovyrtwart the bore he lay. *across*
 The kyng sayde, "God reste with the."
 "Lord, wellcome," he seyde, "mote ye be.
 Of thees I yow pray.
 I have so fowghtyn with this bore
440 That, be my feyth, I may no more;
 This ys the fowrthe day."

 The kyng swore, "Be Cristis myghte,
 Here schall no man with the fyght. *fight with you*
 Grett synne it were the to tene; *to anger you*
445 Thou hast sleyn this wylde bare
 That has ben ferre and wyde whare,
 And mony mannys bone has he bene. *man's bane*
 Worshypfully with thy schylde
 Thou hast sleyn hym in the felde —
450 That we have alle sene.
 I have wist, sythen I was mon of aray, *since I was a man of knightly arms*
 That he hath sleyn syxté on a day,
 Well armed men and clene." *upright*

 Ryche metys forth they browghte, *food*
455 The Raynysh wyn forgat they noght, *Rhenish*
 Whyte clothes sone were spradde.
 The kyng sware, "So mote I the,
 I schall dyne for love of the;
 Thow hast be strongly stadde." *beset*

460 Aftyr mete, as I you say,
 The kyng con the knyght pray *did; ask*
 Of what lond he was.
 He sayde, "My name ys Antorus, *Adventurous*
 I dwelle with Syr Prins Amorus
465 The Erle of Artas."
 Knyghtes nere the kyng drowgh:
 "Thys ys he that Arrok slowgh,
 The gyaunt brodyr Marras." *The brother of the giant Marras*
 The kyng prayes the knyght so fre
470 Thoo dayes with hym to be
 Or that he dede ferrere pas. *further*

"Ther ys a gyaunt here besyde;
My dowghtyr that ys so mykyll of pride
 He wolde have here me fro,
475 And I dar no where ryde out
Butt men of armes be me abowt;
 Selden have I don so.
This wylde bore that thou hast slyen here *slain*
He has ben fedde this fyftene yere
480 Crysten men to slo.
Now ys he gon, with care inowgh, *enough*
To bery hys brodyr that thou slowgh;
 That evyrmore be hym woo."

To byrten the bore they went tyte; *brake (cut up); quickly*
485 Ther was no knyfe in hym wold byte
 So hard of hyde was he.
"Sir Antours," seyde the kyng, "thou hym slowgh;
I trow thy knyfe be good inowgh
 Yyf thy wyll be."
490 The knyghte is to the bore gon
And cleves hym be the rygge bon, *neck*
 Grett joye hyt was to se.
"Lord," seyd the knyght, "I gart hym falle: *made*
Gyfe me the hed and take the alle, *all the rest*
495 Ye wotte yt ys my fee." *know*

Aftyr cartus have they sent, *For carts*
Agayn the none hom they went, *At noon*
 The cyté was them full nere.
All the comenté was full fayn *populace; glad*
500 That the wykkyd bore was sleyn;
 They made full good chere.
The qwene seyd, "God schild us fro shame.
When Marras the gyaunt cometh han
 Newe tydynd gete we here." *tidings*

505 Syr Eglamour, the nobyll knyght,
Was set with the kyngus dowghtyr ryght,
 For that he schulde be blythe.
The maydens name was Organate,
Sche prays the knyght good chere to make
510 And hym besekys fast mony a sythe. *steadfastly; time*
Aftyr mete sche gon hym telle
How a gyaunt wolde them qwelle, *kill*
 And he begynus to lythe. *listen*
"Damysell," he seyde, "so mote I the,

515 Yyf he come whylys I her be
 I schall hym swythe." *kill*

 Ageyn the evyn the kyng gart dyght *had made ready*
 A bath for the gentyll knyght
 Of erbys that were goode; *herbs*
520 And all the nyght therinne he lay
 Tyll on the morn that hyt was day,
 That men to matens yode. *went*
 Be that the kyng had herd his masse *By [the time]*
 The fowle gyaunt comen wasse *foul*
525 And cryed as he were wode. *crazy*
 "Syr kyng," he sayd, "send out to me
 Organate, thy dowghtyr fre,
 Or I schall spylle thy blode!"

 Syr Eglamour, the nobyll knyght,
530 Armes hym anon ryght
 And to the walles wendes he;
 The bores hed he dyde forth bere
 And sette hit upon a spere,
 That Marras myght hyt se.
535 The gyaunt loked upon the hed:
 "Allas, my bore, art thou ded?
 My trust was mykyll in the.
 Be the lawe that I lefe inne, *By; law (religion); believe in*
 My lytyll spotted hogelynne, *piglet*
540 Dere bowght thy lyfe schall be!" *Dearly*

 The gyaunt on the walles dong; *struck*
 At ylke a stroke the fyre out sprong *each*
 For nothyng wold he spare.
 Into the cyté he cast a crye,
545 "Theves, traytours, ye shall abye *atone*
 For sleyng of my bare.
 The ston wallis I woll down dynge, *batter*
 And with my hondis I wyll you hynge *hang*
 Or that I fro you fare!" *Before*
550 Thorowgh the grace of God, or hyt were nyght,
 The gyant had his fyll of fyght
 And sum dele mare. *somewhat more*

 "Syr Awntours," seyd the kyng then,
 "I rede we armes all men *advise*
555 Yondyr fend wyll felly fyght." *fiercely*
 Tho swere he, "Be the Rode, *Then; Cross*
 I schall asaye hym were he wode. *attack*

 Full mykyll ys God of myght."

 Syr Eglamour was noght abasth: *abashed*

560 The help of God was all his trast, *trust*

 And on his swerde so bryght.

 He rydes a cours to sey his stede; *assay (test)*

 He toke hys helme and forth he yede. *went*

 Alle they prayde for that knyghte.

565 Syr Eglamour the felde has tane: *taken*

 The gyaunt hym sey and thedur ys gane *sees*

 And seyde, "Art thou comen, my fere? *companion*

 I trow thou helped my bore was sleyn: *believe; to slay*

 Thow schalt abye or thou fare hen, *atone before; hence*

570 And that ryght dere!"

 Syr Eglamour wendes well to tho: *that one*

 Wyth a spere he rydes hym to

 As man of armes clere. *shining*

 The gyaunt made hym bowne: *prepared himself*

575 Hors and man he smote downe

 The knyght was dede full nere.

 The knyght sawe no bettyr rede *course of action*

 When hys nobyll stede was dede *dead*

 But on fote to he ys gon. *him*

580 Forth to hym he gan go,

 Hys ryghte arme he stroke hym fro

 Faste by the schulder bon.

 All if the lordan had lost hys hand, *Although*

 All day stondes he fast fyghtand

585 Tyll the sonne to reste was gon;

 Then was he so wery he myght no more,

 The blode ran so faste hym fro

 That lyf dayes had he non.

 All that in the cyté ware,

590 When they herde the thefe rare, *roar*

 For joye the bellys gon rynge.

 Edmund was the kynges name

 "Syr Aunterus," he seyd, "be Seynt Jame,

 Here shalt thou be kynge!

595 Tomorn schall I crowne the,

 And thou schalt wedde my dowghtyr fre

 With a full ryche ryng."

 He answered with wordys mylde,

 "God gyfe the joye of thy chylde

600 For here may I not lyng." *linger*

"Syr knyght, for thy dowghty dede
I schall the gyfe a nobyll stede,
 Als reed as any ron. *roan*
In justenyng ne in turnament
605 Thow schalt suffre no dethes dent *death blow*
 Why thou fyghtys hym on." *while*
Then seyde Organate, the swete thyng,
"I schal you gyfe a good gold ryng
 Wyth a full ryche ston;
610 Whethur ye be on watyr or on lond,
And this rynge be on your hond,
 Ther schall no dede you sclon." *deed; slay*

He seyd, "God yelde you, lady clere!" *protect*
"Ye, syr, I schall abyde you fyftene yere, *wait for*
615 Tyll ye wyll me wedde."
The knyght seyde, "Per ma fay, *By my faith*
Be fyftene yere I schall you say *In*
 How that I have spedde."
The knyght takes hys lefe to fare, *fared*
620 With the gyaunt hed and the bare, *go*
 The wey our Lord hym lede. *giant's*
This ys the secund fytte of this: *part*
Makes mery, so have Y blys!
 For thus ferre have I red.

625 Or that fyftene wekys wer comen to ende
In the lond of Artas he gon lende,
 Ther the Erle was.
All the comynté wer full fayn *populace*
That he in qwarte was comen agayn, *court*
630 And all that he fonde in that place.

Cristabell herd of his comynge home:
Agayn the knyght sche ys gon: *Towards*
 "Syr," sche sayde, "how have ye fare?"
"Damysell," he sayd, "well, and traveled sare *travailed sore*
635 To bryng us both out of care."
 Ther he kyssed the lady full yare. *eagerly*

Now into the halle ys he wente
The Erle to good entent,
 To the he des alle bedene. *high dais all together*
640 The hedes two the knyght down leyde:
"Lo, lord" the knyght seyde,
 "In Sydon have I bene."
Therfor was the Erle full woo,

And sayde, "Ther may no devell the slo, *devil slay you*
645 Be Mary, so I wene! *suppose*
Thow art abowte, I undirstande,
To wynne all Artas of my honde
 And my dowghtyr schene!" *lovely*

The knyght seyde, "So mote I the,
650 Not but I wordy be. *Not unless I am worthy*
 Help God, that ys best."
"On schall come and pay for all,"
The Erle seyd. "So hit schall befall,
 Yyf thou be nevyr so prest." *smart*
655 The knyght prayes the Erle so fre
"Twelfe wykes that thou graunt me,
 My bones for to reste."
And for the prayng of gentyllmen
Twelfe wykes he graunt hym then —
660 No lenger wolde he hym frist. *delay*

Aftyr sowper, as I you tell,
He wendys to chaumbyr with Cristabell,
 Ther were lampus brennyng bryght.
The lady was not to hyde,
665 Sche sette hym on here ryght syde
 And seyde, "Wellcome, syr knyght!"
"Damysell," he seyde, "so have I spedde,
With the grace of God I shall you wedde."
 Thereto here trowthes they plyght. *their*
670 So gracyus he con here tell *graciously he began to tell her*
A poynt of armes that hym befell
 And there he dwelled all nyght.

So be twenty wykys were come and gon, *by [the time that]*
Cristabell, as whyte as fom,
675 All fallen was here hewe.
Sche prayes here gentyllwymmen so fre
That they wolde leyne here privyté, *keep her secrets*
 And to here for to be trewe. *her*
The Erle brennes as fyre in care; *burns like a fire with anxiety*
680 "Have don, sir knyght, and make the yare *ready*
 Thy jurnay comes all newe!"
When Cristabell herd therof sey *talk thereof*
Sche mornys therfore nyght and day,
 That all wyttes may rewe. *people*

685 "Syr, at gret Rome, as I the tell,
Ther lyves a dragon, fers and fell,

Herken what I schall the say.
That fend is of so grett renown
Ther dar no man neygh the town *approach*
690 Be seven myle of way.
Arme the, sir knyght, thedur to wende: *go*
Loke thou sle hym with thy honde
Or els say me nay!" *tell me no*
He sayde, "I have don poyntes two, *feats*
695 With the grace of God I schall do mo
Or els ende for ay." *(once) for all*

Aftyr mete, as I you telle,
He toke hys lefe at Crystabell, *leave from*
Als feyre as flour in felde.
700 "Damysell," he seyd, "ther is a poynt undon: *one task*
I wyll wend, and com agayn full son
Wyth the help of Mary mylde.
A good ryng I schall gyfe the:
Kepe hyt well, my lady fre,
705 Yyf God send the a chylde."

Forth he wente, as I you say:
To grete Rome he takes the way
To seke that worme so bolde. *dragon*
Tokenyng of hym sone he fonde: *Signs*
710 Sleyn men on ylke a honde,
Be hunders he them tolde. *By hundreds; counted*
Yyf he wer never so nobyll a knyght,
Of the worme when he had a syght
Hys herte began to colde. *grow cold*
715 Hyt was no wondur thogh he were wroth:
He stroke his stede and hymself both *He (the dragon); his (Eglamour's)*
That to the ground they wolde.

The knyght arose and his scheld up sett,
This wykked worme on hym bett *beat*
720 Byttur dyntes and felle. *Bitter blows; fierce*
He kest out mony fyre brondes thore, *brands there*
Evyr nere the nyght the more, *Always more as night neared*
As hyt walled owt of helle. *welled*
Syr Eglamour, forsoth I sey,
725 Half hys tonge he stroke away; *its tongue*
The fend began to yelle.
With the stump that hym was leved
He stroke the knyght on the hed
A depe wonde and a felle. *wicked*

730 The knyght seyde, "Now am I schent!" *lost*
 Nere the wykked worme he went,
 Hys hed he stroke away.
 And then so nere hym ys he gon
 He cleves hym by the rygge bon. *back bone*
735 The felde he wan that day.
 The Emperour stode in a towre,
 And sygh the fyght of Sir Eglamour, *saw*
 And to hys men he gan say,
 "Gart crye in Rome, 'The dragon ys sleyn!' *Have pronounced*
740 Tha has a knyght don with all his mayn *There; strength*
 Wurthely, per ma fay!"

 In grett Rome he gart crye
 Ilke an ofycer in his baylye, *bailiwick*
 "The worme has evyll endyng!"
745 The Emperour has taken the way
 To the knyght, ther he lay
 Besyde that dredfull thyng.
 And all that myght ryde or gon *walk*
 To Sir Eglamour hyed they thon; *hastened; then*
750 With blys they gon hym hom bryng.
 They are so fayn the worme ys sleyn *glad*
 With processyon they come hym agayn; *towards*
 Radly the bellys they rynge. *Quickly*

 The Emperour has a dowghtur bryght:
755 Sche has unduretane the knyght — *undertaken (the care of)*
 Hyre name was Dyamuntowre.
 There sche saves hym fro the deed, *death*
 With here handys sche helys hys heed *head*
 A twelfmonyth in hyr bowre.
 chamber
760 Thys ryche Emperour of Rome
 Sent aftyr the dragone
 That in the feld was deed. *dead*
 Hys sydys hard as balayne was, *whalebone*
 Hys wynges were grene as any glas,
765 Hys hed as fyre was reed. *red*

 When they sawe the hydowes best *hideous beast*
 Mony awey then ronne fest *fast*
 And from hym fled full sone.
 They metyd hym, forty fote and mo, *measured*
770 The Emperour commanded they schuld hym do;
 Hys wyll most nede be done.

To Seynt Lawrans kyrke they hym bare *church*
And ther schall he lye evurmare
 To the day of dome. *judgment*
775 When the remeved that fowle thyng *they removed*
Mony men fell in swonyng *swooning*
 For stynke that from hym come.

Letters come to Artas
That the dragon of Rome dede was;
780 A knyght has hym slon. *slain*
So long at lechecraft gon he dwelle, *He stayed so long being healed*
A knave chyld has Crystabelle, *male*
 As whyte as whalys bon.
The Erle gaf to God a vowe:
785 "Dowghtyr, into the see schalt thowe
 In a schyp alone,
And that bastard that ys the dere
Cristundam schall non have here!" *Baptism*
 Hyr maydens wepte ylkon.

790 Yf sche were nevur so fayr ne whyte,
Yt was the schip all redy made tyte *quickly*
 That sche schulde in fare.
Sche lokes on hir child with here ye, *eye*
"My sone," sche seyde, "we most nede dye!"
795 Sche hadde full mykyll care.

The lady that was in care clad,
To the schyp they her lad, *led*
 Sche and hyr frely fode. *noble son*
Hyr chambir wymmen in swonyng gan fall
800 And so dyde hyr fryndes all *did her friends*
 That wolde hyr any good. *Who wished her*
Sche seyde, "Fadyr, I you pray
That a prest myght me a gospell say
 For fendes in the flode." *Against fiends; sea*
805 Sche prayde here gentyllwymmen fre,
"Grete well my lord, when ye hym se." *Greet*
 They wepped as they were wode.

The lady syked with herte sare, *sighed*
The wynd rose and to a roche here bare *rock*
810 And thereon gon sche lende.
Sche was full fayn, I undurstonde,
Sche wend hyt had be byggyd londe *thought; inhabited*
 And there up gan sche wende.
Nothyng ellys sygh sche dere *saw; there*

815 Butt see fowles that wylde were *sea birds*
 That fast flew here hende. *fast flew [from] her quickly*
 A grype come in all hyr care, *griffin*
 The yong chyld away he bare
 To a countré unkende. *foreign*

820 Then the lady sayde, "Allas
 That evyr I born was!
 My chylde ys tane me fro!" *taken*
 In the lond of Israell gon he lyght; *alight*
 That wroghte the lade both day and nyght *lady*
825 Sorow and mykyll wo.
 The kyng of Israell an huntyng went;
 He sygh where the grype was lent *saw; griffin landed*
 And thedur rode with othur mo. *more*
 He strok on the chylde with his byll;
830 The chyld scryked that greved hym yll — *shrieked*
 He rose and lefte hym so.

 A skwyere to the chyld gon passe, *squire*
 In a skarlet mantell wonden he was *wound*
 With a full ryche pane, *lining*
835 In that skarlet mantell wounden,
 With a gyrdyll of golde fast bounden.
 Hys yen were clere as cristall stane. *eyes*
 All they swere be the Rode *Cross*
 The child was comen of gentyll blode,
840 Where evur he was tane. *taken [from]*
 For that he fro the grype fell *griffin*
 They named hym Degrebell,
 That wylsome was of wane. *homeless; dwelling*

 The kyng leves huntyng that tyde,
845 Home with the chyld gon he ryde,
 That from the grype was hent. *taken*
 "Dame," he seyde unto the qwene,
 "Mykyll of solas have I sene —
 Thys chyld God has me sent."
850 Thereof sche was both glad and blyth
 And sent aftur a nurce full swyth. *quickly*
 Hys sydus were long and gent. *sides*
 Leve ye the chyld with mykyll honour
 And speke we of his modur whyte as flour,
855 What weys our Lord here lent.

	All nyght on the roche sche lay,	*rock*
	A wynd rose agayn the day	
	And fro the lond here dryves.	
	Sche had nothere mast ne rothere	*rudder*
860	Butt ylke storme strengere then odur	*the other (i.e., the previous one)*
	Strongly with her stryves.	
	As the boke of Rome sayes,	
	Sche was meteles syx dayes:	*without food*
	Hyr herte for care hyt clevys.	*breaks*
865	Butt the sixte day or none	*sixth; before noon*
	God sent here socoure sone:	*succor*
	In Egypte up sche ryves.	*arrives*

	The kyng of Egypt stod in a toure	
	And sygh the lady whyte as floure,	
870	Was wroken on the sonde.	*wrecked; sand*
	He commaundyd a sqwyere to go and se	
	And loke what in the schyp may be;	
	The wynd has dryven hit to londe.	
	For feyntenes sche spake no worde;	
875	The lady lyfte up hyr hode	
	And made sygnes with here hond.	
	To the schyp sche come full tyte,	*quickly*
	And on the syde gan he smyte:	
	The lady gan up stonde.	
880	Makes mery, for yt ys beste!	
	For this ys the laste geste	*last [part of the] poem*
	That I now take in honde.	

	He wyste never what sche ment;	
	Agayn to the kyng ys he went	
885	And kneled on hys knee.	
	"Lord, in the yondur schip nothyng ys	
	But a woman in lykenes	*likeness*
	That rose and loked on me.	
	A fayrer thyng sawe I never non,	
890	Nothere of flesch, blode ne bon,	*neither*
	But hyt were Mary fre.	
	Sche makes me synes with her hond	*signs*
	As sche were of another lond	
	Beyonde the Grekus see."	

895	"Be Jhesu!" sayde the gentyll kyng,	
	"I wyll se that swete thyng."	
	And thethureward he gose.	
	Into the schip he goth anone	
	And bad here speke in Goddys nome.	*name*

900 Agayn the kyng sche rose: *Before*
 The damysell that was so mylde
 Had so greet for here chylde *grieved*
 That sche was waxen hose. *hoarse*
 To a chaumbur they here ledde,
905 Good mete they here bede; *They invited her to a good dinner*
 With good wyll sche with hem gose.

 Aftyr mete then freynes the kyng, *asks*
 "When art thou, my swete thyng? *Whence*
 For thou art bryght of ble."
910 Sche sayde, "I was born in Artas,
 Syr Prynsamour my fadyr was,
 The lord of that countré.
 Sythen it befell, on a day,
 I and my madyns went to play
915 Be a syde of the see.
 The wedyr was lythe and a bote ther stode; *gentle*
 I and my sqwyer therin yode — *went*
 Uncristen man was he! *Unchristian (Unchristened)*

 "On lond I leved my maydenes alle,
920 My sqwyer on slepe gon falle,
 A mantyll over hym I drewe.
 A wynd rose and tyll a roche us bare,
 A fowle come to my sqwyere thare
 And swyftly away hym threwe."

925 The kyng sayde, "Make good chere,
 Thow art my brodyr dowghtyr dere!" *brother's*
 For joye of hym sche lowgh. *laughed*
 Leve this lady whyte as floure
 And speke we more of Sir Eglamour:
930 Now comes to hym care inowgh.

 When Sir Eglamour was hole and sownd
 And well covered of hys wond *recovered*
 He buskes and makes hym yare. *prepares; ready*
 He thankes the Emperour of thys,
935 Hys dowghtyr that was the Emperysse
 And all that he fond thare.
 Crystabell was in hys thowght;
 The dragones hed forgat he noght —
 On a spere he hyt bare.
940 Be that seven wykes were come to ende
 In the lond of Artas gon he lende,
 To hym come letters of care.

	The countré herde, I undyrstand,	people
	That Sir Eglamour was comand	coming
945	With the dragons hed.	
	A sqwyer went agayn hym sone,	
	"Lo, lord, what the Erle has done:	
	Fayre Crystabell ys ded!	
	A knave chyld had sche with hyre borne,	male; carried
950	Thay have both here lyves lorne —	lost
	He was both whyte and rede.	
	He has don in the see them two	
	And with the wynd lett hem go."	
	The knyght swoned in that stede.	

955	"Lord!" seyde the knyght so fre,	
	"Where evyr the gentyllwymmen be	
	That in chambur with here was?"	
	The sqwyer answered hym full sone,	
	"Lord, in the see when sche was done;	sea; put
960	Ylkon ther way gon passe."	
	Into the halle gan they fare	
	Among the grete lordes that there ware	
	Before the Erle of Artas.	
	"Have here this dragons hed.	
965	All ys myn that here ys leved —	left
	Thow syttys in my plas!"	place

	A gret rewthe yt was to here	sorrow
	How he called aftur Cristabell his fere	mate
	And sayde, "Art thou in the see?	
970	God that dyede on the Crosse	
	On thy sowle have mercy	
	And on thy yong sone so fre."	
	The Erle was ferd of Sir Eglamour:	afraid
	He rose up and toke a towre,	went to
975	That evyrmore woo hym be.	
	"Gentyllmen, so God you save,	
	All that odure of knyght woll have	order
	Ryse up and take at me!"	take (it) from

	Gentyllmen come hym tyll;	
980	They were fayn to do his wyll —	
	He gaf them orders sone,	
	And in the halle when he was stad	
	Fyve and thretty knytes he mad	
	Be that othur day at none.	
985	And sythen, I understond,	then

He takes the wey to the Holy Lond
 Ther God on Cros was don. *Where; put*

Syr Eglamour, as ye may here,
Dwelled in the Holy Lond fiftene yere
990 The heden men among. *heathen*
Full dowghtyly he hym bare
There ony dedes of armes ware
 Agayn them that lyved wrong. *lived*
Be that the fiftene yere were come and gon,
995 The chyld that the grype had tane *griffin; taken*
 Was both stren and stronge.

In justenyng nore in tornament
Ther myght no man sytte his dent[1]
 Butt he cast hem to the ground.
1000 Syr Degrebell was wyse and wyghte; *valiant*
The kyng of Israell made hym knyght
 And prynce with hys honde.
Lestenes lordynges, both lefe and dere,
What armes the chyld bare ye schal here *hear*
1005 And ye wyll undyrstond.
He bare in armere a grype of golde *on his coat of arms; griffin*
Rychely betyn in the molde. *engraved; background*
 In hys clothys wavond *banners*
A knave chyld in a mantyll wondyn
1010 And with a goldyn gyrdull bowndyn,
 As he was browght to the lond.

The kyng of Israell was old;
To Degrebell hys sone he told,
 "I wold thou haddest a wyfe;
1015 For I trow thou art me dere.
When I am dede thou getys no pere,
 In rychesse thou art so ryfe." *well endowed*
A messyngere stode by the kyng:
"In Egypt wones a swete thyng, *dwells*
1020 The fayrest that ever bare lyfe. *had*
The kyng hath hys othe sworne
Ther schall no man hyre have that ys born
 Butt he wynns hyre with stryfe!" *combat*

He sware then, "And sche bo good *If she be*
1025 Therfore I woll not let, Be the Rode. *stay; Cross*

[1] *There might no man remain on horseback through his attack*

	Han don and buske the swythe!"	*make yourself ready quickly*
	He commanded a messynger to gon	
	To byd hys knyghtys everylke on	
	That they be there belyve.	*at once*
1030	They busked hem with ryall fare;	*embraced*
	Armoure to schip they bare	
	And passed the watyr blythe.	
	Be thre wykes were come to ende	*By [the time that]*
	In the lond of Egypt con they lende	*they landed*
1035	Therefore for to kythe.	*Their expedition to make known*
	A messyngere went before to tell,	
	"Here comes the kyng of Israell	
	With a fayre semble!	*assembly*
	The prins ys comme, with many a knyght,	
1040	For to wynne your dowghtyr bryght,	
	Yyf your wyll be."	
	He sayde, "Be God, I trowe I schall	*By*
	Fynd redy justyng for them all.	
	Dere wellcome schall they be."	
1045	Trumpes in topcastels rose,	*trumpets (see note)*
	The ryche kyng to londe gose,	
	His knyghtus were clad in pall.	
	The chyld that was of fiftene yere,	
	He gose among hem as ye may here:	
1050	A fote above hem all.	
	The kyng of Egypt agayn hem gose,	
	The kyng be the hond he tase	*takes*
	And ledde hym to the halle.	
	"I pray you swythe, yf that ye myghte,	
1055	Of your dowghtyr to have a syghte,	
	Als whyte as bon of whall."	
	Tyll a chambur they have here browght,	
	With mannes hond as sche were wroght	*As if she were wrought by man's hand*
	Or corven on a tre.	*carved from a tree*
1060	Hys sone stode styll and hyre behelde,	
	"Well were hym that the myght welde!"	*control*
	To hymself sayde he.	
	The kyng of Israell asked that lady fre	
	Yyf sche myght passe the Greces see	*cross*
1065	Hys sones wyfe to be.	
	Sche seyde, "Ye, yf that he may	
	Sytte for me a stroke or tway,	*two*
	Thy askyng graunt I the."	

Grete lordes were at on assent;

1070 Waytes blewe; up to mete they went *Watchmen*
 With a full ryall chere.
 Two kynges the dese bygan, *sat at the head of the table*
 Syr Degrebell and Crystabell than,
 Yyf they were sybbe full nere. *kin*
1075 Knyghtes wente to sette, iwys, *indeed*
 Ilke a sqwyere in hys offys *place*
 To serve hys lorde there.
 Aftyr mete then weschen they; *washed*
 "Deus pacis" clerkes gon sey *God's peace*
1080 That all men myght hyt here.

 On the morn the day sprong,
 Gentyll to there armour throng, *Nobles; thronged*
 Syr Degrebell was dyght. *dressed*
 And trumpes in the feld rose,
1085 Ilke a lorde tyll othyr gose —
 Hyt was a semyly syght.
 Grete lordes made this cry,
 "What manere of man, sykurly,
 That berys a grype full bryghte?" *griffin*
1090 Herodes of armes gon them telle, *Heralds*
 "That ys the pryns of Israell,
 Be well ware for he ys wyghte." *aware*

 The kyng of Egypte tase a schafte, *takes a lance*
 That sawe the chylde and anothur rawght, *took*
1095 Yyf he were nevere so kene. *As he was ever so bold*
 Agayn the kyng the chylde gon fare,
 Hors and man adown he bare
 Strongly on that grene. *field*
 The kyng seyde, "So God me save,
1100 Thow art best worthy here to have!" *her*
 Thus seyde they all bydene. *together*
 Lordes then justed they, *jousted*
 Sqwyeres on that othure day,
 Dowghty men and kene.

1105 Two kynges that were of myght
 Toke Crystabell that was so bryght,
 To the kyrke they here lede.
 Thus gracyously he hase sped
 Hys owen modyr hase he wed,
1110 As I herde a clerke rede.
 Hys armes they bare hym beforn —
 Sche thynkes how hyre chyld away was born,

Therfore sorow sche hade.
Sche grette therfore and sorow gan make *wept*
1115 And all was for hyr sones sake;
A grett swonyng sche made.
"What now," sayde he, "my lady clere,
Why makes thou so sympull chere?
Me thynkes thou art not glade."

1120 "Lorde, in thyn armes a fowle I se *winged creature*
That sumtyme raft a chyld fro me *That once took from me a child*
A knyght dere hym bowghte." *That a knight had dearly paid for*
The kyng swere, "Be Crystus myght!
In my forest gon he lyght; *he alighted*
1125 A grype to londe hym browghte."

He commanded a sqwyere that was hende
Aftur the cofure for to wende *coffer*
Thereinne hyt was ledde. *laid*
I wote he toke hem out full rathe *quickly*
1130 And a goldyn gyrdull bathe *both*
Full rychely were they redde. *decorated*
The lady seyde, "Full wo ys me!
They were fro me rafte in the see." *reft*
O swonynge down sche brayde. *In; sank*
1135 "How longe sythen?" The kyng gon sey.
"Fyftene yere," sche sayde, "per ma fay!"
They graunted alle to that sche sayde. *agreed*

"Lo, sone, all that we done hade: *Look, son, at all that we have done*
A sybbe maryage han we made *incestuous*
1140 In spryngyng of the mone.
I rede we loke, so God me save, *advise; look (find)*
The gre in feld ho so may have, *victory in tournament who*
And in haste that hyt be done."
"Ye, fadur, I holde your counceyll good,
1145 So do I my modyr, by the Rode.
I wedded hyre byfore the none.
Ther schall no man have here, be Seynt Mary,
Butt he wynne here als dowghtyly
As myself have done!"

1150 Grete lordes ylkon tyll othur gon sey,
"For hyr love we wyll turnay
With swerd scharp on end. *(i.e., not blunted)*
He that wynnes this lady clere
He schall wedde hyre tyll hys fere, *as his mate*
1155 There hym loves best to lende." *Where he likes best to live*

	Herodes of armes forth they went	*Heralds*
	To dyscrye thys turnament	*recount*
	In all londys hende.	
	Syr Eglamour was homwarde bowne	*bound*
1160	And herd of that dede of grete renowne,	
	And thythure gan he wende.	
	For Crystabell was don in the see	*since*
	No armes bare he.	*New (see note)*
	Lystyn and I wyll you say sykurly.	
1165	He bare a schyp in armes of gold[1]	
	And a lady drownyng as sche schold,	
	A chyld lyand hyr by.	
	The chyld was butt a nyght old.	
	Hys mast was of sylvyre and gold	*Its*
1170	In every poynte to the ye.	*Wherever the eye might see*
	Of reed gold was hys fane,	*ship's pennant*
	Hys sales and hys ropes ylkane	*sails*
	Was purtred varely.	*portrayed accurately*
	Gentyllmen that herd that cry	
1175	Thethur went they ryally,	
	They that dowghty ware.	
	The kyng of Sydon come full sone	
	With many a knyght, full hard bone,	*of very hard bones*
	That ryche colours bare.	
1180	Renges they made in the felde	*Rings*
	That grete lordes myghte them welde:	*use*
	Full faste they turneyd thare.	
	Syr Eglamour, yf he come last,	
	Yyt he was not away to cast —	*Yet he was not turned away*
1185	The knyght was cladde in care.	
	Crystabell that lady small,	
	Sche was browght to the wall	
	There the crye was made.	*proclamation*
	The chyld that was of fiftene yere eld,	
1190	He was aunterus in the feld.	*daring*
	In that stowre he rade.	*combat; rode*
	When Degrebell began to smyte,	
	From his handis they went ful tyte:	*quickly*
	Wold non hys dynt abyde.	*blow*
1195	He sees a knyght hovande full stylle,	*standing*

[1] *He bore on his arms a ship of gold (Lincoln MS has this phrasing)*

Syr Degrebell rydes hym tylle
 And sayde, "Wylt thou not ryde?"

He seyde, "Hit ys for werynesse,
For I am come out of hethennesse —
1200 Grete syn it were me to tene." *disturb*
Hys owen sayde, "So mote I the, *own (son)*
Then shuld thou not han armed the!
 More worschyp had hyt bene."

The knyght smylyd and on hym lowgh, *laughed*
1205 "Hase thou not turneyd yyt inowgh
 Butt thou of more me pray?"
He sayd, "No, Mari! I am aunterus in stowre[1]
For a lady, as whyte as flowre,
 To wynne here yyf I may."
1210 "Be Jhesu!" swere the knyght than,
"I schall asaye yyf I can *see*
 Ony thyng turnay. *tourney at all (ironic understatement)*
Be God, som tyme have I sene,
In all so hard sement have I bene *contest*
1215 And wan full wele away." *And escaped harm completely*

Grete lordes with wepens long,
Gentyllmen her horses sprong,
 Dowghty men everylke on.
Syr Eglamour has turned the flatt: *flat edge of his sword*
1220 He gafe his sone syche a patt —
 To the erthe ys he gon.
All they sware, "Upon the molde, *ground*
He that berys a schyp of golde
 Has wonne here full gayne."
1225 The lady sayde, "Full wo ys me.
My sone ys deed, be Cristus pyté!
 Yondure knyght has hym slayne."

Herodes of armes cryed then *Heralds*
Yf ther were any gentyllmen
1230 To make his body goode. *To take up the challenge*
Grete lordes sayd now,
"Best wordy art thow *worthy*
 To welde yond frely fode" *govern; young man*
To unarme hym the knyght gose

[1] *He [Degrebelle] said, "No, by Mary! I am ready to fight in battle."*

1235 Kyrtels and surcotis and other close *kirtles; surcoats; clothes*
 That dowghty were in dede.
 Two kynges the dese began,
 Syr Eglamour and Crystabell than.
 Jhesu us all spede!

1240 Sche asked be what cheson he bore *chance*
 A schyp of gold, maste and ore
 Fro the see drowned was done. *Was drowned in the sea*
 The knyght sone gon answere,
 "Thay made the endyng ryght there,
1245 My lemman and my yonge sone." *lover*

 The lady letted for no schane, *stopped; shame*
 "Gode syr, wat ys your name?
 Telles me in thys stownde!" *instant*
 "Men called me ther I borne was
1250 Syr Eglamour of Artas,
 Tho of a worme had a wonde."

 There was mony a robe of palle,
 Then servyd the chyld in the halle
 Of the fyrst messe that day.
1255 Pryvyly sche to hym spake,
 "This ys thy fadyr that the gate!" *begot*
 Therewith say I not nay.

 A grete joye hyt was to se
 When he kneled on hys knee;
1260 There was a hert full sore.
 Hyt is soth sayd, be God of heven,
 "Mony meten at unsett steven," *Many meet through unexpected events*
 And so befell hyt thore. *there*

 The kyng of Israell gon hym telle
1265 How he fond Syr Degrebell;
 Knytes lystend thanne.
 Syr Eglamour kneled on hys kne,
 "And, lord, Gode yelde hyt the; *grant*
 Ye have made hym a manne."
1270 The kyng sayde, "I schall hym geve
 Half my londes whyle I leve,
 My sone as whyte as swanne."
 The kyng of Sydon sayd also,
 "And my dowghtyr Organate to —
1275 Me mynnes his fadure hyr wan." *I remember*

Syr Eglamour prayd the lordys all
Hom into Artas hym wend withall
 And at hys bredale to be. *wedding*
They grauntyd that there were alle,
1280 They busked them with ryall *readied themselves; royal*
 Fare and sythen passed the see.

Shyppus ley wroken on the sond,
Ilkon toke othur be the hond, *Each one (lord) took the other by the hand*
 Knaves there hors gon dryve. *Men*
1285 This olde erld, Sir Prynsamoure, *earl*
Fell down bakward of a towre
 And brake hys nekke belyve. *instantly*
A messengere come before to tell
What kyns aunterus the Erle befell. *kinds of adventures*
1290 Wyth God may no man stryfe! *strive*

All nyght there they lay
Tyll on the morn that hyt was day
 To wedde that lady bryght.
There was mony a lord of pride,
1295 Kyngus led hyre on every side.
 Hyt was a semmyly syght!
Sythen a byschop gan hem wedde;
They thanked God they had so spedde,
And Mary mykyll of myght.

1300 Sythe to wedde gon they go, *Then*
Syr Degrebell and Organato,
 He was a full fayr knyght.
There was drowen in that stownd *drawn; time*
The mowntans of a thowzand pownd, *sum*
1305 Gete hyt wo so myght.
Mynstrelles come fro fere lond, *minstrels*
Thay hadde ryche gyftes, I unthurstond,
 In hert they were lyght.
Sythen to the castell gon they wende
1310 To holde the brydale to the ende, *wedding festivities*
 Hyt lasted a fowrtenyght. *fortnight*
When the brydale was all don
Ilke a lorde toke his lefe full son,
 Thedur there they schuld lend all nyght. *spend*

1315 Mynstralles that were ther in that stownd
Ther gyftus were worth an hondred pownd,
 The boldere myght they spende.
In Rome this gest cronyclyd ys, *story chronicled*

Jhesu brynge us to hys blys
1320 That nevyr schall have ende!

Explicit Eglamour of Artas

19, 20, 28 The characters' names, like those in similar romances, are a kind of pseudo-French. Prynsamour (prince love) and Eglamour are compounds with *amour*, the latter perhaps arrived at by conflating something like OF *egaré*, "lost one," as in the names Egaré and Degaré (found in *Emaré* and *Degaré*, respectively). Cristabelle suggests "clear or bright beauty" and Degrebelle, "lost beauty." See Ramsey ("Chivalric Romances," p. 166) for an allegorical interpretation of these names.

31–36 The manuscripts exhibit a good bit of variation in the characters mentioned in this passage. In the sixteenth- and seventeenth-century versions, line 31 refers to Cristabelle, line 32 to the earl. This sets up the incest theme, as do similar alterations in lines 40 and 47.

54 Richardson suggests that the sense of this line is "you meet a lot of people" (*Sir Eglamour*, p. 99). That is, because the squire travels widely and comes in contact with a lot of people he would have many opportunities to divulge Eglamour's counsel were he not charged with secrecy.

64–84 This awareness of the potential for Eglamour to advance his position within society by marrying an heiress, Cristabelle, is reflective of what Riddy calls a "crisis in male succession" (*Middle English Romance*, p. 245) at the time of the poem's composition. According to Charbonneau, the Black Death heightened an already high rate of failure of inheritance through a direct male line "so that less than half of landowners had sons to inherit" between the late 1370s and early 1380s ("Trangressive Fathers," p. 247). Conditions were, therefore, favorable for succession through the female line that, in turn, resulted in an increasing number of opportunities for men of lesser social status to advance themselves through marriage. The potential for incest and the earl's desire to block Eglamour's more appropriate suit of marriage to his daughter further threaten the already fragile sociopolitical family unit.

66 A proverbial expression (also see lines 70–71): "For much would have more." The sense seems to be "People who are wealthy (have much land or property) want more." Richardson says the phrase refers to the earl or the wealthy suitors of Cristabelle (*Sir Eglamour,* p. 100), but it seems just as likely that the squire could be referring to Cristabelle herself, who might reject the suit of a knight of little land like Eglamour.

70 The Cambridge text omits lines 70–72, perhaps because the proverb was unfamiliar, or too homely. It substitutes three rather padded lines in which Eglamour addresses his squire:

> "Dere frende Y prey the that thou me behete
> That thou wylt that lady in this maner grete
> What some evyr happe to be hur answere,"

and then goes on to create a name (for the squire?) — *Syr umbe than thenke on thys thyng* — out of the unfamiliar verb form *umbythynk* found in Thornton.

81 *lufe*. The Cotton MS reading *lyfe* makes little sense in this context (Cristabelle would not marry Eglamour if he were an old man). It may be a scribe's attempt to make sense of a flawed exemplar. The Egerton MS reads *lyuf*, an odd form, perhaps a corruption (*Sir Eglamour*, ed. Richardson, p. 100). The Thornton MS reads *lufe* and the Cambridge MS *love*, so I have emended to this more appropriate reading "Cristabelle would only marry him if their love were well-established."

106–07 Manuscript variations in these lines suggest rather different conceptions of marital bliss. The Thornton MS reads, *And rejoyse hir all my lyfe*; the Cambridge MS reads, *And sethen reches in my lyfe*.

138 At this point, the Thornton and Egerton manuscripts include the lines

> For na man ne wald scho spare
> Till his chambir for to fare,
> Whare that he gan lende.
> The sqwyere sayd, "Maystir, ma gud chere:
> Here commes the erls doghetir dere.
> Cryste len that ye part frende."

Thus the squire serves (briefly) as a mediator between the lady and the knight, making their exchange less abrupt and more courteous. The omission of these lines explains such awkward features as why Cristabelle identifies Eglamour to himself in line 140 of the Cotton MS. In the Thornton and Egerton manuscripts, it is the squire who responds to Cristabelle in line 143 saying his master is *bowndyn for the luf of the*.

148 *unto*. Cotton MS: *utto*. Richardson's emendation.

158 In the Thornton MS, Cristabelle tells Eglamour to find out from her father what his will is.

162 In the Thornton MS, the word *fude* (human being, creature) appears at the end of the line, giving the reading "I will fail you for no one." This seems more chivalric than Cotton's reading.

170 In the later Middle Ages particularly, when there were many more marriageable women than men, the awarding of dowries to women of lesser means was regarded as an especially charitable act.

172 *her*. Cotton MS: *he*. Richardson's emendation.

189 Thornton includes three lines which establish the time and place of the hunt:

> Appon the morne when it was daye
> Sir Eglamour tase the waye
> Till a revere full ryght

226 Cypress trees, associated with death, were often planted in graveyards.

251 Cristabelle's gifts to Eglamour before his departure are conventional chivalric
 endowments. The hounds and the sword are necessary for those quintessential
 knightly activities, hunting and fighting. These are not specifically magical gifts,
 though the sword found by St. Paul in the Greek sea certainly has an aura. The
 sword from the sea is a traditional motif, compare Arthur and Lancelot's gifts
 from the Lady of the Lake.

288 The exact meaning of this line is not clear, and the manuscripts are not in agree-
 ment. Richardson prefers the reading, "And roused himself with a rush," based
 on translations of the same formula in *Sir Tristrem*. Schleich takes Thornton *repid*
 (Cotton *repys*) to be a form of the verb *rape* ("grasp"), rather than *rouse*. Cook
 takes *rese* to be an idiosyncratic scribal spelling of the noun *rest*; this is the way the
 Cambridge scribe rendered it, though it may be a form of OE *raes* ("course," as
 in millrace). The translation given here follows the sense of Thornton in using
 the preposition *of* rather than *on*. Thus, "The barking of the hounds grabbed him
 from (deprived him of) his rest" (*Sir Eglamour*, ed. Richardson, p. 104).

300 Eglamour is honoring hunting law and protocol by blowing his horn to an-
 nounce a legally taken prey. The *prise* is the "hunting call blown when game is
 taken" (*MED*).

344 This is the first of three fitt divisions marking Eglamour's feats. The others occur
 at lines 622 and 882. Richardson (*Sir Eglamour*, p. 106) suggests that these were
 in the original (now lost) version of *Eglamour*. Though regarded by some as clumsy
 intrusions in the middle of scenes, this one does mark the turning point between
 Eglamour's report of his victory and the earl's announcement of the next task.

349 Sidon, on the Mediterranean in what is now Lebanon, was important in the
 Crusades.

408 Many romances refer to a "book of Rome" as their source, but there is little evi-
 dence to suggest that this is anything more than a common formula. The title
 of the famous story collection, *Gesta Romanorum*, may have suggested or been
 suggested by this conventional attribution.

414 Thornton reads, *I drede full lange we duelle*; i.e., "I fear we stay too long" ("we will
 not find him in time to help him").

417 *swerd*. Cotton MS: *swere*.

425–29 Azure (blue) and sable (black) are heraldic colors, though Eglamour's device is
 not particularly authentic. The word *sperys* in the phrase *sperys of sabull* may be
 a corruption of *sporys* ("spurs"). The Thornton MS has *bagges of sabyll*. Richard-
 son notes that Cook suggests that the *bagges* are badges which knights affixed to

their pennons (*Sir Eglamour*, p. 108). Such decorations are more fittingly described by heraldic colors than the spears or spurs.

460 Here Thornton includes the lines:

> "Ya, so helpe me God!" the knyght says,
> "I hafe foghetyn foure dayes
> And never a fote I flede."
> "Sir Knyght," the kyng says,"I pray the
> All nyght that thou wold duelle wyth mee,
> And riste the in a bed."

463 Eglamour gives a nickname, meaning "Adventurous." This kind of disguise is common among knights on quests; and Sir Degrevant uses a similar name. In some romances such sobriquets are part of a theme of character development and self-discovery.

496 Here Thornton includes the lines:

> The kyng said, "So God me save,
> Of the bare what thou will have,
> Thou hast it boghte full dere."

594–97 This offer of kingship through marriage to his daughter establishes the king of Sidone as the earl of Artas' foil given his willingness to reward heroic behavior properly. As Charbonneau notes, "The villainous father of Cristabelle eventually flees to a tower — a phallic structure symbolizing his virility perhaps — but in its isolation and prison-like qualities, it becomes a symbol of his impotence as a man and ruler. . . . Appropriately, he falls backwards to his death — his desires were after all regressive as he symbolically proves himself incapable of moving forward in accepting his daughter's suitor and planning for appropriate succession and transfer of power" ("Transgressive Fathers," p. 258).

605 The horse and ring are magical gifts that insure his life, though we do not see him use them. Such magical gifts are the stuff of folktale. See note, line 251.

615 Here Thornton includes three lines:

> Trewly and so God me save,
> Kynge ne duke nane for to have,
> Thofe thay be comly clede.

624 *red.* The implication seems to be that the narrator is reciting from a written text. See note to line 344.

628 Thornton reads: *Alle bot the erle were full fayne.* This gives more and earlier indication of the earl's treachery.

632 Thornton reads: *Till his chambir scho mad hir yare.* The chamber, a private place, was the conventional setting for such meetings between lovers. The hall (line 637), by contrast, is a public place and the domain of the earl. In line 697, Cotton also lacks the reference to chamber contained in Thornton.

638 Thornton reads: *The erle for to tene*. This is more negative than Cotton, which emphasizes Eglamour's good intentions and, by implication, the earl's evil ones.

652 Lines 652–54 have no counterpart in Thornton, though they appear in other manuscripts. In Cambridge the order is reversed, which gives a better reading. The first line is proverbial.

669 This betrothal, the consummation that follows, and Eglamour's gift of a ring constituted a valid marriage, according to canon law. Such unions were considered clandestine and punishable by penance, but they were not invalid.

673 *Twenty* is a mistake for *twelve*. See line 656.

676 *Sche*. Cotton MS: *sch*. Richardson's emendation.

694 The Cambridge manuscript inserts these lines here:

> Syr that was nevyr my purpos
> For to leve oon soche a trase [undertaking]
> Be nyght nor be day
> Wyth the grace of God almyght
> Wyth the worme yyt schall y fyyght
> Thowe he be nevyr so wylde.

705 That the departing knight worries that he might be leaving his girlfriend pregnant, even though they are informally married, is most unusual in medieval romances.

706 The Thornton manuscript includes a redundant transition not found in Cotton:

> And, als the buke of Rome says,
> To grete Rome he tase the wayes
> To seke that worme so wylde.

> The knyght wendis on his waye —
> Herkyns, now; I sall yow saye —
> To seke that dragone bolde.

725 The Thornton text has Eglamour cut off the dragon's tail, and it makes better sense in line 727 for the dragon to strike Eglamour with the stump of his tail than the stump of his tongue, as in Cotton. Taking the dragon's tongue for a trophy is, however, a traditional feature appearing in the Tristran story and elsewhere.

754 The Thornton manuscript includes six lines:

> The emperour wyth hym tuke hym hame
> Octoveane was his name,
> A lord of gret honour.
> Bot alle that ever saw his hede
> Thay sayd that he was bot dede,
> This knight Sir Eglamour.

Octavian was a conventional name for a Roman emperor, so this is not a reference to the character in the Middle English romance *Octavian*.

760 The two stanzas describing the dragon are not present in the Thornton text. Elements of description are conventional: the stench, the similes (hard as balayne, green as glas, red as fire), the forty-foot length (though this seems short beside the fifty-foot measurement of the giant Marrass in line 330).

772 St. Lawrence was well known in England. Tradition had it that he was buried outside Rome, so the reference to his church would have seemed appropriate to medieval audiences. See *Sir Eglamour*, ed. Richardson, p. 117.

785–89 This willingness to kill not only his own daughter but also her child and his only male heir further exemplifies the extent to which the earl's trangressive desires threaten to destroy the social order he is supposed to uphold (Charbonneau, "Transgressive Fathers," p. 257).

788 Without baptism, the soul could not ascend to heaven.

790 The Thornton version includes three lines:

> Scho wappid hym in a mantill of skarelett rede
> "My dere child, dighte es oure dede.
> Thi fadir seese us na mare."

This is the first reference to Degrebelle's mantle, a token which later identifies him to his mother.

795 The Cambridge text inserts six lines here:

> Hur chaumburwomen that be hur con stonde
> They weptyn faste and wrang ther hande
> They had full mekyll care
> When they wyste that sche schoulde forthe passe
> Then they cryed and seyde "Allas.
> Now are we lafte full bare."

808 The Thornton manuscript includes the conventional transition formula:

> Now leve this knyght, Sir Eglamour,
> And speke we of this lady whytt als flour,
> So wilsome wayes scho yode.

829–31 The three lines describing the griffin attack are not in the Thornton version, where the infant is merely dropped. This detail accords with the Cotton text's attention to fabulous creatures elsewhere; it also heightens Degrebelle's plight. Richardson thinks it impedes the narrative (*Sir Eglamour*, p. 118).

837 Thornton has an additional line: *The childe was large of lym and lythe.*

842 *Degrebell.* The name means "lost beautiful one" (see note to line 19), an apt description of his situation.

852 Long sides are not appropriate for an infant, but they are conventional in descriptions of noble personages. Richardson (*Sir Eglamour*, p. 118) suggests that *his* is a mistake for *her*, referring to the nurse, though all the manuscripts have *his*.

856 The number *iiii* appears here in the margin and space between the lines in the margin of the manuscript, indicating a division in the text — the fourth fitt (see note to lines 880–82, below).

874 Lines 874–76 and 877–79 are reversed in the other manuscripts, which makes more sense as the squire strikes the ship to determine if anyone is aboard before the lady speaks.

880–82 These lines are not in Thornton, and they make for a long stanza. They set off the last section of the narrative, but Richardson suggests they are in the wrong place, since the Cotton manuscript shows the number *iiii* beside line 855, a more suitable place for such a division (*Sir Eglamour*, p. 119). There is also a mark beside line 880.

917 Cristabelle's retelling winks at the truth, omitting all reference to her angry father and relationship to her *sqwyer*.

976 *Gentyllmen*. Cotton MS: *entyllman*. Richardson's emendation.

985 Here Thornton includes the lines:

> Alle that were sembled, ylke one,
> He gaf tham for to lyfe appone
> For Cristabelle saule to mone.

Cambridge begins, *And he that was the porest of them all*, reverses Thornton's lines 986–87, and then includes the following lines:

> Yn the halle that he there hadd.
> V and thretty knyghtys he madd
> Be that odur day abowte none
>
> And he that was the porest of them all
> He gaf for Crystabellys soule
> Londys to leve upon.

This material, omitted by the Cotton scribe, provides important details: that Eglamour is able to provide livings for his knights, as a lord should, and that their function is a pious one. One half-expects them to accompany him to the Holy Land, but there is no further reference to them. By remaining in Artois, they could assert Eglamour's claim to that land pending his return. Eglamour has clearly assumed power in Artois when he stands in the hall to formally dub his knights. Richardson notes that Eglamour follows standard procedures for making knights (*Sir Eglamour*, p. 120).

997–1000 These lines are not in the Thornton text.

1012 *kyng*. Cotton MS: *knyg*. Richardson's emendation.

1023 *Wynns hyre with stryfe* is a formulaic expression in which *strife* has a narrow, idiomatic meaning, indicating specifically a combat in which a bride is to be won.

1037 Thornton reads: *That thare come the kyng of Iraelle / Wyth a full riche nave*, which follows from the preceding description of the voyage. Five lines later, Thornton

includes lines similar to those found at 1036–37 in Cotton. This variation seems to be due to the proximity of similar lines: the Cotton text conflates them, omitting intervening material.

1044 Here Cambridge inserts:

> And yf they come on gode array [order]
> To ther mete y schall them pray
> As mote y thryve or the.

1045 Topcastles were platforms with battlements at the tops of ship's masts from which missiles could be fired (*OED*).

1060 *Hys*. In Thornton the pronoun is *Hir*, which points to the incest theme and makes better sense. *Hys* may refer to the king of Israel who speaks next.

1063 It is a bit unorthodox for Degrebelle's guardian to ask Cristabelle herself if she will marry. In Thornton, the king of Israel asks *hir eme*, that is, her uncle the king of Egypt, if he is willing for Cristabelle to marry.

1070 In aristocratic households *waytes* functioned as watchmen as well as musicians who played horns of various types at ceremonies and to announce meals. Their name seems to be derived from *wayt*, a kind of pipe. See Rastall, "Minstrels of English Royal Households," p. 5.

1079 *Deus pacis* were the first words of the blessing for dinner on days which were not fast days (*Sir Eglamour*, ed. Richardson, p. 122).

1085–87 Here Thornton includes the lines:

> The kyng of Egippe gun hym hy
> Into a faire felde, wittirly
> Wyth many a doghety knyghte.

Cotton lines 1083–85 appear later in Thornton, after what is line 1091 in Cotton. Thornton's arrangement is more coherent: The king of Egypt first rides into the field to meet Degrebelle. The men ask who he is, the heralds tell them, then blow the trumpets to announce the tournament. The teams then ride together and finally the king and Degrebelle confront one another.

1122 Thornton includes the lines:

> In a skarelett mantill was he wonden
> And with a gold girdill bownden
> That full richely was wroghte.

This formulaic description appears several times in the romance (see Cotton line 832), though more often in Thornton than Cotton.

1142 Thornton reads: *Whilke of myn erles scho will have*. This is more specific, but less courtly than Cotton. Degrebelle rejects his stepfather's plan simply to give Cristabelle to one of his men; she must be won in combat as he has won her.

1157 *dyscrye*. Cotton MS: *decrye*. Richardson's emendation.

| 1163 | Thornton reads *New*; Cambridge reads *Now soche armes beryth he*. Cotton's *No* makes little sense, as a description of the arms follows, and they are different from the ones he wore when fighting with the boar (line 428). |

1163 | Thornton reads *New*; Cambridge reads *Now soche armes beryth he*. Cotton's *No* makes little sense, as a description of the arms follows, and they are different from the ones he wore when fighting with the boar (line 428).

1168 | Thornton reads: *In the see so grym and balde*.

1170 | Thornton reads: *And evir in poynte to dy*, which is more appropriate than the Cotton reading.

1172 | *sales*. Cotton MS: *fales*.

1186 | Here Thornton includes the lines:

> Hawrauds of armes bygan to crye
> Grete lordis full rathely
> Into a felde so brade.

1195 | Here Thornton includes the lines:

> His fadir hovede and byhelde
> How he fellid in the felde
> The knyghtis all bydene.
> His sonne hym sawe and rade hym till;
> Said, "Sir, why hovys thou sa stille
> Amange thir knyghtis kene?"

1201 | Thornton reads: *"Sir," he said than, "So mot I the."* Cotton's *Hys owen* is more ironic in pointing out their relationship.

1214 | *sement*. Richardson suggests that this is a mistake for *semblee*, meaning assembly or meeting (*Sir Eglamour*, p. 125). Thornton has *auntirs*.

1222–27 | The Thornton text reverses the order of the two units of this stanza.

1231 | The Thornton version is different and includes the lines:

> Say forthe whils he was thare,
> That will juste or turnay any mare —
> He wold be auntirous, by the rode!
> His sone said, "Ne ware his swerd so brighte,
> Alle the day myght I wyth hym fyght,
> Thofe he were werse than wode."

1234–37 | In Thornton, it is the lady who goes to disarm the knight:

> To unarme hym the lady gase;
> A surcott vuerte [green] the knyght tase.
> To mete than gan thay wende.

Cotton line 1235 is a tag line inserted for rhyme.

1246–60 | The Thornton text's version of the reunion scene is different, probably original.

> Knawlege of hym gun scho taa,
> "Swete sir, how felle it swa
> That thay were broghte to grownde?"

"Dameselle, I was in a ferre contré,
Hir fadir dide tham to the see
 Wyth the wawes to confounde."

In swounynge than felle that lady free,
"Welcome, Sir Eglamour, to me;
 Dere hase thou boghte me are."
Grete lordis than told scho sone
How that scho to the se was done.
 Thay wepede, both lesse and mare.
"In the wawes grete and gray
A gryffon bare my childe awaye."
 Gentillmen than syghede sare.

Cotton and Cambridge show the influences of another variant of the reunion episode where father and son are reunited when the son kneels to serve his father in the hall. Perhaps this shows the influence of *Emaré*, which makes its only appearance in the Cambridge manuscript.

1276–84 The Thornton manuscript includes a different, longer narration of the return home:

Sir Eglamour prayed the kynges three
In Artasse at his weddynge to be,
 His lykynge for to have.
Thay graunted hym bathe mare and lesse,
The gret lordis that thare was,
 Thare Jhesu Crist tham save!
Kynges and dukis, I undirstande,
And gret lordis of othir lande,
 Thaire stremours made thay full rathe.
Trompis in topcastells thay rase,
Alle maner of men to schippe gase;
 A comly wynd tham drave.

Thorow the myght of God this fayre nave
Alle in lykynge passed the see,
 In Artasse up thay raffe.
The erle in his castelle stode;
Gentillmen sone to lande yode
 Knyghtis to horse gan dryve.

1291–1312 The wedding episode is narrated differently in Thornton, where it is a bit shorter. Cotton stresses minstrels and gifts, adds a bishop to perform the ceremony and a tournament to celebrate it. Thornton repeats the investiture scene from lines 1270–71. Forty- and fourteen-day feasts are conventional.

And thus in Artasse are thay lent,
Eftir the emperour thay sent
 To that mangery so free
And in alle the lande garte thay crye

> Wha that wolde com to that mangerye
> Dere welcome solde thay be.
> Sir Eglamour to the kirk gun ga,
> Sir Degrebelle and Organata,
> The ladys bryghte of blee.
> The kyng of Iraelle sayd, "I yow gyffe
> Halfe my kyngdome whils I lyffe —
> Brouke alle wele aftir me."
>
> With myrthe that mangery was made,
> Fowrtty dayes it habade
> Amange thase lordis hende.

1306 *come*. MS: *cone*.

1321 *Explicit*. Cambridge adds: *Here endyth Syr Egyllamowre of Artas and begynneth Syr Tryamowre*.

In *Sir Tryamour*, as in *Octavian*, the story of the calumniated queen is developed to feature the career of her son. The poem was composed in the northeast Midlands toward the end of the fourteenth century. No immediate source is known — the romance seems to be of English origin. The first third of the story, concerning an exiled queen, old knight, and faithful dog, resembles the widely-known legend of Sibille, Charlemagne's queen. Similar legends of canine fidelity are found in folktale and ballad (*Sir Aldinger*). Most of *Sir Tryamour* is devoted to the combats of the son as he wins his bride, and it is this attention to fighting that distinguishes the romance from other treatments of the formulaic separation and reunion plot.

The romance begins with the predicament of Ardus, king of Aragon, and his queen, Margaret. As they are childless, Ardus vows to journey to the Holy Land in hopes that God will send him an heir, and before he departs, Tryamour is conceived. The king appoints his steward, Marrok, to protect the queen and kingdom during his absence. Marrok, however, attempts to seduce Margaret and is rebuffed. When Ardus returns, happy to find his wife pregnant, Marrok takes revenge by telling him the child was fathered by a knight discovered sleeping with the queen. Without consulting Margaret, Ardus agrees to the steward's plan to banish the queen and sends her forth under the escort of an old knight, Sir Roger.

Marrok secretly arranges to ambush the queen. Roger is killed in the attack and buried by his faithful dog, True-love; Margaret escapes to Hungary where she gives birth to Tryamour in a forest. She is discovered by Sir Barnard, who recognizes her noble bearing, brings her into his household, and fosters her son. True-love guards his master's grave for seven years, then, to avenge his death, returns to Ardus' court and kills Marrok, revealing the steward's treachery. The repentant king attempts to find his queen.

Meanwhile, the king of Hungary has died, leaving a young daughter, Helen, as his sole heir. War breaks out in her kingdom and she is advised to marry someone who can rule, so a tournament for her hand is announced. Tryamour hears of it and, though he is young and inexperienced, hastens to attend. Barnard accompanies him; Ardus is there as well. On the first day of the tournament, Tryamour fights on the side of his father, jousting with James, son of the German emperor, among others. On the second day Tryamour overcomes Ardus and gains Helen's attention. On the third day he defeats James and is recognized as victor. However, James does not accept the decision and attacks Tryamour after the tournament, when he is unarmed. Barnard and Ardus come to Tryamour's aid; he is able to kill James, but not before being wounded. Tryamour returns home to recuperate while Helen, unable to find her champion, is granted a two-year delay of marriage.

The German emperor besieges Ardus to avenge his son's death, sending his champion, the giant Moradas, to challenge the king. Tryamour, recovered from his wounds, sets out to claim Helen. As he journeys through Aragon, he is arrested for poaching and brought

before Ardus, who recognizes him from their encounters in Hungary. Tryamour gladly fights as Ardus' champion since he is responsible for James' death. Ardus knights him and makes him his heir on the eve of the combat. Moradas is vanquished, the Emperor accepts defeat, and Tryamour continues on his journey to Helen.

Next, the knight encounters two giants, brothers of the slain Moradas, who seek to avenge his death. A fourth brother, Burlond, is laying claim to Helen. After killing the giants, Tryamour arrives at the Hungarian court on the very day of Burlond's challenge. The knight defeats the usurper and for the second time is recognized as Helen's fiancé. Tryamour has his mother brought to meet his bride; at this point Margaret reveals his father's identity and Ardus is invited to the wedding. There recognition takes place and the son reunites his parents. All live happily ever after, Tryamour leaving two sons to succeed him.

Though the romance concerns the separation and reunion of a family, family relations are not as problematic as in some similar romances. Adultery, illegitimacy, and patricide are threatened, but there are no generational conflicts, and the villain is not a member of the family; indeed, he is an outsider who has been entrusted with familial responsibilities and has betrayed that confidence by usurping his lord's place. Ardus, by trusting an outsider rather than his own spouse, temporarily loses the heir who can continue the family. The point seems to be family cohesiveness — Tryamour and his mother remain together, and he is in contact with his father during most of the romance, though they are unaware of their relationship.

The father-son relationship is particularly important. The hero is motivated in his adventures by a desire to learn his father's identity. Margaret withholds this knowledge from her son until he has proven himself worthy. Tryamour encounters his father immediately upon entering the world of chivalry, fighting on Ardus' side in the melee on the first day of the tournament. Two complementary episodes develop the relationship: Ardus' rescue of Tryamour from James, and Tryamour's rescue of Ardus from the Emperor. In *Tryamour*, father and son are not in competition, though Tryamour does defeat him in the tournament; rather, their relationship is one of natural affinity and mutual help. Bernard, another father figure, aids Tryamour throughout the romance.

In contrast to the treatment of father and son, the romantic relationships are undeveloped.[1] There is a tender moment in the initial dialogue of Ardus and Helen, but Tryamour and Helen barely have an opportunity to exchange words. They hardly seem to fall in love — we are told Helen admires Tryamour's performance in the jousts, but there are no courtship scenes like those of *Eglamour* and *Octavian*. The most deeply felt emotions seem to be those of Roger's dog, True-love. Since the dog's name is the English equivalent of the hero's, they should in some sense be understood as parallels. The dog is important to the action, for his revelation of his master's murder causes Ardus to realize his wife's innocence and to expose the treachery of Marrok, bringing an end to the first action of the story and preparing the way for the next.

If *Tryamour* does not give much attention to matters of love, it includes many episodes of war and combat. There are seventeen in all. The three-day tournament is comprised of ten individual combats, followed by James' ambush, the encounter with Ardus' foresters, the battles with Moradas, with his two brothers, and, finally, with Burlond. The major combats are formal tournaments, judicial in nature. The basic episode consists of a sequence of

[1] Ramsey, *Chivalric Romance*, pp. 264–65.

charge/blows/unhorsing, which may require only three lines, but the three main combats — the tournament for Helen's hand, the battle with Moradas, and Burlond's challenge for Helen — are all fully developed. The combat with Moradas includes comments on the troops as they arrive on the field, the knighting of the hero, the drawing up of forces, the onlookers' reactions to the combat, boasts by the main combatants, mounted attacks with spears, unhorsings, attacks with swords on foot, and exchanges of wounding blows, culminating in victory for the hero. Tryamour's victories are often preceded by a mistake which puts him at a momentary disadvantage (a badly aimed blow kills Moradas' horse, not the giant; the knight loses his sword to Burlond). But these are also occasions for displays of wits, as in Tryamour's rejoinder to Moradas' jibe about killing the horse (lines 1225–27), and his taunts to Burlond as he literally cuts him down to size (lines 1555–57). All this is related with relish; these scenes of combat are among the more impressive in tail-rhyme romance.

The presentation of the villain is also effective. While the treacherous steward is a favorite stock character of romance, Marrok's characterization is elaborated in dialogues with the queen and king. Not only does Marrok try to seduce the queen; he lies to her about his intentions and pretends to be loyal, then lies to Ardus about her behavior, going to some lengths to invent a story putting himself in the best light and her in the worst. He finally incites the king to banish the queen while secretly planning to kill her and the innocent, elderly Sir Roger. His deceit and treachery do not go unpunished, for Ardus has his corpse publicly hanged, drawn, and quartered. This desecration is in contrast to Roger's proper funeral.

The romance's composer has not developed certain themes latent in the conventional material. *Tryamour* raises no questions about social class, as do other narratives of its type. No character changes his or her social status; all belong to some noble stratum. Sir Bernard is the only exception, but he lacks none of the accoutrements of status and easily provides arms and horses to equip young Tryamour for tournaments. Though the romance is certainly moral, it is not particularly pious. Tryamour is conceived by divine intervention, and he and his mother prevail through divine providence, but none of the characters' adventures show spiritual growth such as we see, for example, in *Isumbras*. Nor are there any of the supernatural motifs common in romances such as monstrous opponents or mythological child-snatching animals. Instead, we have the marvelous fidelity of True-love and Roger's preserved corpse.

Sir Tryamour survives complete in a late fifteenth-century manuscript (Cambridge MS Ff. 2.38), two printed texts, and the seventeenth-century Percy Folio, as well as in several fragments. The present edition is based on the Cambridge text, as that is the only complete medieval copy to survive. The basic verse pattern is the twelve-line tail-rhyme stanza, though there is much variation, including many six- and some nine-line stanzas. Some features of the poem suggest loose transmission: variations in stanza length, a tendency to redundancy and repetition, paratactic style, and "variations and transpositions of the traditional tail-rhyme phraseology."[2] The dialect is predominantly East Midland, with some Northern forms, like the *-r* plural in the noun *chylder*. The inflected forms are those of early Modern English: the present participial ending is *-yng*; the third-person feminine singular nominative pronoun is *s(c)he*, though the Northern form *scho* is also present; the third-person plural pronouns take the *th* forms, *they*, *them*, etc.; no past participles begin *w/y*.

[2] Pearsall, "Development of Middle English Romance," p. 112.

MANUSCRIPTS AND PRINTS

Indexed as item 1177 in Boffey and Edwards, eds., *New Index of Middle English Verse*:

- Cambridge, Cambridge University Library MS Ff. 2.38 (1450–70), fols. 79v–90r. [Base-text for this edition.]
- Oxford, Bodleian (Rawlinson) MS (a sixteenth-century fragment, now missing).
- Percy Folio MS (London, British Library MS Addit. 27879) (c. 1650), pp. 210–32.

- *Syr Tryamour*. London: R. Pynson, n.d. [1503?]. [Only fragments of this print (*STC* 24302.5) survive.]
- *Syr Tryamour*. London: Wynkyn de Worde, n.d. [c. 1530]. [Only fragments of this print (*STC* 24302) survive.]
- *Syr Tryamoure*. London: Wyllyam Copland, n.d. [1561?]. [This print (*STC* 24303) contains the complete text of the poem.]

SIR TRYAMOUR

1	Heven blys that all schall wynne,	
	Schylde us fro dedly synne	
	And graunte us the blys of hevyn!	
	Yf ye wyll a stounde blynne,	*while pause*
5	Of a story Y wyll begynne,	
	That gracyus ys to nevyn;	*tell*
	Of a kyng and of a quene,	
	What bale and blys was them betwene,	*sorrow*
	Y schall yow telle full evyn.	*exactly*
10	A gode ensaumpull ye may lere,	*example; learn*
	Yf ye wyll thys story here	*hear*
	And herkyn to my stevyn.	*listen; voice*
	He was the kynge of Arragon,	
	A nobull man and of grete renown,	
15	Syr Ardus was hys name.	
	He had a quene that hyght Margaret,	*was named*
	Trewe as stele Y yow behett,	*promise*
	That falsely was broght in blame.	
	The kyngys steward Marrok hyght;	
20	False and fekyll was that wyght	*fickle; person*
	That lady for to fame.	*defame*
	He lovyd well that lady gente;	*very much; gentle*
	For scho wolde not to hym assente	*Because she*
	He dud hur mekyll schame.	*did; much*
25	The kyng lovyd well the quene,	
	For scho was semely on to sene	*pleasing; look*
	And trewe as stele on tree.	*steel in wood (see note)*
	Ofte tyme togedur can they meene,	*did; lament*
	For no chylde come them betwene,	
30	Sore syghed bothe sche and hee.	
	Therfore the kyng, as Y undurstonde,	
	Hath made a vowe to go in to the Holy Londe	
	To fyght and not to flee,	
	That God almyghty schulde helpe them so	

35 A chylde to gete betwene them two
 That ther heyre myght bee. *heir*

 When the kyng hys vowe had maked
 And at the pope the cros takyd, *from*
 To bedd then were they broght;
40 That nyght on hys lady mylde, *gentle*
 As God wolde, he gate a chylde, *begot*
 But they of hyt wyste noght. *knew*
 Sone on the morne, when hyt was day,
 The kyng wolde forthe on hys way
45 To the londe there God us boght; *(see note)*
 Than began the quene to morne; *mourn*
 For he wolde no lenger soyorne, *sojourn*
 Prevy sche was in thoght. *Privately; worried*

 The kyng bad ordeygne hys armoryes;[1]
50 Knyghtys, squyers and palfrays,
 All redy for to goo.
 He toke hys leve at the quene, *from*
 At erlys and barons all bedene, *From; together*
 And at Syr Marrok alsoo.
55 He comawndyd Marrok, on hys lyfe,
 That he schulde kepe wele the quene hys wyfe, *guard well*
 Bothe in wele and in woo. *good fortune*
 Betwene the quene and the kyng
 Was grete sorowe and mornynge,
60 When they schulde parte in twoo. *part company*

 Now ys the kyng passyd the see, *has; crossed*
 To hys enemyes gon ys he,
 And warryth there a whyle;
 But than Syr Marrok, hys steward,
65 Was faste abowtewarde *attempting*
 To do hys lady gyle. *evil*
 He wowyd the quene bothe day and nyght, *wooed*
 To lye hur by, he had hyt hyght, *vowed*
 He dredyd no peryle. *feared; peril*
70 Feyre he spake to hur aplyght; *indeed*
 Yf he hur thoght turne myght *If he might change her mind*
 Wyth wordys, hyt was hys wylle.

 The quene was stedfaste of wylle;
 Sche herde hys wordys and stode styll

[1] *The king ordered his armed forces to prepare*

75 Tyll he all had sayde.
 Sche seyde, "Traytur, what ys thy thoght?
 All that thou spekyst hyt ys for noght.
 Owt upon the, thefe!" sche seyde in that brayde. *altercation*
 "My lorde, when he went to the see,
80 For specyall tryste he toke me to the *trust; entrusted*
 To have undur holde; *protection*
 And now thou woldyst wondur fayne *gladly*
 Be the furste to do me trayne! *treason*
 How darste thou be so bolde?"

85 He seyde, "Ye be my lady gente
 For now ys my lorde wente
 Agayne hys fone to fyght; *foes*
 And but the more wondyr bee
 Ye schall nevyr more hym see;
90 Therfore Y rede yow ryght. *advise*
 Now ys he gone, my lady free, *liberal*
 In hys stede ye schall take me;
 Am Y not a knyght?
 And we schall do so prevely
95 That whethyr he leve or dye *live*
 Ther schall wete no wyght." *know; person*

 Then was the quene wondur wrothe
 And swere mony a grete othe,
 As sche was woman trewe!
100 "Yf ye be so hardy
 To wayte me wyth velanye *lie in wait for*
 Fowle hyt schall the rewe.
 Y trowe Y schall nevyr ete bredd
 Tyll thou be broght to the dedd, *death*
105 Soche balys then schall Y the brewe. *inquiries; prepare you*
 Y may evyr aftur thys *wish*
 That thou woldyst tyse me to do amys *entice; amiss*
 No game schulde the glewe." *No pastime shall amuse you*

 Marrok seyde, "Madam, mercy,
110 Y seyde hyt for no velanye
 But for a fondynge; *test*
 For Y wolde wytt yowre wylle *know*
 Whethur that hyt were gode or ylle
 And for no nothyr thynge.
115 And now, madame, Y may see
 That ye ar trewe as stele on tree
 Unto my lorde the kynge;
 And that ys me wondur lefe *pleasing*

Wherefore taketh hyt to no grefe *offense*
120 Or wyckyd askynge." *wicked*

So excusyd he hym tho, *himself then*
The lady wende hyt had byn soo *believed*
 As Syr Marrokk sayde.
He goth forthe and holdyth hys pese,
125 More he thenkyth then he says,
 He was full evyll payde. *extremely ill satisfied*

Of the quene let we bee
And thorow the grace of the Trynyté
 Grete wyth chylde sche was!
130 And of Kyng Ardus speke we,
Farre in hethennes ys he *pagan realm*
 To werre in Goddys grace. *war in behalf of*

There he had grete chyvalry, *knightly prowess*
He slewe hys enemyes wyth grete envy *fierceness*
135 Grete worde of hym aroos. *fame*
In hethennes and yn Spayne, *heathen lands*
In Gaskyn and in Almayne *Gascony; Germany*
 Wyt they of hys loos. *Knew; glory*

When he had done hys pylgrymage
140 And maked all hys message *accomplished; mission*
 Wyth wordys that ware not wyckydd,
To Fleme Jordon and to Bedlem, *River; Bethlehem*
And to the borogh of Jerusalem, *town*
 There God was dede and qwykk, *dead; alive*

145 Then longed he at home to bene
And for to speke wyth hys quene
 That hys thoght was evyr upon.
And he gate schyppys prevay *ships secretly*
And to the schypp on a day
150 He thoght that he flewe anon.

So longe they drove upon the fome *sea*
That at the laste they come home
 To hys owne lande
When the kyng and the quene were togedur agayne
155 They made mekyll joye, gle and game,
 Then tolde the kynge hur tythande. *[she] told; tidings*
The kynge behelde the quene mylde
And sawe that sche was wyth chylde,
 Then made he glad semland. *semblance*

160 Twenty tymys he dud hur kysse,
 Then made they game and blysse
 And he toke hur be the hande.

 But sone aftur come tythyngys,
 Marrok mett hys lorde kynge
165 And faste he can hym frayne. *inquire*
 "Syr," he seyde, "for Goddys pyne, *pain*
 Of a thyng that now ys ynne,
 Whareof be ye so fayne?[1] *pleased*
 Ye wene the chylde yourys be; *believe*
170 Hyt ys not so, so mote Y the, *thrive*
 The quene hath done the trayne! *you treachery*
 Another knyght, so mote Y spede, *prosper*
 Gat the chylde syth thou yede *after you went*
 And hath the quene forlayne!" *seduced*

175 "Allas," seyde the kyng, "What may that be?
 Betoke Y not hur to the *Entrusted*
 To kepe hur in weyle and woo?
 Sche was undur thy kepeyng
 Why letyst thou hur do that wyckyd thynge
180 Alas! Why dud sche soo?"
 "Syr," seyde Syr Marrok, "Wyte not me *Blame*
 For grete moone sche made for the *moan*
 As sche had lovyd no moo. *As if*
 Y trowed in hur no falsehedd *believed*
185 Tyll Y fonde them wyth the dede *in the act*
 Togedur betwene them two.

 In the fyrste fourtenyght that ye were went, *two weeks*
 Y fownde them togedur verament *truly*
 Or they ther wylle had done. *Before*
190 To hym Y ran wyth egur mode *I ran angrily*
 And slewe the knyght there he stode *where*
 Be myn owne dome! *judgment*

 Then wende sche, sche schulde be schente, *thought; shamed*
 And me behett londe and rente *promised me land and rent (income)*
195 And hyght me to do my wylle: *bid*
 But Y myselfe wolde noght;
 Ye were evyr in my thoght
 Bothe lowde and stylle. *aloud; silently*

[1] *Why are you so happy about this thing that has happened?*

	"Allas," seyde the kynge; "now Y wondur;	
200	For sorowe my herte brekyth in sondyr.	
	Why hath sche done amys?	
	Y wot not to whom Y may meene,	*complain*
	For Y have loste my comely quene	
	That Y was wonte to kysse!"	
205	"Marrok," he seyde "What ys thy rede	*advice*
	Whether that sche be done to dedd	*put to death*
	That was my blysse?	*Who*
	For sythen sche hath forsaken me	*since*
	Y wylle hur no more see	
210	Nor dwelle wyth hur, ywys."	*certainly*

	"Syr," seyde Marrok, "Ye schall not soo;	
	Ye schall hur nother brenne nor sloo	*burn; slay*
	For dowte of synne.	*Because it might be a sin*
	Bettyr hyt ys, syr, be my rede,	*by; advice*
215	Owt of yowre londe sche be flemyd in dede,	*exiled indeed*
	And faste ye schall hur comawnde to wynne.	*depart*

	"But take hur an oolde stede,	*give; steed*
	And an olde knyght that may hur lede	
	Tyll sche be paste yowre realme,	*beyond*
220	And gyf them some spendynge,	*money*
	That them owt of thy londe may brynge;	
	Y can no bettyr deme.	*judge*

	"For, syr," he seyde, "Hyt were not feyre,	*just*
	A horcop to be yowre heyre,	*bastard; heir*
225	But he ware of yowre kynne."	*Unless*
	Then seyde the kynge, "So mote Y the,	
	As thou haste seyde, so schall hyt bee,	
	Arste y schall not blynne."	*I will not cease until it is accomplished*
	Then exylyd the kyng the quene.	
230	Sche had wondur what hyt myght meene,	
	What made hym so to begynne:	
	No lenger he wolde gyf hur respyte	*rest*
	Nor no worde he wolde speke hur wyth,	
	And that was grete synne.	

235	He let clothe hur in sympull wede	*had her dressed; clothes*
	And set hur upon an olde stede	
	That was bresyd and blynde;	*shaggy*
	And toke to hur an olde knyght	
	That Syr Roger hyght,	*was named*
240	That curtes was and kynde,	*courteous*
	And gaf them twenty dayes to passe;	

And ovyr that tyme hys wylle was,
 Yf men myght hur fynde,
Sche schulde be takyn and be brente, *burned*
245 And the knyght, be there assente, *by their agreement*
 Schulde wayne wyth the wynde. *go*

Thretty florens to there spendynge
He gaf them, wythowte lesynge, *He gave them, [I tell you] without lie*
 And comawnded them to goo.
250 The qwene for sorowe wolde dye
For sche wyste not wherefore nor why
 That sche was flemed soo. *banished*
Therfore sche had grete drede
And sche swownyd on hur stede; *fainted*
255 Hyt was no wondur thogh sche were wo.
Syr Roger comfortyd the quene
And seyde, "At Goddys wylle muste hyt bene,
 What helpyth hyt yow yf ye youreselfe sloo?" *slay*

Knyghtys, squyers and ladyes gente
260 Morned for the quene was wente; *Mourned because*
 The kynge had no chesowne, *cause*
And the quene had grete care
For sche schulde fro hur lorde fare
 Wythowte ony resowne.
265 But then they wente fro that stede, *place*
On ther way forthe they yede *went*
 Ferre fro every towne
Into a grete wyldurnes;
Full of wylde bestys hyt was,
270 Be dale and eke be downe. *also*

Marrok thoght utturly
To do the quene a velanye, *villainy*
 Hys luste for to fulfylle.
He ordeygnyd hym a companye *organized himself*
275 Of hys owne meynye *retinue*
 That wolde assente hym tylle. *obey him*
To a wode they wente in hye, *haste*
There the quene schulde passe by,
 And there stode they all stylle.
280 There had he thoght redyly *readily*
To have do the quene a velanye —
 Fayne he wolde hur spylle. *Very much he would like to kill her*

The quene and Syr Roger come into the wode,
Wote ye wyll thay thoght but gode *Know well*

285	To passe wythowtyn dowte.	*fear*
	Then were they war of the steward	*aware*
	Come rydyng to them warde	*toward them*
	Wyth a grete rowte.	*mob*
	"Here ys treson," seyde the quene.	
290	"Allas!" seyde Roger, "what may that bene?	
	We here be sett all abowte!	
	Syth we here schall dye,	*Since*
	Oure dedys full sore they schall abye,	*deaths; pay for*
	Be they nevyr so stowte!"	*strong*
295	The steward Roger can ascrye,	*challenge*
	And seyde, "Yylde the, for thou schalt dye.	*yield*
	To us thou haste no myght!"	
	Syr Roger seyde, "Traytur forthy	*therefore*
	My dethe schalt thou dere abye,	*dearly pay for*
300	Yf that Y wyth the fyght."	
	There come they to hym in hye;	*haste*
	Syr Roger, wyth grete envy,	*fierceness*
	Kydd he was a knyght.	*Proved*
	They hewe on hym full boldely.	
305	Ther was none of all that company	
	So bolde nor so wyght.	*strong*
	Syr Roger smote them on the hede	
	That to the gyrdyll the swerde yede.	*girdle*
	Of hym were they qwyte.	*They were requited of (revenged on) him*
310	They hewe on hym faste as they were wode,	*chopped; crazy*
	On eche syde then sprong the blode	
	So sore on hym they dud smyte.	
	Trewe-love, hys hownde so gode,	*hound*
	Halpe hys maystyr and be hym stode.	*Helped; by*
315	Byttyrly he can byte.	*Fiercely*
	Whyll they were togedur bestedd,	*beset (under attack)*
	The quene passyd awey and fledd	
	On fote and lefte hur stede.	*horse*
	Sche ranne to a thorne grene;	*hawthorne bush*
320	Tyl sche come thedur sche wolde not blyn	*cease*
	And daryth there for drede.	*hid*
	Syr Roger sche dydd beholde;	
	He hewe on ther bodyes bolde,	
	Hys hownde halpe hym at nede.	*helped*
325	Os hyt ys in the story tolde,	*As*
	Forti Syr Roger downe can folde	*Forty; did throw*
	So qwyt he them ther mede.	*paid; reward*

	Had he ben armyd, ywys,	*in armor; certainly*
	All the maystry had byn hys.	*victory*
330	Allas! why wantyd he hys wede?	*lacked; armor*
	As Syr Roger gaf a knokk,	
	Behynde hym come Syr Marrok —	
	Therfore evyll mote he spede.	*may evil come to him*
	He smot Syr Roger wyth a spere,	
335	Thorow the body he can hym bere,	*thrust*
	Faste then can he blede.	*Quickly*

	He hath an evyll wounde —	
	That dynte hath broght hym to the grounde	*blow*
	And fellyd hym on the grene.	
340	Than he was slayne certenly,	*When*
	They rode forthe wyth grete envy	*malice*
	To seke aftur the quene;	
	But they wyste not what they myght sey —	
	Hur stede they fonde, sche was awey —	*horse*
345	Then had that traytur tene.	*anger*
	Ther jurney then they thoght evyll sett,	*ill conceived*
	But they wyth the lady not mett,	
	They wyste not what to mene.	*knew not how to proceed*
	Ovyr all the wode they hur soght	
350	But, as God wolde, they fonde hur noght;	
	Then had they grete tene.	*anxiety*

	When he myght not the lady fynde,	
	He wente away as knyght unkynde	*wicked*
	To Syr Roger there he lay.	
355	Thryes he styked hym thorowowt,	*Thrice*
	Of hys dede he had no dowte.	*death*
	Allas that ylke day!	*very*
	When that traytur had done soo,	
	He turynd ageyne there he come fro,	
360	Unmanly for to say,	*Dispirited*
	For hys company was all gon,	
	Forty he had chaunged for oon:	*exchanged*
	Ther skaped but two away.	*escaped*

	The quene was aferde to be schente	*injured*
365	Tyl sche sye that they were wente	*saw; had gone*
	And passyd owt of the slogh;	*swamp*
	Then rose sche up and come agayne	
	To Syr Roger and fonde hym slayne —	
	Then had sche sorow ynogh.	

370 "Allas!" sche seyde, "Now am Y spylte; *lost*
 Thys false thefe, wythowtyn gylte *provocation*
 Why dyd he the to-slon? *you kill altogether*
 Syr Roger, thys haste thou for me: *you have done this for me*
 Allas that evyr Y schulde hyt see!"
375 Wyth that sche felle in swowne.

 When sche myght ryse sche toke hur stede;
 Sche durste no lenger dwell for drede *remain*
 That no man schulde fynde hur thore. *there*
 Sche seyde, "Roger, Y see the blede.
380 Allas who may me wys and lede? *advise; guide*
 For certen thou mayst no more."

 Hys gode hownde, for weyle nor woo, *loyal dog*
 Wolde not fro hys maystyr goo
 But lay lykyng hys woundys. *licking*
385 He wende to have helyd hym agayne; *thought; healed*
 Therto he dyd all hys mayne — *all he could*
 Grete kyndenes ys in howndys.

 He lykkyd hym tyll he stanke, *licked*
 Than he began and konne hym thanke *bethought himself*
390 To make a pytt of ston;
 And to berye hym was hys purpos, *bury*
 And scraped on hym bothe ryn and mosse, *buried him; bark*
 And fro hym nevyr wolde gon;
 Than levyd they stylle thare. *Then remained; there unmoving*
395 The quene faste can sche fare *go*
 For fere of hur foon; *foes*
 Sche had grete mornyng in hur herte
 For sche wyste not whedurwarde
 That sche was beste to goon.

400 Sche rode forthe, noght forthy, *nevertheless*
 To the londe of Hongary,
 Tyll sche come thedur wyth woo.
 When sche come undur a wode syde
 Sche myght no lenger abyde, *endure*
405 Hur peynys were so throo; *pains; fierce*
 Sche lyghtyd downe, that was so mylde, *lay*
 And there sche travaylyd of a chylde, *gave birth to*
 Hyrselfe allon, wythowtyn moo.
 Forthe sche went wyth sorowe ynogh
410 And tyed hur hors to a bogh, *bough*
 Tyll the throwes were all ydoo. *pains; done*

A feyre sone had sche borne, *fair*
When sche herde the chylde crye hur beforn
 Hyt comfortyd hur full swythe; *very quickly*
415 So when sche hurselfe myght styr,
Sche toke up hur sone to hur
 And lapped hyt full lythe. *embraced; gently*

What for febulnes, wery and woo, *exhaustion*
Sche felle aslepe and hur sone alsoo;
420 Hur stede stode hur behynde. *horse*
There come a knyght them full nere
That hyght Syr Barnard messengere, *Who was called*
 Huntyng aftur an hynde, *female deer*
And founde that lady lovely of chere *countenance*
425 And hur sone slepyng in fere, *together*
 Lyeng undur a lynde. *linden*
He put upon that lady bryght, *approached*
And sche loked upon that knyght,
 And was aferde full sore of hys comyng. *extremely*

430 He seyde, "What do ye here, madam?
Fro whens come ye? What ys yowre name?
 Why lye ye here nowe?"
"Syr," sche seyde, "yf ye wyll wytt, *know*
My name at home ys Margaret,
435 Y swere be God a vowe.

Here have Y mekyll grefe;
Helpe me now at my myschefe, *misfortune*
 At some towne that Y were."
The knyght behelde the ladyes mode *manner*
440 And thoght sche was of gentyll blode,
 That in the foreste was bystadd there. *beset*

He toke hur up full curtesly
And hur sone that lay hur by
 And home he can them lede.
445 He let hur have wemen at wylle *servants as she wished*
To tent hur, and that was skylle, *tend; right*
 And broght hur to bede.
Whatsoevyr sche wolde crave
All sche myght redyly hyt have,
450 Hur speche was sone spedd. *Her bidding was quickly accomplished*

They crystenyd the chylde wyth grete honowre
And callyd hyt Tryamowre;
 Of hyt they were full gladd.

	A norse they gatt hyt untyll	*nurse*
455	Sche had mekyll of hur wyll;	*much of what she wanted*
	They dud as sche them badd.	
	Sche was bothe curtes and hynde,	*gracious*
	Every man was hur frynde	*person; friend*
	And of hur was full gladd.	
460	There dwellyd that lady long,	
	Moche myrthe was them amonge	
	But ther gamyd hur no glewe.	*pleased her; merriment*
	Of hyr they were nevyr yrke,	*annoyed*
	Sche techyd hur sone for to wyrke,	*taught*
465	And taght hym evyr newe;	*always new (things)*
	Hur sone that then dwellyd hur wyth,	
	He was mekyll of boon and lyth,	*great; bone; limb*
	And feyre of hyde and hewe.	*fair of skin; color*
	Every man lovyd hym aftur ther estate;[1]	
470	They had no cheson hym to hate,	*cause*
	So seyde all that hym knewe.	
	Leve we stylle at the quene	
	And of the greyhound we wyll mene	*tell*
	That we before of tolde.	
475	Seven yere, so God me save,	
	Kepyd he hys maystyrs grave	
	Tyll that he wexyd olde.	*grew*
	Evyr on hys maystyrs grave he lay;	
	Ther myght no man gete hym away	
480	For oght that they cowde do,	
	But yf hyt were onys on the day,	*once*
	He wolde forthe to gete hys praye,	*prey*
	And sythen ageyne he wolde goo.	*then; go (return)*
	Seven yere he levyd there,	*lived*
485	Tyll hyt befell agenste the Youle	*at; Yule*
	Upon the fyrste day;	
	The hounde, as the story says,	
	Ranne to the kyngys palays	*palace*
	Wythowt ony more delay.	
490	As the kyng at the mete was than,	*dinner*
	Into the halle the hound can ren	*run*
	Amonge the knyghtys gay.	
	All abowte he can beholde	

[1] *Every man showed him love, in a manner befitting their station in life*

And when he sawe not that he wolde
495 He dyd hym faste away. *went*

The hound rennyth evyr, ywys,
Tyl he come there hys maystyr ys;
 He fonde not that he soght.
The kynge wondurth in hys wede *(see note)*
500 Fro when he come and whedur he yede, *went*
 And who hym thedur broght. *thither*
He thoght that he had sene hym thare
But he wyste not when nor whare,
 Forthy then seyde he noght;
505 But faste bethenkyth he hym then,
For he thoght he schulde hym kenne — *know*
 So syttyth he in a thoght.

The tother day on the same wyse, *in; manner*
As the kynge fro the borde can ryse *table*
510 The hownde spedd not thoo. *then*
All abowte the halle he soght,
But at that tyme he fonde hym noght,
 Than dyd he hym faste to goo.
Then seyde the kyng that ylke stounde, *very moment*
515 "Me thynkyth that was Syr Roger hounde
 That wente wyth hym thoo
When the quene was flemed owt of my londe." *exiled*
"Syr," they seyde, "we undurstonde
 For sothe that hyt ys soo!"

520 The kyng seyde, "What may thys mene? *mean*
Y trowe Syr Roger and the quene
 Be comen to thys londe,
For nevyr syth they went, ywys,
Sawe Y Syr Roger hounde or thys. *before now*
525 That ys wondur tythand! *marvelous tidings*

When he goth, pursewe hym then,
For evyrmore he wyll renne
 Tyll he come there hys maystyr ys."
The tothyr day among them all *next day*
530 To mete as they were sett in halle
 Syr Marrok was there ferre wythynne, ywys. *far inside*

And the hounde wolde nevyr blynne, *cease*
But ranne abowte faste wyth wynne *joy*
 Tyll he wyth hym metyth. *meets*
535 He starte up verament, *leapt*

	The steward be the throte he hente:	*by; seized*
	The hownd wrekyd hys maystyrs dethe.	*revenged*
	The stewardys lyfe ys lorne —	*lost*
	There was fewe that rewyd theron	*regretted*
540	And fewe for hym wepyth.	

	The greyhownde dyd hym sone to go	
	When hys maystyrs dethe he had venged soo	
	On hym that wroght hym trayne.	*treachery*
	All they folowed hym in that tyde	*time*
545	Some on horsys and some besyde,	
	Knyghtys, squyers and swayne.	
	Reste wolde he nevyr have	
	Tyll he come to hys maystyrs grave	
	And then turned he agayne.	
550	They myght not gete hym therfro;	
	He stode at fence ageyn them tho,	*defense against*
	But they wolde hym have slayne.	

	When they sawe no bettyr bote	
	They turned ageyne on hors and fote,	
555	Wyth grete wondur, Y wene.	
	They tolde the kyng all thus,	
	"Allas!" seyde kyng Ardus,	
	"What may thys be to meene?	
	Y trowe Syr Marrok, be Goddys payne,	
560	Have slayne Syr Roger be some trayne	*treachery*
	And falsely flemyd my quene.	*banished*
	The hound had not Syr Marrok slayne	
	Had not some treson byn,	*been*
	Be dereworth God, as Y wene!"	*By precious; suppose*

565	They wente agayne, bothe knyght and knave,	
	And founde Syr Roger in hys grave	
	As hole as he was layde.	*As intact as when he was buried*
	They toke hym up and leved hym noght,	*left*
	The corse before the kyng was broght,	
570	That made hys herte sory, as men sayde.	
	Hys hownde wolde not fro hym fare.	
	"Allas!" seyde the kyng, "now have Y care,	
	Thys traytur hath me betrayed.	
	For he hath slayn an awnturs knyght	*adventurous*
575	And flemyd my quene wythowten ryght	*banished*
	For false tales that he hath me telde."	

| | The steward also tyte | *at once* |
| | The kyng let drawe hym, wyth grete dyspyte, | *had him drawn; hatred* |

Wyth horsys thorow the towne,
580 And hanged hym on the galowe tree
That al men myght hyt see,
That he had done treson.
Syr Rogers corse wyth nobull delay *corpse; great pomp*
They beryed hyt the tothyr day, *buried it; next*
585 Wyth many a bolde baron.
Hys hownde wolde not fro hym away
But evyr on hys grave he lay
Tyll deth had broght hym downe.

The kyng let sende a messengere
590 Fro towne to towne, ferre and nere, *far and near*
Aftur the quene to spye;
For nothyng that they cowde spere *find out*
They cowde nevyr of hur here.
Then was the kyng sory:
595 He seyde, "Now can Y no rede,
For well Y wot that Y am but dedd,
For sorowe Y wyll now dye!
Allas! that sche evyr fro me wente,
Owre false steward hath us schent *ruined*
600 Wyth hys false traytory."

Thus leveth the kyng in sorowe;
Ther may no blys fro bale hym borowe *No happiness could sway him from grief*
Tyll he be broght to grounde.
Soche lyfe he leved many a yere,
605 Wyth mekyll sorowe and evyll chere; *unhappy expression*
Nothyng may make hym sounde. *healthy*
Hyt dothe the kyng mekyll payne
When he thenkyth how Syr Roger was slayne,
And then halpe hys hownde; *And how his hound then helped him*
610 And of hys quene that was so mylde,
How sche went fro hym grete wyth chylde;
He swownyd that ylke stownde.

And at Syr Roger yende we wyll dwelle, *death (end); stop speaking*
And of the quene we wyll telle,
615 And of hur chylde Tryamowre; *child*
He was a moche man and a longe, *large; lean*
In every lym styff and stronge, *limb powerful*
And semely of colowre. *pleasing*
Men and wemen dwellyd he among
620 Yyt wrethyd he nevyr non wyth wrong; *Yet angered*
That was hys owne honowre.

In that tyme certaynly
Dyed the kyng of Hungary
　　And was beryed, ywys.
625 He had no heyre hys londys to welde *heir; rule*
But a doghtyr of seven yerys elde;
　　Hur name Helyn ys.
Sche was whyte os blossom on flowre, *as*
Mery and comely of colowre,
630 　　And semely for to kysse.

When hur fadur was dede
Moche warre began to sprede
　　Yn hur lande all abowte.
Therfore sche ys gevyn to rede *is advised*
635 To take a lorde to rewle and to lede
　　Hur londe, wyth hys rowte. *troop*
A nobull knyght that cowde or myght *knew how to or was able to*
Rewle hur londe wyth gode ryght *rightfully*
　　That men myght drede and dowte. *fear*

640 Hur cownsell wyll that sche do soo,
For grete nede cawsyth hur therto,
　　And sche answeryd them there on hye *loudly*
That they schulde faste hur wyth no fere, *tie; mate*
But he were prynce or prynceys pere, *Unless; equal*
645 　　Or ellys chefe of chyvalry.
Therfore that lady feyre and gente,
Wyth them wolde sche assente
　　A justyng for to crye; *A tournament to be announced*
And at that justyng schall hyt bee
650 Who so evyr wynneth the gree *prize*
　　Schall wedde hur wyth ryalté. *splendor*

A day of justyng was ther sett;
Halfe a yere, no lenger, they lett *allowed*
　　To be thore at that day *there*
655 That they myght have there a space, *a while*
Knyghtys of dyvers a place, *diverse*
　　And no lenger delay.
Knyghtys of dyvers londys,
When they harde of these tythandys *heard*
660 　　They gysed them full gay. *dressed themselves*

Of every londe the beste,
Thedur they rode wythowten reste,
　　Full wele arayed and dyght; *clothed*
Some therselfe for to assay, *test*

665	And some to wynne that feyre may	*lady*
	That semely was in syght.	
	Mekyll was the chevalry	
	That then come to Hungary,	
	To go juste wyth ther myght.	
670	When Tryamowre herde telle of thys tythand,	*news*
	Of that justyng in that londe	
	Schulde hastely begynne,	*soon*
	Yf he wyste that hyt wolde gayne,	*be of use*
	He wolde purvey hym full fayne	*prepare; gladly*
675	That lady for to wynne.	
	He had nothyr hors nor spere	*neither*
	Nor no wepyn hym wyth to were;	*fight*
	That brake hys herte wythynne.	
	Faste he bethynkyth hym bothe evyn and morow	*evening; morning*
680	Where hym were beste to borowe,	
	Arste wolde he not blynne.	*Until [then]; cease*
	To hys lorde he can meene,	
	And preyed hym that he wolde hym leene	*loan*
	Wepyn, armowre and stede,	
685	"For at the justyng wolde Y bene	*be*
	To kythe me wyth the knyghtys kene,	*prove myself*
	My body for to blede!"	
	Syr Barnard seyde, "What haste thou thoght?	
	Of justyng canste thou ryght noght,	*know*
690	For thou art not of age."	
	"Syr," he seyde, "what wott ye	*know*
	Of what strenkyth that Y bee	*strength*
	Or Y be provyd in felde wyth the sage?"	*experienced*
	Barnarde seyde also hynde,	*courteously*
695	"Tryamowre, syn ye wyll wynde,	*go*
	Ye schall wante no wede	*lack; armor*
	For Y schall lende the all my gere,	
	Hors and harnes, schylde and spere,	*shield*
	And helpe the at thy nede."	
700	Then was Tryamowre full blythe;	*happy*
	He thanked Bernard fele sythe	*many times*
	Of hys feyre proferynge.	*offer*
	Before the justyng schulde bee,	
	The chylde wente to hys modur free	
705	And preyed hur of hur blessynge.	
	Sche wolde have had hym at home fayne,	

But ther myght no speche gayne,
 Ther myght be no lettynge. *There was no stopping him*

Sone on the morne when hyt was day
710 Tryamowre was gysed full gay,
 Redyly armyd and dyght. *prepared*
When he was armed on a stede
He was a mykell man of brede *breadth*
 And also moche man of myght. *great*
715 Tryamowre to the felde rydeth;
Barnard no lenger abydeth
 But rode wyth hym full ryght.
Ther was no prynce that day in felde
That was so semely undur schylde
720 Nor bettur besemyd a knyght. *more handsome*

Then was that lady sett
Hye up in a garett, *upper floor*
 To beholde that play. *fighting*
There was many a nobull knyght
725 And prynceys proved in that fyght
 And themselfe to assay. *test*
Wyth helmes and armowre bryght
That felde schon as candull lyght,
 So were they dyght gay. *armed*

730 There was mekyll pres in pryde *throng; pomp*
When eche man began to ryde —
 Knyghtys of grete renowne.
Hyt befelle Tryamowre in that tyde
To be on hys fadurs syde,
735 The kyng of Arragon.
The fyrste that rode noght forthy *(see note)*
Was the kyng of Lumbardy,
 A man of grete renowne,
And Tryamowre rode hym ageyn: *against*
740 Thogh he were mekyll man of mayne, *great; strength*
 The chylde broght hym downe. *youth*

The kyngys sone of Armony, *Armenia*
On a stede, wyth grete envy,
 To Tryamowre he ranne;
745 And Tryamowre turnyd forthy
And justyd wyth hym pertly *boldly*
 And downe he bare hym than.

Then seyde Barnard wyth gret honowre
"A Tryamowre! A Tryamowre!" *For*
750 That men myght hym kenne. *know*
Maydyn Elyn, that was so mylde, *Helen*
More sche behelde that chylde *courtly youth*
 Then all othur men. *Than*

Then was ther a bachylere,
755 A prowde prynce wythowtyn pere, *peer*
 Syr James he hyght, *was called*
The emperoure sone of Almayne. *Germany*
He rode Syr Tryamowre agayne, *against*
 And he kepyd hym full ryght; *warded him off*
760 Ayther on other sperys braste *Either one; broke*
But neyther to the grounde was caste,
 Bothe ware they men of myght.
But Syr James had soche a chopp *blow*
That he wyste not, be my toppe, *head*
765 Whethur hyt were day or nyght.

Thus they justyd tyll hyt was nyght
Then they departyd in plyght: *under oath*
 They had nede to reste.
Sone on the morne, when hyt was day,
770 The knyghtys gysed them full gay *arrayed themselves*
 And proved them full preste. *eagerly*
Then, wythowtyn more abode, *waiting*
Every knyght to odur rode
 And sykurly can they stryke and threste. *thrust*

775 Tryamowre rode forthe in haste
And prekyd among the oost *galloped; host*
 Upon the tother syde;
The fyrste that rode to hym thon *then*
Was the kynge of Arragon
780 He kepeyd hym in that tyde.
He gaf hys fadur soche a clowte *blow*
That hors and man felle down wythowt dowte
 And sone he was dyscryed. *noticed*

Syr Asseryn, the kyngys sone of Naverne, *Navarre*
785 Wolde nevyr man hys body warne,[1]
 He come hym ageyne. *He (Asseryn)*
He hyt hym on the helme soo, *He (Tryamour); hym (Asseryn)*

[1] *Whenever a man protected his body (i.e., put on armor)*

Soche a strokk he gaf hym tho,
 That all men hyt syen. *saw*
790 The blode braste owt at hys eerys *burst*
 And hys stede to grownde he berys —
 Then was Syr Barnard fayne!

 Then that lady of grete honowre,
 Whyte os lylly flowre, —
795 Hur love was on hym lente. *placed*
 They sesyd not tyll hyt was nyght *ceased*
 And then they departyd them in plyght
 And to ther ynnys they wente. *inns*

 The nyght was paste, the day was come, *past*
800 Every knyght hys hors hath nome, — *taken*
 Some were wey and on wylde. *Some [horses] were far away; running free*
 The Dewke of Sysell, Syr Sywere, *Sicily*
 He was the furste in that were *battle*
 That fared forthe to the felde.
805 Syr Tryamowre toke to hym a spere,
 To the dewke he can hyt bere,
 And hyt hym on the schylde
 And togedur they wente,
 That hyt bowed and bente, *it (the spear)*
810 So ferse he was in felde! *fierce*
 And at that tyme, as Y yow hente, *inform*
 Many a lovely lady gente
 Full faste them behelde.

 The Dewke of Lythyr, Syr Tyrre, *Lithuania*
815 He prekyd forthe full pertly
 Tryamowre to assayle.
 Tryamowre turned hym belyve, *quickly*
 To the dewke can he dryve
 But lothe he was to fayle;
820 Soche a strokk he gaf hym then
 That the dewke bothe hors and man
 Turned toppe ovyr tayle!
 Then rode to hym the Dewke of Aymere;
 He servyd hym on the same manere, —
825 Ther myght no thyng avayle! *help*

 Kyng Ardus rode forthe in pres;
 The Emperours sone, Syr James,
 A spere spendyd he thare.
 He prekyd to the kyng wyth fors

830	And bare hym downe of hys hors	*from*
	And hath hym hurted sare.	*sorely*
	Then Tryamowre was fayne.	*glad*
	Then he pryked to James of Almayn	*rode*
	As kene as ony bore.	*boar*
835	So harde to hym can he caste	*throw*
	That schylde and spere all to-braste;	*burst asunder*
	Then myght James no more.	
	Tryamowre wolde nevyr have reste	
	But bare hym boldely to the beste —	
840	That was moost of honowre.	
	To ylke a prynce he was preste,	*For every; ready*
	Hors and man downe he caste,	
	So styrde he hym in that stowre.	*he stirred himself; battle*
	Ther was none so gode as he,	
845	Therfore they grauntyd hym the gree,	*victory*
	That hyght Tryamowre.	*That one was called*
	Than hath that lady gente	
	Chosyn hym wyth comyns assente	*common*
	To be hur governowre.	
850	Than began the justyng to cese	
	And Tryamowre wened to have had pese,	*expected*
	And onarmed hym also tyte.	*unarmed; quickly*
	The Emperours sone, Syr James,	
	Wyth grete pryde aftur hym can pres,	
855	Of hym he had grete dyspyte;	*resentment*
	To Tryamowre can he crye,	
	"Yelde the thefe, or thou schalt dye.	
	Thou schalt not go qwyte!"	
	Tho seyde Tryamowre wyth grete envy,	
860	"Syth Y am demed to dye,	*doomed*
	Some stroke wyll Y smyte."	
	Ther was no lenger let;	*pause*
	On ylke a syde they hym beset	*each*
	And gaf hym many a wounde.	
865	Tryamowre sturde hym so there	*stirred; occasion*
	That whosoevyr he come nere	
	He was nevyr aftur sownde.	*sound (healthy)*
	Syr Barnard was of myght	
	And halpe Syr Tryamowre to fyght,	
870	And styrde hym in that stownde.	*stirred*
	Kyng Argus of Arragon	
	Come rydyng to the towne	

And sawe them fyght in fere. *together*
Hyt dud the kyng mekyll grefe
875 When he sawe the chylde at myschefe *in danger*
That was hym leve and dere. *beloved; precious*
Than halpe he Tryamowre *helped*
And broght hym gode socowre.
Men that of myght were
880 Then began a strong stowre; *fierce battle*
Ther was no lenger socowre
But every man to hys pere. *equal (i.e., single combats)*

Syr James was prowde and preste, *eager*
Among the knyghtys can he thruste —
885 At Tryamowre had he tene. *anger*
Styfly he stroke in that stownde *Sturdily*
And gaf Tryamowre a wyckyd wounde
Thorowowt the flanke, Y wene.

Then was Tryamowre owt of hys wytt.
890 Syr James on the hedd he hytt
Tyll he felle downe at that stede.
When Syr James to the grownd was caste,
Hys men were aferde and fledd faste
And morned for drede.
895 Tryamowre was hurte sore
That fyght myght he no more,
So byttyrly can he blede. *heavily*
Tryamowre made no lenger lettyng *delay*
But takyth hys leve at the kyng *from*
900 And thankyd hym for hys feyre dede.
And nevyr wolde he blynne *cease*
Tyll he come to Syr Barnardys town wythynne,
And to hys modur he yede. *went*

That lady sorowed in hur wede
905 When sche sawe hur sone blede,
That all wan was hur blee and hur blode. *pale; complexion*
Tryamowre kyssed hys modur in hye *in haste*
And seyde, "Modur, let be yowre crye;
Me eylyth nothyng but gode." *Nothing afflicts me*
910 A leche was sent aftur in that stownde *doctor (leach)*
For to serche the chyldys wounde
And for to stawnche the chyldys blode.
Tryamowre he undurtoke belyve *quickly*
To save hym upon hys lyfe,
915 Then mendyd hys modurs mode. *mood*

The tother knyghtys, the boke says, *other*
Prekyd to the palays *Rode*
 The lady for to here.
Knyghtys apperyd to hur prest, *presented themselves*
920 Then myght sche chose of the beste
 Whych that hur wylle were.
Tho knyghtys behelde that free *noble (lady)*
But Tryamowre can sche not see,
 Then chaungyd hur chere.
925 Sche seyde, "Lordyngys, where ys hee
That yysturday wan the gree? *victory*
 I chese hym to my fere." *choose; mate*

All that stode there thay soght
But Tryamowre fonde they noght;
930 Then was that lady woo.
Hur barons were before hur broght
Sche prayed them to graunt hur hur thoght:
 Respyte of yerys two. *years*
Sche seyde, "Lordyngys, so God me save *lords*
935 He that me wan, he schall me have.
 Ye wot wele yowre crye was so." *proclamation*
The lordys assentyd wele ther tylle *to*
For sche seyde nothyng but skylle *but what was reasonable*
 And that sche wolde no moo. *she wished for nothing else*

940 When thys was grauntyd verament, *truly*
Of all the folke the lady gente
 Wolde none but Tryamowre. *Wanted*
Every prynce in hys present *presently*
Home to mete there thay went; *dinner*
945 There dyd they lytyll honowre.
Syr James men were not fayne
For ther lorde was slayne
 That was so strong in stowre. *battle*
And in a chare they hym layne *wagon*
950 And ladd hym home into Almayne *led*
 To hys fadur the Emperowre.

The Emperowre felle downe in swown
When they hys sone broght hym beforn
 And seyde, "Who hath hym slayne?"
955 They seyde, "We wott not what he ys,
But Tryamowre he hyght, ywys. *is called*
 Ther was none there so moche of mayne. *great of strength [as he]*

The kyng of Arragon alsoo
He halpe hym yowre sone to sloo *slay*
960 And also all hys pres!" *force*
"Allas!" seyde the Emperowre,
"Tyll Y be venged of Tryamowre
 Schall Y nevyr cese!
Kyng Ardus and Tryamowre
965 They schall abye full sore *pay for*
 The dethe of Syr James!"
The Emperowre verament *indeed*
Aftur helpe he hath sente
 Prynces proved in pres. *battle*

970 The kyng then was sore adredd,
For the Emperowre soche power hadd
 And wolde hym batayle bede. *would offer him battle*
He sawe hys londe ovyr spradd; *land over-run by a hostile force*
To a castell hymselfe fledd
975 And vetaylyd hyt for drede. *provisioned*

The Emperowre was full stowte
And beseged the castell abowte
 And spradd hys baners in haste,
And gaf a sawte to the holde. *assault*
980 Kyng Ardus was stowte and bolde
 And defendyd hym full faste.
Kyng Ardus fendyd hys wonys — *defended; dwelling*
Wondur grete were the stonys
 That they there owt cowde caste;
985 They brake of some bothe back and bonys,
So they farde every day onys. *once*
 The sawte dud six dayes laste. *assault did*

The kyng thoght that full stronge *severe*
To be beseged so longe
990 That he wyste not what to do; *knew*
Two barons on hys message he sente
And to the Emperowre they went
 And prayed hym of reste thoo. *then*

"Syr, ye wyte owre kyng wyth wronge, *accuse*
995 For he nevyr Syr James slowe at none honde, *in any way*
 He wyll hymselfe qwyte full fayne;
Nor he was not in present,
Nor wyth hys wylle, nor wyth hys assent,
 Was not Syr James slayne.

1000	That wyll he do betwene yow two,	
	Yowreselfe and he, yf ye wyll soo,	
	Yf ye hyt on hym wyll say;	*If you will say it to him (i.e., speak the agreement)*
	Or ellys to take yow a knyght,	
	And he to take anodur to fyght,	
1005	Be a certayne day:	*By*
	And yf yowre knyght happyn soo	
	To be scowmfetyd or be sloo	*discomfited; slain*
	Os hyt wyll be may,	*will*
	He wyll put hym yn yowre wylle,	*power*
1010	To make yowre pees, as hyt ys skylle,	*appropriate*
	Wythowtyn more delay.	
	And yf hyt so betyde,	*happens*
	That the knyght of owre syde	
	May sle yowrys wyth chawnce,	*yours*
1015	He preyeth yow that ye wyll cese	
	And let owre londys be in pees	
	Wythowtyn any dystawnce."	*disagreement*
	The Emperowre, wythowt fayle,	
	Toke the day of batayle	
1020	Wyth the kyng at that chawnce,	
	For he had a champyon,	
	In every londe of moste renown, —	
	In hym was hys fyawnce.	*trust*
	When pese was cryed and day tan,	*peace; arranged*
1025	Kyng Ardus was a joyfull man;	
	He trystyd on Tryamowre.	*trusted*
	He sende to seke hym wythowtyn fayle	
	Agayne the day of batayle,	
	For hys dere socowre.	
1030	The messengere ys come and gone	
	But tydyngys of Tryamowre herde he none;	
	The kyng began to lowre.	*frown*
	"Yf he be dedd," he seyth, "allas!	
	Who schall fyght wyth Moradas,	
1035	That ys so styffe in stowre?"	*fierce; battle*
	Whan Tryamowre was hole and sownde	
	And coverde of hys grevus wounde,	
	He busked hym to fare.	*readied*
	"Moder," he seyde wyth mylde chere,	
1040	"Wyste Y who my fadur were,	*If I knew*
	The lasse were my care!"	*less*

"Sone," sche seyde, "wele schalt thou wytt *know*
When thou haste done that thou hett, *what you promised*
 Be God that for us dye can!" *did die*
1045 "Modur," he seyde, "yf ye wyll soo,
Have gode day, for Y wyll goo
 And speke wyth my lemman." *beloved*

Tryamowre rode ovyr dale and downe
Into the londe of Arragon,
1050 Awnturs to seke and see. *Adventures*
As he come rydyng in a foreste
He sawe many a wylde beste, *beast*
 And had howndys thre. *And [Tryamour]*
To a herte he let renne; *After; hart; gave chase*
1055 Twelve fosters dyscryed hym then, *foresters*
 That were kepars of that fee. *keepers; herd*
They lapped hym in on every syde; *surrounded*
Ther was no bote but to abyde, *recourse*
 But loth was hym to flee. *unwilling*

1060 He bad a wedd nevyrthelesse *asked a pledge*
And preyed them that he myght passe
 Yf he had trespaste oght. *at all*
Then swere the fosters all twelve,
They wolde no wedd but hymselfe, *would receive no pledge*
1065 Othurwes be hyt noght; *It may not be otherwise*
"Soche ys the lawe of thys londe
That ye muste lese yowre ryght honde,
 Othur may hyt be noght!"
Then seyde Tryamowre, wyth herte throo, *fearless*
1070 "That wedd ys me lothe to forgoo,
 But hyt be dere boght." *Unless*

There was noght ellys to say,
But all the fosters to hym cun lay *attack*
 Wyth sterne worde and mode; *spirit*
1075 But sone of pees they hym pray.
Ther wente but oon on lyve away; *alive*
 There had they lytyll gode.

When they were betyn to the growndys,
Tryamowre wente to seke hys howndys
1080 And wolde not leve them soo,
Tyll he come to a watur syde —
There he sawe the beste abyde, *beast*
 And had slayn hys howndys twoo.
The thrydd hownde fyghtyng he fyndys, *third*

1085	The beste stroke hym wyth hys tyndys	*tusks*
	And Tryamowre was full woo.	
	He stroke hys hors into the rever,	*river*
	Ho socowrd hys hownde and slew the dere.	*wild animal*
	Hys bewgull blewe he tho.	*bugle; then*

1090	The kyng soyournyd in that tyde	*remained*
	At a maner there besyde,	*manor*
	And herde a bewgull blowe.	
	All that were in the halle	
	Wondurd, bothe gret and small,	*lowly*
1095	For no man dud hyt knowe!	
	Wyth that come a foster,	
	Certenly wyth a fowle chere,	*unhappy*
	Into the kyngys halle, Y trowe;	
	The kyng at hym can frayne,	*asked*
1100	"Syr," he seyde, "yowre men ar slayne,	
	Alle nyn on a rowe!"	

	Than he tolde a tale trewe,	
	That was he that the horne blewe	
	That thys wondur hath wroght.	
1105	"Twenty men were full fewe	
	To take the knyght, he ys soche a schrewe,	*fierce fighter*
	But hyt were dere boght!"	*the victory would cost a lot of lives*
	Kyng Ardus seyde then,	
	"Y have mystur of soche a man;	*need*
1110	God hath hym hedur broght.	*hither*
	Full well Y am begone,	
	Y trowe God hath me sent won	*one*
	That shall Moradas bryng to noght."	

	The kyng callyd knyghtys fyve	
1115	And bad them go belyve	*immediately*
	And fynde hym at hys play;	
	"No evull worde to hym ye nevyn	*give*
	But sey to hym wyth mylde stevyn,	*voice*
	He wyll not sey yow nay!"	

1120	Anon the knyghtys ther horsys hente	*took*
	And to the wode then they went	
	To seke aftur the chylde.	
	They fonde hym be a water syde;	
	He sate and fedd hys howndys in that tyde	
1125	Wyth the beest so wylde.	
	They seyde, "God be at yowre game."	
	He seyde, "Welcome all same."	

He lete hym selfe then be gylyd. *beguiled*
They seyde, "Syr, ys hyt thy wylle
1130 To come and speke owre kyng tyll,
 Wyth wordys meke and mylde?"

Tryamowre asked them full hende,
"Syr," he seyde, "what hyght yowre kyng *is called*
 And what hyght hys londe?"
1135 "Thys londe," they seyde, "hyght Arragon,
The kyng hyght Ardus wyth crowne,
 Hys place ys nere-honde." *near by*

When Tryamowre come into the halle
He haylesed the kyng and sythen all; *greeted; then everyone else*
1140 He knewe hym at that syght.
The kyng toke hym be the hande
And made hym glad semelande *looked pleased*
 And asked hym what he hyght.
"Syr," he seyde, "Y hyght Tryamowre,
1145 Ye halpe me onys in a stowre, *helped; battle*
 Ye feynyd yow not to fyght; *You did not shirk*
Had ye not byn, Y had be slayne
Wyth the Emperowrs sone of Almayne. *By*
 Ye knewe wele that knyght."

1150 The kyng wyste wele that hyt was he,
He kyssyd hym tymes thre;
 And terys let he falle; *tears*
He seyde, "Welcome ye bee!
Grete blame Y have sofurd for the." *suffered*
1155 And sythen he tolde hym all.
"Wyth the Emperowre Y have takyn a day *set*
To defende me yf Y may.
 To Jhesu wolde Y calle;
Os Y nevyr Syr James sloo, *As; slew*
1160 He delyvyr me of woo,
 And so Y trowe He schall."

Tryamowre seyde, "Y am full woo
That thou art for me anoyed soo, *harassed*
 Yf Y myght hyt amende. *set right*
1165 At the day of batayll forthy
Ther schall no man fyght but Y,
 Take the grace that God wyll sende."
Then was the kyng bothe blythe and gladd,
And seyde, "For Moradas Y am not adrad *Because of; afraid*
1170 To batayle when he schall wende.

Ofte Y made men aftur yow to spere *inquire*
But myght Y not of yow here —
 My ryght schall thou defende."

Than dwellyd they togedur same *together with each other*
1175 Wyth mekyll joye and game,
 Therof they wantyd ryght noght. *lacked nothing*
They went on hawkyng be the rever *one*
And other whyle to take the dere *wild game*
 Where that they gode thoght, *Where they pleased*
1180 Tyll the day of batayll was comen
That they had before nomen, *appointed*
 Then the Emperowre thedur soght. *went*
Wyth hym he broght kyng and knyght;
And Moradas that was so wyght, *bold*
1185 To batayle was he broght.

Bothe the partys there were harde *brave*
And sythen to the felde they farde *fared*
 The place was barryd and dyght. *barred (see note)*
The kyng comfortyd Tryamowre.
1190 For sothe, or he went to the stowre, *before; battle*
 He made hym a knyght.
The kyng kyste hym and seyde hym full feyre,
"Tryamowre, Y make the myn heyre, *heir*
 And for me thou schalt fyght!"
1195 "Syr," he seyde, "have thou no drede,
Y tryste in God that He schall me spede, *protect*
 He standyth wyth the ryght."

Then bothe the partyes swore
To holde the covenaunt they made before;
1200 To Jhesu can they calle.
Syr Tryamowre and Moradas
Wery redy armed in that place *Were*
 And broght among them all.
Ayther were armed on a stede;
1205 Of Tryamowre was grete drede —
 Ther was non so hynde in halle. *able*
Moradas was so styff in stowre *hardy*
Ther myght no man hys dyntys dewre, *endure*
 But he made them to falle.

1210 Than rode they two togedur aryght,
Wyth scharp sperys and swerdys bryght
 Thay smote togedur sore.
Ther sperys they spendyd and brake schyldys; *spent*

The pecys flewe into the feldys —
1215 Grete dyntys dud they dele thore. *blows; gave*

All had wondur that there were,
Olde, yonge and chylde, Y swere,
 So sore they dud smyte.
Tryamowre thoght hyt schulde be qwytt, *avenged*
1220 He faylyd of hym, hys hors he hytt, *missed*
 To hys herte hys spere can byte.
Moradas seyde, "Hyt ys grete schame
On a hors to wreke thy grame!" *avenge; anger*
 Tryamowre seyde as tyte:
1225 "Levyr Y had to have hyt the. *I'd rather have hit you*
Have my hors and let me bee, *Take; remain*
 Y am lothe to flyte." *flee*

Moradas seyde, "Y wyll hym noght *I do not want him*
Tyll thou have that strok boght, *payed for*
1230 And wynne hym wyth ryght." *[I] win*
Than leved Tryamowre hys stede; *left*
He lyghtyd downe and to hym yede — *went*
 On fote can they fyght;
Tryamowre sparyd hym noght
1235 But evyr in hys hert he thoght,
 "Today was Y maked knyght!
Owthyr schall he sle me sone, *slay*
Or on hym Y schall wynne my schone, *shoes (spurs)*
 Thorow the grace of God almyght."
1240 Grete wondur hyt was to see them two,
The strokys that were betwene them tho,
 So harde on helme they hewe.
Moradas was forfoghtyn and forbledd, *had fought and bled a lot*
Therfore ho was nevyr so sore adredd; *he; ever*
1245 Hym gamed lytyll glewe.
Tryamowre was then ferse: *fierce*
Thorowowt the armour into the flesche
 He gaf hym a wounde newe.
Thorow hys herte the swerde ranne;
1250 The Emperowre was then a sory man
 And Moradas asked trewe. *truce*

He kyssyd the Kyng and was hys frende *He (the Emperor)*
And toke hys leve for to wende,
 No lenger wolde he dwelle. *remain*
1255 Kyng Ardus and Tryamowre
Were ledd home wyth honowre,
 For sothe as Y yow telle.

All that yn that cyté were,
Bothe lesse and more, *Both of the lower and higher classes*
1260 Hym presed for to see. *thronged*
There were they wythowtyn care,
Wyth glad semeland and welfare; *happiness*
 Ther myght no bettur bee.

Grete was the honowre and the renowne
1265 That he had in Arragon
 For hys feyre dede.
The Kyng profurd hym full feyre, *offered*
"Tryamowre, Y make the myn heyre
 Of londe and of lede." *people*
1270 "Syr," he seyde, "gramercy, nay, *thank you*
Efte togedur speke we may, *Another time*
 Y aske yow but a stede: *horse*
To other londys wyll Y spere, *go*
More of awnturs for to here *adventures*
1275 And who dothe beste yn dede."
There he dwellyd whyll he wolde;
The Kyng gave hym bothe sylver and golde
 That ryche gyftys were.
Gode horsys wantyd he noght
1280 To take or to leve whethur he thoght,
 And all hys other gere.

He toke hys leve at the kynge
And kyssed hym at hys partyng;
 The Kyngys herte was full sore.
1285 He seyde, "Tryamowre, all that ys myne,
When thou wylt, hyt schall be thyn,
 My londe lesse and more."

Now ys Tryamowre wente,
Hym selfe ys in gode atente *intent (disposition)*
1290 For every man ys hys frende.
Yn to every londe, ferre and nere,
Where he myght of awnturs here,
 Thedur can he wende.
In all londys he had the gree, *victory*
1295 Ther was none so gode as hee
 Of all the knyghtys hende.
Therfore gate he grete name
Yn every londe there he came,
 In all placys where he can wende.

1300	Justyng and turnamentys let he bee	*he left off*
	And in to Hungary wende wyll hee,	
	For no man wyll he lett.	*stop*
	Betwene two mowntayns was hys way;	*mountains*
	He went forthe as the strete lay,	*road*
1305	Wyth a palmer he mett;	
	He askyd hym gode for charyte,	*money*
	Tryamowre gaf hym wyth hert free.	
	The palmer for hym can grete;	*call out to*
	He seyde, "Syr, turne agayne,	
1310	For or ye passe the mowntayne	
	Ye schall be slayne or bete!"	

	Tryamowre asked hym, "How soo?"	
	"Syr," he seyde, "for brethur twoo	
	That on thys mowntayn can dwelle.	
1315	Therfore Y prey yow wyth herte fayne	
	That ye wyll turne ageyne,	
	For drede hyt ys wyth them to melle!"	*fight*
	Then seyde Tryamowre, "But they were moo,	*Even if; more*
	Owt of my wey wyll Y not goo,	
1320	Yf they were devyls of helle!"	

	He seyde, "Palmer, have gode day."	*Pilgrim*
	And went forthe on hys way	
	Os faste os he cowde ryde.	
	He had not redyn but a whyle,	
1325	Not the mowntans of a myle,	*duration (see note)*
	Two knyghtys sawe he hove and abyde;	*halt*
	The toon rode hym untyll,	*The one*
	The tother hovedd on an hylle	
	A lytull there besyde.	

1330	The toon hoved and behelde	*watched*
	The strokys they gaf undur schylde;	
	Gret wondur had hee!	
	Betwene them can he ryde	
	And preyed them to abyde	
1335	And sone then let they bee.	*they left off*
	To Tryamowre he seyde anon,	*quickly*
	"So strong a knyght sawe Y nevyr non,	
	Thy name anon telle thou me."	
	Seyde Tryamowre, "Then wolde Y fayn wytt	
1340	Why ye two kepe thys strett,	*guard this road*
	And sythen Y schall telle the."	

The tother brothur seyde, "We schall yow tell,

For thys cheson here we dwelle, *reason*

 And wroght all thys woo.

1345 We had a brodur they callyd Moradas,

Wyth the Emperowre he was

 A stalworth man ynogh.

In Arragon, for the Emperowre,

A knyght they callyd Tryamowre

1350 In batayll dud hym sloo! *slay*

Yf we wyth hym mett, *In the hope that; might meet*

Therfore kepe we thys strett."

 And Tryamowre logh thoo. *laughed*

"And also, Y say another: *another [reason]*

1355 Burlonde owre other brother,

 The man moost of myght,

He besegeth a lady, *besieges (tries to win)*

The kyngys doghtyr of Hungary,

 To wedd hur hath he hyght. *promised*

1360 And so well then hath he spedd,

That for sothe he schall hur wedd, *truly*

 Syr Burlonde that knyght,

But yf sche fynde may

To defende hur, os Y yow say, *as*

1365 A man of armes bryght;

Therfore sche hath takyn a day, *set*

Certenly, os Y yow say,

 And waged hur glove for to fyght. *issued a challenge*

And that same Tryamowre

1370 Loveth that lady peramowre, *for love's sake*

 As hyt ys me tolde,

And sche hath aftur hym sente

And we have waytyd hym verament *awaited*

And slayne hur barons bolde;

1375 And yf he wyll to Hungary,

Thus forthe schall hys way lye,

 And sle hym fayne we wolde. *slay*

He hath hur socowre hett *He has promised aid to her*

Yf we may, we schall hym lett,

1380 Y trowe hyt schall not holde.[1]

And yf sche at hur day fayle, *fail*

Ther schall no thyng hur avayle *help*

[1] *I think it (Tryamour's promise of aid) will not hold good*

But Burlonde schall hur wedd,
And Tryamowre noght, we kenne.
1385 Wherefore ther passyth here no men
 Wyth strenkyth but they be kedd. *unless; proved*
Now have we the cheson tolde, *reason*
Thy ryght name wytt fayne we wolde *know*
 And be thou not adredd. *If you are not*
1390 Thou schalt dwelle here wyth us twoo
And yf thou wylt not soo,
 Evyll then haste thou spedd!"

"Spede," seyde Tryamowre, "as Y may,
Whyll Y have behett yow for to say *promised*
1395 My name schall Y not layne. *conceal*
Yowre jurnay may ye thynk well sett: *task; undertaken*
Wyth the man have ye mett
 That yowre brothur hath slayne.
And ye wyll geve me leve to goo, *If*
1400 Wyth Burlonde wyll Y fyght so,
 For hur love that ye sayne!"
"Welcome," they seyde, "Tryamowre,
Hur love thou schalt bye full sore, *pay for*
 Nothyng may the gayne!"

1405 They smote togedur wyth hert throo *fierce*
And he allone ageyne them twoo, *against*
 To fyght he was full preste. *ready*
Ther armowre myght not gayne, *not serve its purpose*
Bothe thorowowt back and bone
1410 He made the blode to owtbreste. *burst out*
Grete strokys they gaf amonge *gave each other*
And that lasted wondur longe
 Wythowtyn any reste.
So faste abowte conne they goo
1415 That they wroght hym mekyll woo,
 As Y yow say, be Goddys est! *grace*

Tryamowrs hors was sekur, ywys, *trustworthy*
And hys schylde flewe all to pecys,
 So harde to hym they yede. *they went at him*
1420 In that tyme ther was not soche thre,
Gret wondur hyt was to see,
 So doghty they were in dede. *valiant*
But Tryamowre, at the laste,
The too brothur downe he caste, *The one*
1425 Then had the tothur mekyll drede.
No lengur there then wolde he byde

But rode forthe there a lytull besyde
 And hovedd on hys stede. *hovered about*

Sone had Tryamowre slayn the tother,
1430 A sory man was hys brothur
 And wolde be venged fayne;
"Take the grace that God wyll sende me,
Me ys levyr to dye then flee." *I would rather*
 Wyth that he turned agayne.
1435 Wyth hys swerde to hym he yede, *went*
And slew Syr Tryamowrs stede, *horse*
 Full mekyll was hys mayne. *great; strength*
Syr Tryamowre faght on fote, *fought*
What schall we more of hym mote? *tell*
1440 The tothur brothur was slayne.

Tryamowre takyth the knyghtys stede,
For that lady he was in drede
 For sche besegedd lay. *besieged*
The lady had so grete thoght *worry*
1445 For Tryamowre came noght,
 Sche wyste not what to say. *knew*
The day was come that was sett,
Lordus come, as they hett, *promised*
 Many oon stowte and gay.
1450 Burlonde was there redy dyght
And bad hur brynge forthe hur knyght
 And sche seyde schortly, 'Nay."

In the castell had sche hyt hyght *promised*
To defende hur wyth all hur myght,
1455 So as hur counsayle radd; *advised*
"Certys, yf Tryamowre be on lyfe, *alive*
Wyth Goddys grace he schall come belyve; *quickly*
 Wyth enemyes Y am bestadd! *beset*
For Y trowe he loveth me wele
1460 And trewe he ys as any stele. *steel*
 In worlde where evyr he be bestedd, *situated*
And he wyste of thys case, *If*
Hyddur he wolde take hys pase — *make his way*
 My lyfe dar Y lay to wedd." *I dare pledge my life on it*

1465 And ryght wyth that come Tryamowre
ln the moost of that stowre, *the thickest; battle*
 Then gamed hym no glee. *enjoyed; delight*
He asked a man what hyt myght meene
And he tolde hym all bedeene *continuously*

1470	How the batayle schulde bee.	
	He sawe Burlonde on hors hove,	*mounted*
	He rode to hym and waged hys glove;	
	That lady chalenged hee.[1]	
	Sayde Tryamowre, "Who so wyll fyght,	
1475	Y am redy in my ryght	
	To slee hym or he mee!"	

The lady on a towre stode
And sche wende that he had ben wode *thought; mad*
 For sche knewe not hys myght.
1480 Sche asked Barnarde then,
"Syr, can not ye a knyght kenne *recognize*
 That ys to batayle dyght? *in battle dress*
A kreste he beryth in blewe." *crest; wears; blue*
Syr Barnarde then hym knewe
1485 And seyde at that syght,
"Madam, God hath sent yow socowre,
For yondur ys Syr Tryamowre,
 That wyth Burlonde wolde fyght."

Then was that lady full fayne,
1490 Bothe to Jhesu can they prayne *pray*
 To gyf hym grace to spede. *succeed*
Tryamowre to hym berys, *bears down on*
And they all to-braste ther sperys,
 That bothe to the grownde they yede.
1495 That ylke metyng was so throo *fierce*
When bothe to the grownde conne goo,
 The rychest in wede. *in armor*
They settyd strokes of mode, *dealt; violence*
When they bothe to the grownde yode,
1500 They were bothe doghty in dede. *bold*

They start up bothe wythyn a whyle,
Ther stedys on the grownde lay full styll;
 On fote they faght in fere. *fought together*
Ther was none in felde thoo *then*
1505 That cowde chese the bettur of them twoo,
 So boldely they them bere. *conduct themselves*
The batayle lasted wondur longe,
They seyde, "Be Burlonde nevyr so stronge,
 He hath fonde hys pere." *his match*
1510 Wyth swerdys scharpe the faght faste, *they fought earnestly*

[1] *He (Tryamour) issued a challenge for (the hand of) the lady*

At ylke stroke the fyre owt braste — *sparks flew*
 They nyghed wondur nere.

Tryamowre at hym conne mynte; *did aim a blow*
Hys swerde felle fro hym at that dynte.
1515 To the grownde can hyt goo.
Then was Burlonde full gladd
And that lady was sore adradd,
 Knyghtys were full woo!
Tryamowre asked hys swerde agayne
1520 But Burlonde faste can hym frayne, *ask*
 Then seyde he to hym soo:
"Telle trewly what thou hyght, *are called*
And why thou chalangyst that lady bryght,
 And take thy swerde the too." *And [then you can]*

1525 Sayde Tryamowre, "On that covenaund
My ryght name schall Y not wande *refuse*
 Ware thou the devyll of helle!
Men calle me Syr Tryamowre,
Y wanne thys lady in a stowre, *won; battle*
1530 Wyth tonge as Y the telle!"
Then seyde Burlonde, "Thou hyt was
That slewe my brodur Moradas;
 A feyre chawnce there the befelle."
Tho seyde Tryamowre, wyth hert throo, *fearless*
1535 "So Y dud thy brethur twoo
 That dwellyd upon the yondur hylle.'"

Then was Burlond all preste, *plenty eager*
"Tryamowre have thou no reste.
 Now am Y well bethoght; *resolved*
1540 Thy swerde getyst thou nevyr agayne,
Tyll Y be venged or be slayne,
 Sorowe haste thou soght!"
Tho seyde Tryamowre, "Holde thou thy pese,
That schall the rewe or that we cese. *before*
1545 Go forthe! Y drede the noght!"
Burlond to fyght was bowne; *prepared*
Hys fote schett and he felle downe, *slipped*
 And Tryamowre wylyly wroght. *craftily*

Tryamowre hys swerde he hente *seized*
1550 And agayne to Burlond he wente
 And servyd hym on the newe gyse. *manner (i.e., with sword)*
He smote Burlond of be the kneys *at the knees*
And hewe hys leggys all in pecys

	Ryght as he schulde ryse.	*Just as he was about to*
1555	"A lytull lower, syr," seyde hee,	
	"And let us small go wyth thee;	*let us make you become small*
	Now are we bothe at oon assyse!"	*size*
	A lowde laghtur that lady logh	*laughed*
	And Syr Barnard was prowde ynogh	
1560	And thanked God fele sythes.	*many times*

	Burlonde on hys stompus stode,	*stumps*
	Wyte hym not yf he were wode,	*Blame; furious*
	Then faght he wondur faste!	
	Tryamowre on the hedd he hytt;	
1565	He had gevyn hym an evull smytt	*would have; blow*
	But hys swerde braste.	*broke*
	Tryamowre seyde to hym full sone:	
	"Thy gode dayes are nere done,	
	Thy power ys nere paste!"	*nearly over*
1570	Tryamowre at hym can stryke	
	That hedd and fete lay bothe in lyke,	*alike (i.e., cut off)*
	To grownde was he caste.	

	Now ys Burlonde slayne,	
	And Tryamowre, mekyll of mayne,	
1575	To the castell ys he wente.	
	That lady that was so mekyll of myght,	
	At the gate she kepyd the knyght	*met*
	And in hur armes hym hente.	*took*
	Sche seyde, "Welcome, Syr Tryamowre,	
1580	Ye have boght my love full sowre!	
	My love ys on yow lente!"	*is fixed on you*
	Then seyde all the barons bolde,	
	"Of hym we wyll owre londes holde	
	Be the comyns assent."	

1585	Then was ther no nother to say	*nothing more*
	But takyn they have another day	*appointed*
	That he schulde hur wedd.	
	Tryamowre had aftur hys modur sente;	*for*
	Barnard aftur hur was went	
1590	And to the cowrte hur ledd.	
	Tryamowre seyde to hys modur then,	
	"Now Y wolde my fadur kenne,	*know*
	For now have we well spedd!	*prospered*
	Telle me now, modur free,	
1595	Who ys my fadur and what hyt hee?	*what is he called*
	For nothyng be ye adredd."	*concerned*

Hys modur togedur hur fyngers can folde
And all togedur sche hym tolde
 And mekyll sche can hym meene. *tell*
1600 "Kyng Ardus of Arragone,
He ys thy fadur, and thou art hys sone,
 And Y was hys weddyd qwene;
And afturward Y was delefully demydd, *wrongfully judged*
And owt of that londe Y was flemydd. *banished*
1605 Y nevyr wyste what hyt myght meene, *knew; signify*
Why hyt was, nothur wherefore,
Nothur myght hyt wete lesse nor more, *understand*
 But Y was broght in tene!" *grief*

When Tryamowre thys tale herde,
1610 How he wyth hys modur farde,
 Letturs he dudd wryte;
To the kyng he sente them tylle
And preyed hym, yf hyt were hys wylle,
 That he faylyd hym not at that tyde,

1615 But that he wolde come to Hungary
For to worschyp that mangery; *honor; feast*
 Therof he hym besoght.
Then was the kyng wondur gladd,
The messengere gode gyftys hadd
1620 That the tythyngys broght. *news*

The day was come that was sett
The kyng come as he hadd hett, *promised*
 Wyth mekyll pres in pryde. *great entourage*
The lordys wolde no lenger lett; *delay*
1625 The maydyn forthe was fett *brought*
 And erlys on ylke a syde. *each*
The lady to the churche they ledd,
A byschopp togedur them to wedd,
 Yn herte ys not to hyde; *There is no hiding it*
1630 And sone aftur the weddynge
They crowned Tryamowre kynge;
 They wolde no lenger abyde.

Ye may well wytt certeynly
That there was a grete mangery, *feast*
1635 There as so many were mett:
Qwene Margaret began the deyse, *dais*
Kyng Ardus, wythowtyn lees, *without lie (certainly)*
 Be hur was he sett. *By*
The kyng behelde the qwene,

1640 Hym thoght that he schulde hur have seene, *must have seen her before*
 Wyth glad chere he hur grett:
 "Yf hyt be yowre wylle," he seyde, "Madam,
 Telle me what ys yowre name,
 For nothynge that ye lett." *delay*

1645 "Syr," seyde the qwene then,
 "Some tyme was ye cowde me kenne, *There was a time; recognize*
 And ye were well bethoght." *If; mindful*
 The kyng spake not oon worde
 Tyll men had etyn and drawen the borde, *eaten; removed; table*
1650 But stylle he satt in thoght.

 Then the kyng toke the lady gente
 And to a chaumbur anon they went.
 Syr Tryamowre dud they calle.
 Sche seyde, "Here ys yowre sone,
1655 Knowe hym yf ye konne."
 And sythen sche tolde hym all.

 Sche tolde how Marrok wowyd hur in dede *wooed*
 Aftur that hur lorde yede, *left*
 For nothyng wolde he spare.
1660 "Y seyde he schulde be drawe *he (Marrok); drawn*
 For hys sory sawe, *vile speech*
 And he seyde he wolde no mare!
 Aftur that, in that wode so wylde,
 He mett me and Y wyth chylde;
1665 To fordo me thoght he thare, *murder*
 And Syr Roger slewe of hys men fiftene.
 And Y went away full clene, *completely*
 They wyste nevyr whare.
 Sone aftur in a wode so wylde
1670 Y was delyvyr of a chylde,
 Wyth mekyll sorowe and care;
 Then come Syr Barnard
 Aftur a dere full harde,
 And of me he was ware. *aware*

1675 "He seyde, 'Dame, what doyst thou here?'
 And hym Y tolde of my matere; *story*
 Then syghed he full sore
 He toke up my sone and mee
 And ledd us home wyth herte free
1680 And evyr sythen have we byn thore." *since*

Then was there joye and blys,
To see them togedur kysse
 Full ofte, or they cowde cese. *before*
Kyng Ardus was nevyr so blythe,
1685 He kyssyd Tryamowre twenty sythe, *times*
 And for hys sone he hym chese. *accepted*
Then the qwene was full gladd,
That sche soche a lorde hadd,
 Ye wott, wythowtyn lees.
1690 Sche seyde, "Y have well spedd
That soche a lorde hath me wedd
 That beryth the pryce in prees." *who wins victory in combat*

Then dwellyd they bothe in fere *together*
Wyth all maner deynteys that were dere, *dainties; expensive*
1695 Wyth solas on every syde. *happiness*
Kyng Ardus toke hys leve and wente
And ledd wyth hym hys lady gente,
 Home rychely conne they ryde.
All hys londe was full fayne
1700 That the qwene was come ageyn,
 The worde spronge full wyde. *spread*
Kynge Ardus and hys wyfe
Wyth joye and blys they ladd ther lyfe,
 Yn hert hyt ys noght to hyde.

1705 Kyng Tryamowre and hys qwene,
Mekyll joye was them betwene;
 Man chylder had they twoo. *Male children*
Aftur that hys fadur was dedd
Then he cowde no nothur redd, *he didn't know what to do*
1710 Ywys he was full woo! *he was so unhappy*

Hys yongyst sone then ordeygned hee *ordained*
Aftur hys fadur kynge to bee,
 God grawnt hym wele to rejoyse!
Here endyth Syr Tryamowre,
1715 That was doghty in every stowre,
 And evyr wanne the gree, as the boke seys. *won the prize*
God bryng us to that blys
That evyr schall laste wythowt mys. *fail*
 Amen, amen, for charytee!

 NOTES TO *SIR TRYAMOUR*

Before 1	A colophon appears on the leaf preceding the romance: *Here endyth Syr Egyllamowre of Artas and begynneth Syr Tryamowre.*
19	The name Marrok and the name of the giant, Moradas, are similar to the names of the giant brothers, Marras and Arrok, in *Sir Eglamour of Artois.*
27	A proverbial expression meaning "as true the steel spear point is to the wooden shaft."
38	Following the tradition established by Urban II, who preached the First Crusade throughout France, knights took vows from the pope to fight the infidel in the Holy Land. As a sign that they were God's soldiers, they wore red crosses sewed to their surcoats.
45	*us.* MS: *was.* Fellow's emendation. Schmidt adheres to the MS but suggests in her note that *us* makes better sense. The idiom refers to Christ's crucifixion which redeemed the souls of humanity.
48	Fellows emends *Prevy* to *Hevy.*
80 ff.	The queen addresses Marrok, an inferior, with the singular pronoun, while he addresses her in the polite plural.
91	*lady free* is a conventional epithet for a courtly lady, one who is liberal in rewarding knights. Here the pun on freedom may be ironic.
103	This is a proverbial expression occurring in *Guy of Warwick* and *Sir Perceval of Galles* (*Syr Tryamowre*, ed. Schmidt, p. 88).
139–41	The sense of these lines is "When he had accomplished all that he had pledged / With words that were true." The list of sites which comes next follows grammatically from line 139, *done hys pylgrymage . . . To Fleme Jordan,* etc. Though Ardus' earlier vow (line 32) refers to crusading, crusading and pilgrimage to the Holy Land were spiritually and geographically analogous, not to mention historically linked.
156	"She told the king her tidings" makes better sense (*Syr Tryamowre*, ed. Schmidt, p. 89).
189	A common euphemism (see *Sir Tristrem* and *Syr Tryamowre*, ed. Schmidt, p. 89).

212	An adulterous queen was legally considered a traitor, and burning was the accepted punishment.
246	*wayne wyth the wynde*. I.e., leave with the swiftness of the wind (*Syr Tryamowre*, ed. Schmidt, p. 89).
270	This formula appears in Chaucer's romance parody, Sir Thopas (*CT* VII[B²] 796).
305	I take the sense of the passage to be "There were none of that company, no matter how bold or strong, that Sir Roger did not hit on the head so that his sword split them to the waist. The soldiers requited them, striking Roger rapidly as though they were berserk."
313	*Trewe-love* as a dog's name also occurs in the ballad *Horn Childe*.
343	The line begins with a large capital *B*, marking the beginning of the second section of the story relating the vicissitudes of the queen and the eventual discovery of her innocence.
353	The sense of the line seems to be that the men did not know how they would account to Marrok for their failure to find Margaret. The word *unkynde* here has the sense of "unnatural," i.e., "unknightly." Defacing the body of a fallen adversary was most unchivalric.
392	*hym*. MS: *hy*. Schmidt's emendation.
	ryn and mosse. MS: *ryn mosse*. Schmidt's emendation.
401	Hungary is the setting for the adventures of Sibille, Charlemagne's calumniated queen. It is considerably closer to the frontiers of Charlemagne's empire than to Aragon, but romance need not observe realities of physical and political geography.
422	Barnard is a messenger (i.e., emissary or herald), perhaps for the king. The fact that he is hunting a hart is an indicator of chivalric status.
452	Tryamour is also the name of the fairy mistress in *Sir Launfal*.
485	The first day of Yule is Christmas Day.
499	*in hys wede*. Literally "in his clothes"; a formulaic filler here perhaps best glossed as "at his [the dog's] behavior."
567	Line 388 suggests that the body had begun to decay. An uncorrupted corpse was a sign of special sanctity.
613	Space for a large capital *A* at the beginning of this line marks the end of the calumniated queen episode and the beginning of Tryamour's adventures.
639	Dread and fear were considered appropriate responses to a lord. By cultivating them in his subjects, he would be able to maintain order.
690	Fifteen seems to have been the usual age for knighting of romantic heroes. See Degrebelle (Eglamour's son) and Octavian.

736 *noght forthy* is usually translated "nevertheless," which seems inappropriate here. "Rode forth" would make better sense, though it does not fit the meter or rhyme. See line 400 for a similar locution.

754 A *bachylere* was a novice knight or a knight without vassals who served under the banner of a greater knight.

781 There is a similar formula in the corresponding scene of father-son combat in the Thornton manuscript of *Eglamour* (line 1260) where the father gives the son *swylke a swappe*.

799 In the manuscript, this line begins with a large capital *T*, marking the beginning of the third day of the tournament. From this proceeds James' ambush and the Emperor's revenge on Ardus.

814 Lithuania was an important state in the lands of the Teutonic Knights; see Chaucer's description of the Knight in the General Prologue to *The Canterbury Tales* (I[A]54–55).

832 It seems odd that Tryamour would be pleased (*fayne*) to see James wound Ardus, unless he is pleased to have a reason to attack James.

916 This reference to a book as the source for a romance is highly conventional. There is no reason to believe it alludes to an actual volume.

940–1020 This passage corresponds to the fragment preserved in the Rawlinson manuscript.

943 *in hys present* does not make sense. Schmidt suggests, *in thys present*, i.e., "now."

945 The knights achieved little honor in that the princess would accept none of them.

983 The corresponding line in the Rawlinson fragment reads, *With gunnes and grete stones round*.

997 But in lines 871–78 Argus came to Tryamour's aid against James.

1006 Schmidt (*Syr Tryamowre*, p. 93) notes that *yowre* is "evidently a scribal error for *owre*."

1036 In the manuscript, this line begins with a large capital *W*, marking the episode of Tryamour's departure to claim Helen.

1067 The loss of a hand was a typical penalty for poaching.

1188 *barryd*. The suggestion seems to be that the battlefield was enclosed.

1191 Tryamour is now knighted, having proven himself in the earlier combats and acquired a patron of sufficient status to grant knighthood. He is no longer a bachelor, and is now able to lead men in battle.

1222 Killing a horse was considered to be unchivalric.

1238	An idiom. A new-made knight was said to win his shoes when he performed a gallant deed (*Syr Tryamowre*, ed. Schmidt, p. 94).
1251–52	*Moradas* may be a mistake for Ardus. The following line, including a kiss of peace between Ardus and the Emperor, makes better sense with this reading (see Fellows, *Of Love and Chivalry*, p. 308).
1282	In the manuscript this line begins with a large capital *H* marking Tryamour's departure from Ardus and his journey through the pass of the giant brothers.
1325	*the mowntans of a myle*. That is, the time in which a mile can be traveled.
1368	To wage one's glove was an idiom equivalent to "throw down the gauntlet." The sending of a glove to an opponent was a challenge to combat.
1370	"Love par amours," a French expression, refers to courtly — that is, romantic — love.
1441	In the manuscript, this line begins with a large capital *T*, marking the final episode: the combat with Burlond.
1496, 1499	Such repetition is unusual in *Sir Tryamour* and may be a corruption.
1561	*Chevy Chase*, a fifteenth-century ballad, contains a similar incident (Fellows, *Of Love and Chivalry*, p. 309).
1619	It was traditional to give gifts to messengers and minstrels.
1636	To begin the dais is to sit at the head of the table, the place of honor and high social status.

GLOSSARY

abowne *on top*
abowteward *attempting*
abyde *wait, endure*
agayn *to, at*
al if *entirely*
als *as; as if*
anelase *dagger*
antowre *adventure, exploit*
a-plyght *certainly*
are *before*
arethede *previously*
armoryes *armed forces*
arste *previously; until then*
ascrye *challenge*
asent *agreed*
aspye *notice, see*
assay *test*
assent *obey*
at *from*
atente *frame of mind*
aungyl *angel*
avayle *avail*
awen *own*
ay *always*
ayere *heir*
aythir(e) *either, each*
aythur *either*
aywhere *everywhere*

badd *offered*
balayne *whale bone*
balys *misfortunes*
bar *burn; carried*
barne *child*
barst *beat*
baselarde *dagger*
baylye *baily*

bede *arrange; command*
be-dene *together, continuously*
begyfte *gave*
behett *promised*
belamy *(Fr.) dear friend*
beld *shelter, dwell*
belefte *remained*
berye *bury*
berys *bears down on*
bestedd *beset*
bete *better*
bethought *resolved*
betyde *happens*
bey *ornament*
birdis *ladies*
ble *expression, complexion*
blede *bleed*
bloo *blue*
blynne *pause, stop*
blyschede *started*
blythe *happy*
bodworde *message*
bofete *buffet*
bone *bane; boon*
borde *table*
bote *remedy*
bowden *hastened*
bownke *bank*
brasten *burst*
brayde *altercation*
brede *breadth*
brene *corselet*
brent *burned*
brere *briar*
bretage *barricade*
brome *broom-plant*
brondes *coals*

195

browk *use, possess*
brydale *wedding*
brydyll *reins*
brymly *boldly*
bryne *burn*
bryten *break, cut up*
burdone *club*
burgh *town*
busked *readied, hastened*
byblede *covered*
byde *endure*
bydene *indeed*
byggynges *buildings*
byleves *remains*
bynke *bench*
bystadde *beset*
byttyrly *grievously*

canste *know*
ceté *city*
chare *cart, wagon*
chawndelere *candle-maker*
chese *choose, chose*
chesowne *reason*
childe *noble youth*
chippe *ship*
clappe *embrace*
clene *completely*
clere *valiant; bright, shiny, beautiful*
cleves *cliffs*
cloth *carpet*
clout *blow*
clyppyng *embracing*
comenté *populace*
con(ne) *did, can*
concelle *thoughts*
couthe *know how*
covyre *recover*
cowde *could*
curtes *courteous*
curteysé *courtesy*
cyteles *citoles*

daryth *hid*
debonorly *meekly*
deed *dead*
deernes *favor*

degré *preeminence, status*
delayne *delay*
dele *distress*
delefully *wrongfully*
deme *judge*
dere *do harm; expensive*
derne *secret*
dereworth *precious*
dese *dais*
dewre *endure*
deynteys *dainties*
deyse *dais*
dole *sorrow*
dong *struck*
dool *sad*
dowre *endure*
dowte *fear*
drawen *removed*
dree, dreghe *endure*
drowgh *brought*
druuyye *dreary*
dugty *doughty, valiant*
dulefully *grievously*
dwellyng *delay*
dyghte *struck; prepared; adorned*
dyke *ditch*
dynte *blow*
dyscried *noticed*
dyspyte *hatred*
dystawnce *disagreement*

efte *another time, afterwards*
eghene *eyes*
egre *angry*
elde *age*
envy *enmity, fierceness*
er *earlier*
erste *before*
es *is*
est *grace*
etyn *eaten*
evere *always*
evyn *exactly*
eyleth *troubles*
eyr *heir*

fame *defame*
fande *found*
fare *go*
fast *steadfastly*
faste *go*
fatt *fetch*
fawte *lack*
fe *property*
felide *felt*
fell *skin; dangerous*
fence *defensively*
ferde *fared (went); fear*
fere *mate, companion;* **in fere** *together*
ferly *marvelously*
ferre *far; soon*
ferse *fierce*
fett *brought*
fewle *flying creature, griffin*
feyle *fail*
feynyd *shirked*
feyre *fair*
flemed *banished*
fleygh *fled*
Florynys *Florins*
folde *fall*
fondis *sets out*
fondynge *test*
fone *foes*
fordo *kill*
forfare *destroy*
forlayne *seduced*
forsothe *in truth*
forthi *because, since, on account of*
fownde *go, depart*
frayne *inquire*
fre(e) *generous*
fyance *trust*
fytte *episode, exploit*

gaf *gave*
gamed *enjoyed*
gamen *games*
gan *did; began*
gare *sword*
gate *road*
gayne *benefit; be of use*

gedirynge *gathering*
gle *amusement; joy*
glede *bird of prey*
gle(e)de *ember, burning coal*
glewe *amuse; amusement*
gode *goods, money*
goo *walk*
goven *gave*
grame *anger*
grammercy *thank you; lit. grant mercy*
gre *victory, prize*
grefe *offense*
gret(e) *call out in supplication; weep*
gretheth *grieves*
greve *grove*
gyer *evil*
gyffe *give*

habode *waited*
hafe *have*
halp *helps*
halse *neck*
hare *grey*
hastely *soon*
havene *harbor*
haylsed *embraced, greeted*
heghe *high*
helde *health*
hem *them*
hende *accomplished, skillful; gracious; near*
hente *caught; seized, took*
here *army; their; her; here*
herkyn *listen*
hestes *wishes*
hete *promise*
hethynnes *heathen lands*
heved *head*
heyre *heir*
hit *it*
hode *hood*
holde *follow*
holtes *forests, woods*
hond *hand, side*
hore *grey*
hove *halt*
hyde *skin*

hydowes *hideous*
hye *loud*
hyed *hurried*
hyghte *promised, named*
hym *it; him*
hynde *female deer*
hynge *hang*
hyre *her*
hythen *hence*

ile *island*
ilke *each, every; same*
inowg *enough*
intill *into*
iwhils *meanwhile*

kembe *comb*
kende *recognized*
kene *swift; bold*
kenne *know, recognize*
kepe *intend*
kepeth *cares for*
kepyd *met*
keste *cast*
kevere *recover*
kirnelle *embrasure*
knave *male*
knyfe *sword*
kouthe *fortune*
kreste *crest*
kynde *nature; kinship*
kyrke *church*
kythe *make known; prove; tell*

ladd *led*
laghte *drew*
lapped *surrounded*
lare *belief*
lasse *less*
lawe *low*
lay *law, religion, story*
laykyng *loving behavior*
layn *remain silent*
leach *doctor*
leene *loan*
lees *lies*
lemman *beloved*

lende *remain; leaned*
lente *arrived, come*
lere *learn*
lesynge *lying*
lette *lift*
leve *believe; cease; live*
levyd *left*
loffed *loved*
loffte *lifted*
logh *laughed*
longed *pertained*
lore *lost*
lorn *lost*
lovyd *valued*
lowgh *laughed*
lowse *loose*
lufe *love*
luke *try*
lybard *leopard*
lyghte *alight*
lykes *pleases*
lymes *limbs*
lyre *face*

make *give; make*
mangery *feast*
matere *story*
matins *daybreak*
may(e) *lady; maiden; wish*
mekyl *much*
mene *moan; tell, signify*
message *mission*
messe *mass*
mete *dinner, meat (food, hospitality)*
metyng *meeting*
moch *big*
mode *mind, heart, soul; manner*
molde *background (heraldic), ground*
molettys *bosses*
moo *other; more*
mood *manner; mind, heart, soul*
moone *moan*
mowntayns *mountains*
mykyll *much, more*
mynte *aimed a blow*
myrk *dark*
mys *harm*

mysdo *mistreat*
mystur *need*

nerhande *almost*
nevene *tell; count; name*
nevenede *referred to*
neyg *nigh, come nigh*
noght forthy *nevertheless*
nomen *appointed; took, taken*
none *noon*
noresche *nurse*
noye *trouble*
noyes *noise*

off *of*
oght *any*
on *own*
one *on; one*
only *once*
onsownde *injured*
onys *once*
ordeygn *command, organize*
ore *mercy; previously*
orysoune *prayer*
overtaken *discovered*
ovyr *after*
ovyrdon *excessive*
ovyrtwart *across*

palle *fine cloth*
palmere *pilgrim*
palmes *claws*
par *(Fr.) for*
Paresche *Paris*
pase *course, way*
paveleone *tent*
payde *satisfied*
payneyere *basket*
paynnes *pains*
penys *pennies*
peramowre *(Fr.) par amour, for love's sake*
pere *peer*
per ma fay *(Fr.) by my faith*
pertly *boldly*
peryle *peril*
peté *pity*

petous *pitiful*
play *admire himself; fight*
playe *pleasure*
plyght *obligation*
poynt *deed*
prekyd *galloped*
pres *throng, battle*
preste *eagerly; ready*
pryste *priest*
pryvyté *secret*
purveyyed *arranged, prepared*
pyke *staff*

quysschene *cushion*
qwarte *court*
qwelle *kill*
qwykk *alive*
qwyte *requite(d)*

rase *tear out*
Raynysh *Rhenish*
raughte *wroght*
rebawde *rascal*
rechese *riches*
ren *run*
repys *touch*
rese *rush*
revedde *taken*
rewme *realm*
rewyd *grieved; was/were sorry*
riste *peace*
rode *cross*
rowte *mob; troop*
ryff *well-known*
rygge *neck*
rynnande *running*

sall *shall*
samen *remained; together*
sampnede *assembled*
sare *sore*
sawdon *sultan*
sawte *assault*
sayn *assay (charge)*
schawbereke *scabbard*
schent *shamed, troubled*
schett *slipped*

schewe *reveal*
schill *cold*
scho *she*
schowe *shove*
schrewe *fierce fighter*
schyppys *ships*
sclon *slay*
scownfetyd *discomfited*
scryp *bag*
seche *such*
see *sea*
seghe *saw*
seke *sick*
sekur *trustworthy, sure*
selcouthe *marvelous*
semelande *appearance, looks*
semely *appropriate, pleasing*
sene *apparent*
serkirly *truly*
sesyd *ceased*
share *cut*
siththen *then; afterwards*
skryke *shriek*
skyll *cleverness*
skylle *proper*
slak *ravine*
slogh *ditch*
sloo *slay, slain*
smertly *quickly*
smytt *blow*
socowre *help*
solas *happiness*
somedale *somewhat*
sone *soon; son*
sonne *sun*
sothe *truth*
sowkyde *sucked*
soyournyd *remained*
spere *spare; inquire after*
sprent *leapt*
sprete *pole*
spronge *spread*
spylle *kill*
stele *great; steel*
steryd *governed*
steven *sorrowful*
stevene *voice; command*

stounde *while, time, moment*
stour *place*
stowte *strong*
strenkyth *strength*
strong *great*
stye *path*
styf *fierce, sturdy*
styll *quiet*
swayne *person of servile rank*
swog *whizzing blow; rushing sound*
swoghe *faint*
swownyd *swooned*
swylke *such*
swynkyr *work*
swythe *quickly*
sych *such*
syg *see*
sykud *sighed*
syne *after*

takyn *appointed*
tame *domesticated*
tane *undertaken, taken*
teght *taught*
telde *tent*
tent *tend*
terys *tears*
thay *they*
the *you*
the *prosper, thrive*
thede *country*
thedur *thither*
then *than; then*
ther *where*
thofe *though*
thoo *then, there*
thore *there*
thrange *throng*
threste *thrust*
thro(o) *fierce*
till *to*
tittler *more quickly*
to *at, until*
told *counted; gave*
too *the one*
toppe *head*
trayne *treason, treachery*

trewe *truce*
trowe *believe, think*
trompes *trumpets*
tryste *trust*
tusschus *tusks*
tyde(s) *betides; happens; time*
tyndes *tusks*
tyse *entice*
tyte *quickly, tight*

unclede *undressed*
uncorne *unicorn*
uncouthe *unknown*
undirtake *guarantee*
unfrely *ugly*
unkynde *wicked*
unnethes *with difficulty, scarcely*
unryde *rough*
unryght *injustice*

vataylyd *victualled, provisioned*
velanye *villainy*
venquyscht *won*
verament *truly*

waged *wagered*
walle *stir up*
wande *refuse*
wane *domesticated*
wanne *won*
war *aware*
ward *toward*
warne *protect*
wate *wet*
wayte *await*
wede(s) *clothes, array, gown; armor*
wedir *where*
welfare *happiness*
weme *hurt*
wende *go, turn; thought, understood*
wene *think, doubt*
wepnes *weapons*
were *defend; wear*
werne *refuse*
wery *were*
wete *understand*
wexe *become, grow*

whylke *which*
wilde *would*
with-alle *moreover*
withowtten *outside, without*
wode *went; crazy, mad, insane*
woghe *woe*
wold *protection*
wolde *wanted, took*
won *fortune; one; won*
wonne *come*
wonys *dwelling*
worschyp *honor*
wote *know*
wowyd *wooed*
wrekyd *revenged*
wrethyd *angered*
wrothe *crazy*
wroughte *accomplished*
wroughten *carved*
wunt *accustomed*
wyght *person, man, creature; valiant*
wyll *strength*
wylsome *deserted*
wys *guide, advise*
wyste *knew*

yare *ready;* **full yare** *entirely, eagerly*
yate *gate*
ydoo *done*
yede *went*
yelde *give (up)*
yeme *keep*
yende *end, death*
ylente *arrived*
ylkane, ylkon *each one*
ylke *same; every; very*
ynnys *inns*
ynomyn *taken*
yode *went*
yore *readily*
yowrys *yours*
yrke *irritated*
yron *iron*
ywys *I think; indeed*
yyng *young*

BIBLIOGRAPHY

Barron, W. R. J. *English Medieval Romance*. London: Longman, 1987.

Boffey, Julia, and A. S. G. Edwards, eds. *A New Index of Middle English Verse*. London: The British Library, 2005.

Braswell, Laurel. "Sir Isumbras and the Legend of Saint Eustace." *Medieval Studies* 27 (1965), 128–51.

Brewer, D. S., and A. E. B. Owen, eds. *The Thornton Manuscript*. London: Scolar Press, 1975.

Charbonneau, Joanne. "Trangressive Fathers in *Sir Eglamour of Artois* and *Torrent of Portyngale*." In *Discourses on Love, Marriage, and Transgression in Medieval and Early Modern Literature*. Ed. Albrecht Classe. Tempe: Arizona Center for Medieval and Renaissance Studies, 2004. Pp. 243–65.

Crane, Susan. *Insular Romance: Politics, Faith, and Culture in Anglo-Norman and English Middle English Literature*. Berkeley: University of California Press, 1986.

Evans, Murray. *Rereading Middle English Romance: Manuscript Layout, Decoration, and the Rhetoric of Composite Structure*. Montreal: McGill-Queen's University Press, 1995.

Fellows, Jennifer. "Mothers in Middle English Romance." In *Women and Literature in Britain c. 1100–1500*. Ed. Carol M. Meale. Cambridge: Cambridge University Press, 1993. Pp. 41–60.

Fowler, Elizabeth. "The Romance Hypothetical: Lordship and the Saracens in *Sir Isumbras*." In *The Spirit of Medieval English Popular Romance*. Ed. Ad Putter and Jane Gelbert. Essex, UK: Pearson, 2000. Pp. 97–121.

Guddat-Figge, Gisela. *Catalogue of Manuscripts Containing Middle English Romances*. Münchener Universitäts-Schriften: Philosophische Fakultät, 4. Munich: Wilhelm Fink, 1976.

Halliwell, James Orchard, ed. *The Thornton Romances: The Early English Metrical Romances of Perceval, Isumbras, Eglamour, and Degrevant. Selected from Manuscripts at Lincoln and Cambridge*. London: Camden Society, 1844. [Cambridge text.]

Hopkins, Andrea. *The Sinful Knights: A Study of Middle English Penitential Romance*. New York: Oxford University Press, 1990.

Hudson, Harriet E. "Construction of Class, Family, and Gender in Some Middle English Romances." In *Class and Gender in Early English Literature*. Ed. Britton Harwood and Gillian Overing. Bloomington: Indiana University Press, 1994. Pp. 76–94.

Knight, Stephen. "The Social Function of Middle English Romances." In *Medieval Literature: Criticism, Ideology, and History*. Ed. David Aers. New York: St. Martin's Press, 1986. Pp. 99–122.

Loomis, Laura Hibbard. *Mediæval Romance in England: A Study of the Sources and Analogues of the Non-Cyclic Metrical Romances*. New York: Burt Franklin, 1924. Rpt. 1960.

McSparran, Frances, and P. R. Robinson, eds. *Cambridge University Library MS Ff.2.38*. London: Scolar Press, 1979. [Fascimile.]

Mehl, Dieter. *The Middle English Romances of the Thirteenth and Fourteenth Centuries*. London: Routledge & Kegan Paul, 1969.

Mills, Maldwyn. *Six Middle English Romances*. London: Dent, 1973. [Cotton text.]

———. "*Sir Isumbras* and the Styles of the Tail-Rhyme Romance." In *Readings in Medieval English Romance*. Ed. Carol M. Meale. Woodbridge, Suffolk: Brewer, 1994. Pp. 1–24.

Murdoch, Brian. "Sin, Sacred and Secular: Hartman's *Gregorius, The Incestuous Daughter, The Trenatalle Sancti Gregorii*, and *Sir Eglamour of Artois*." *Blütezeit* 70 (2000), 309–20.

Octavian. In *Octavian: Zwei Mittelenglische Bearbeitungen der Sage*. Ed. Gregor Sarrazin. Heilbronn: Henninger, 1885. [Northern: Lincoln and Cambridge texts; Southern: Cotton text.]

———. In *Six Middle English Romances*. Ed. Maldwyn Mills. London: Dent, 1973. Pp. 75–124. [Northern: Cambridge text.]

———. In *Octovian Imperator: Ed. from MS BL Cotton Caligula A II*. Ed. Frances McSparran. Heidelberg: Carl Winter, 1979. [Southern: Cotton text.]

———. In *Octovian*. Ed. Frances McSparran. EETS o.s. 289. London: Oxford University Press, 1986. [Northern: Lincoln, Cambridge, and Huntington texts.]

Pearsall, Derek. "The Development of Middle English Romance." *Medieval Studies* 27 (1965), 91–116.

Powell, Stephen. "Models of Religious Peace in the Middle English Romance *Sir Isumbras*." *Neophilologus* 85 (2001), 121–36.

Purdie, Rhiannon. "Generic Identity and the Origins of *Sir Isumbras*." In *The Matter of Identity in Medieval Romance*. Ed. Phillipa Hardman. Cambridge: D. S. Brewer, 2002. Pp. 113–24.

Ramsey, Lee C. *Chivalric Romances: Popular Literature in Medieval England*. Bloomington: Indiana University Press, 1983.

Rastall, Richard. "Minstrels of English Royal Households 25 Edward I–Henry VII." *Journal of the Royal Music Association* 4 (1964), 5.

Reiss, Edmund. "Romance." In *The Popular Literature of Medieval England*. Ed. Thomas J. Heffernan. Tennessee Studies in Literature 28. Knoxville: University of Tennessee Press, 1985. Pp. 108–30.

Riddy, Felicity. "Middle English Romance: Family, Marriage, Intimacy." In *The Cambirdge Companion to Medieval Romance*. Ed. Roberta L. Krueger. Cambridge: Cambridge University Press, 2000. Pp. 150–64 and 235–52.

Robinson, P. R. "The Booklet: A Self-Contained Unit in Composite Manuscripts," *Codicologica* 3 (1970), 46–64.

Salter, David. "'Born to Thraldom and Penance': Wives and Mothers in Middle English Romance." In *Writing Gender and Genre in Medieval Literature: Approaches to Old and Middle English Texts*. Ed. Elaine Treharne. Cambridge: D. S. Brewer, 2002. Pp. 41–59.

Severs, J. Burke, et al., eds. *A Manual of the Writings in Middle English, 1050–1500*. Vol. 1: *Romances*. New Haven: Connecticut Academy of Arts and Sciences, 1967.

Simons, John. "Northern *Octavian* and the Question of Class." In *Romance in Medieval England*. Ed. Maldwyn Mills, Jennifer Fellows, and Carol M. Meale. Cambridge: D. S. Brewer, 1991. Pp. 105–12.

Sir Eglamour of Artois. In Halliwell, ed., *The Thornton Romances*. Pp. 121-76.

———. In *Bishop Percy's Folio Manuscript*. Ed. John W. Hales and Frederick J. Furnivall. London: N. Trübner, 1867–68. Pp. 338-89.

———. In *Sir Eglamour: Eine Englische Romanze des 14 Jahrhunderts*. Ed. Gustav Schleich. *Palaestra* 53. Berlin: Mayer & Müller, 1906. [Lincoln Thornton text.]

———. In *Sir Eglamour: A Middle English Romance*. Ed. A. S. Cook and Gustav Schleich. New York: Holt, 1911. [Lincoln Thornton text.]

———. In *Sir Eglamour of Artois*. Ed. Frances E. Richardson. EETS o.s. 256. London: Oxford University Press, 1965. [Egerton, Lincoln, and Cotton texts with other variants.]

Sir Isumbras. In *Here Begynneth the History of Syr Isenbras*. 1550. English Experience Series 245. New York: Da Capo Press, 1970.

———. In Halliwell, ed., *The Thornton Romances*. Pp. 88-120.

———. In *Sir Ysumbras*. Ed. Gustav Schleich. *Palaestra* 15. Berlin: Mayer and Miller, 1901. [Composite edition, based on Gonville-Caius text, with variants.]

———. In *A Critical Edition of the Romance of Sir Isumbras*. Ed. Charles M. Broh. Ph.D. dissertation, Case Western Reserve University, 1969. [Cambridge text.]

———. In *Sir Isumbras*. In Mills, ed., *Six Middle English Romances*.

Sir Tryamour. In *The Romance of Syr Tryamoure*. Ed. J. O. Halliwell. Percy Society 16. London: T. Richards for the Percy Society, 1846. [Includes a transcription of the Rawlinson fragment.]

————. In *Syr Tryamowre: A Metrical Romance*. Ed. Anna Johanna Erdman Schmidt. Utrecht: Broekhoff, 1937.

————. In *Syr Tryamowre*. In *Of Love and Chivalry: An Anthology of Middle English Romance*. Ed. Jennifer Fellows. London: J. M. Dent/Everyman's Library, 1993. Pp. 147–98.

Southworth, John. *The English Medieval Minstrel*. Suffolk, UK: Boydell, 1989.

Trounce, A. McI. "The English Tail-Rhyme Romances." *Medium Ævum* 1 (1932), 87–108, 168–82; 2 (1933), 34–57, 189–98; 3 (1934), 30–50.

Wittig, Susan. *Stylistic and Narrative Structures in the Middle English Romances*. Austin: University of Texas Press, 1978.

Wright, Glenn. "The Fabliau Ethos in the French and English *Octavian* Romances." *Modern Philology* 102: 4 (2005), 478–500.

MIDDLE ENGLISH TEXTS SERIES

The Floure and the Leafe, The Assembly of Ladies, The Isle of Ladies, edited by Derek Pearsall (1990)

Three Middle English Charlemagne Romances, edited by Alan Lupack (1990)

Six Ecclesiastical Satires, edited by James M. Dean (1991)

Heroic Women from the Old Testament in Middle English Verse, edited by Russell A. Peck (1991)

The Canterbury Tales: Fifteenth-Century Continuations and Additions, edited by John M. Bowers (1992)

Gavin Douglas, *The Palis of Honoure*, edited by David Parkinson (1992)

Wynnere and Wastoure and The Parlement of the Thre Ages, edited by Warren Ginsberg (1992)

The Shewings of Julian of Norwich, edited by Georgia Ronan Crampton (1994)

King Arthur's Death: The Middle English Stanzaic Morte Arthur and Alliterative Morte Arthure, edited by Larry D. Benson, revised by Edward E. Foster (1994)

Lancelot of the Laik and Sir Tristrem, edited by Alan Lupack (1994)

Sir Gawain: Eleven Romances and Tales, edited by Thomas Hahn (1995)

The Middle English Breton Lays, edited by Anne Laskaya and Eve Salisbury (1995)

Sir Perceval of Galles and Ywain and Gawain, edited by Mary Flowers Braswell (1995)

Four Middle English Romances: Sir Isumbras, Octavian, Sir Eglamour of Artois, Sir Tryamour, edited by Harriet Hudson (1996; second edition 2006)

The Poems of Laurence Minot 1333–1352, edited by Richard H. Osberg (1996)

Medieval English Political Writings, edited by James M. Dean (1996)

The Book of Margery Kempe, edited by Lynn Staley (1996)

Amis and Amiloun, Robert of Cisyle, and Sir Amadace, edited by Edward E. Foster (1997)

The Cloud of Unknowing, edited by Patrick J. Gallacher (1997)

Robin Hood and Other Outlaw Tales, edited by Stephen Knight and Thomas Ohlgren (1997; second edition 2000)

The Poems of Robert Henryson, edited by Robert L. Kindrick with assistance of Kristie A. Bixby (1997)

Moral Love Songs and Laments, edited by Susanna Greer Fein (1998)

John Lydgate, *Troy Book Selections*, edited by Robert R. Edwards (1998)

Thomas Usk, *The Testament of Love*, edited by R. Allen Shoaf (1998)

Prose Merlin, edited by John Conlee (1998)

Middle English Marian Lyrics, edited by Karen Saupe (1998)

John Metham, *Amoryus and Cleopes*, edited by Stephen F. Page (1999)

Four Romances of England: King Horn, Havelok the Dane, Bevis of Hampton, Athelston, edited by Ronald B. Herzman, Graham Drake, and Eve Salisbury (1999)

The Assembly of Gods: Le Assemble de Dyeus, or Banquet of Gods and Goddesses, with the Discourse of Reason and Sensuality, edited by Jane Chance (1999)

Thomas Hoccleve, *The Regiment of Princes*, edited by Charles R. Blyth (1999)

John Capgrave, *The Life of Saint Katherine*, edited by Karen A. Winstead (1999)

John Gower, *Confessio Amantis*, Vol. 1, edited by Russell A. Peck; with Latin translations by Andrew Galloway (2000; second edition 2006); Vol. 2 (2003); Vol. 3 (2004)

Richard the Redeless and Mum and the Sothsegger, edited by James M. Dean (2000)

Ancrene Wisse, edited by Robert Hasenfratz (2000)

Walter Hilton, *The Scale of Perfection*, edited by Thomas H. Bestul (2000)

John Lydgate, *The Siege of Thebes*, edited by Robert R. Edwards (2001)

Pearl, edited by Sarah Stanbury (2001)

The Trials and Joys of Marriage, edited by Eve Salisbury (2002)

Middle English Legends of Women Saints, edited by Sherry L. Reames, with assistance of Martha G. Blalock and Wendy R. Larson (2003)

The Wallace: Selections, edited by Anne McKim (2003)

Richard Maidstone, *Concordia (The Reconciliation of Richard II with London)*, edited by David R. Carlson, with a verse translation by A. G. Rigg (2003)

Three Purgatory Poems: The Gast of Gy, Sir Owain, The Vision of Tundale, edited by Edward E. Foster (2004)

William Dunbar, *The Complete Works*, edited by John Conlee (2004)

Chaucerian Dream Visions and Complaints, edited by Dana M. Symons (2004)

Stanzaic Guy of Warwick, edited by Alison Wiggins (2004)

Saints' Lives in Middle English Collections, edited by E. Gordon Whatley, with Anne B. Thompson and Robert K. Upchurch (2004)

Siege of Jerusalem, edited by Michael Livingston (2004)

The Kingis Quair and Other Prison Poems, edited by Linne R. Mooney and Mary-Jo Arn (2005)

Chaucerian Apocrypha: Selections, edited by Kathleen Forni (2005)

John Gower, *The Minor Latin Works*, edited and translated by R. F. Yeager, with *In Praise of Peace*, edited by Michael Livingston (2005)

Sentimental and Humorous Romances: Floris and Blancheflour, Sir Degrevant, The Squire of Low Degree, The Tournament of Tottenham, and The Feast of Tottenham, edited by Erik Kooper (2006)

Everyman and Its Dutch Original, Elckerlijc, edited by Clifford Davidson, Martin W. Walsh, and Ton J. Broos (2006)

Dicts and Sayings of the Philosophers, edited by John William Sutton (2006)

DOCUMENTS OF PRACTICE SERIES

Love and Marriage in Late Medieval London, selected, translated, and introduced by Shannon McSheffrey (1995)

Sources for the History of Medicine in Late Medieval England, selected, introduced, and translated by Carole Rawcliffe (1995)

A Slice of Life: Selected Documents of Medieval English Peasant Experience, edited, translated, and with an introduction by Edwin Brezette DeWindt (1996)

Regular Life: Monastic, Canonical, and Mendicant Rules, selected and introduced by Douglas J. McMillan and Kathryn Smith Fladenmuller (1997); second edition, selected and introduced by Daniel Marcel La Corte and Douglas J. McMillan (2004)

Women and Monasticism in Medieval Europe: Sisters and Patrons of the Cistercian Reform, selected, translated, and with an introduction by Constance H. Berman (2002)

Medieval Notaries and Their Acts: The 1327–1328 Register of Jean Holanie, introduced, edited, and translated by Kathryn L. Reyerson and Debra A. Salata (2004)

COMMENTARY SERIES

Haimo of Auxerre, *Commentary on the Book of Jonah*, translated with an introduction and notes by Deborah Everhart (1993)

Medieval Exegesis in Translation: Commentaries on the Book of Ruth, translated with an introduction and notes by Lesley Smith (1996)

Nicholas of Lyra's Apocalypse Commentary, translated with an introduction and notes by Philip D. W. Krey (1997)

Rabbi Ezra Ben Solomon of Gerona, *Commentary on the Song of Songs and Other Kabbalistic Commentaries*, selected, translated, and annotated by Seth Brody (1999)

John Wyclif, *On the Truth of Holy Scripture*, translated with an introduction and notes by Ian Christopher Levy (2001)

Second Thessalonians: Two Early Medieval Apocalyptic Commentaries, introduced and translated by Steven R. Cartwright and Kevin L. Hughes (2001)

The Glossa Ordinaria on the Song of Songs, translated with an introduction and notes by Mary Dove (2004)

MEDIEVAL GERMAN TEXTS IN BILINGUAL EDITIONS SERIES

Sovereignty and Salvation in the Vernacular, 1050–1150, introduction, translations, and notes by James A. Schultz (2000)

Ava's New Testament Narratives: "When the Old Law Passed Away," introduction, translation, and notes by James A. Rushing, Jr. (2003)

History as Literature: German World Chronicles of the Thirteenth Century in Verse, introduction, translation, and notes by R. Graeme Dunphy (2003)

VARIA

The Study of Chivalry: Resources and Approaches, edited by Howell Chickering and Thomas H. Seiler (1988)

Studies in the Harley Manuscript: The Scribes, Contents, and Social Contexts of British Library MS Harley 2253, edited by Susanna Fein (2000)

The Liturgy of the Medieval Church, edited by Thomas J. Heffernan and E. Ann Matter (2001); second edition (2005)

TO ORDER PLEASE CONTACT:

Medieval Institute Publications
Western Michigan University
Kalamazoo, MI 49008-5432
Phone (269) 387-8755
FAX (269) 387-8750

http://www.wmich.edu/medieval/mip/index.html

Medieval Institute Publications is a program
of The Medieval Institute, College of Arts
and Sciences, Western Michigan University

Typeset in 10/13 New Baskerville
with Golden Cockeral Ornaments display
Designed by Linda K. Judy
Manufactured by McNaughton-Gunn, Inc. _____

Medieval Institute Publications
College of Arts and Sciences
Western Michigan University
1903 W. Michigan Avenue
Kalamazoo, MI 49008-5432
http://www.wmich.edu/medieval/mip

 WESTERN MICHIGAN UNIVERSITY